ST/LIB/SER.B/E.92

# Index to Proceedings of the Economic and Social Council

## 2015 session

Dag Hammarskjöld Library     New York, 2016     United Nations

DAG HAMMARSKJÖLD LIBRARY
Bibliographical Series, No. E.92

ST/LIB/SER.B/E.92

UNITED NATIONS PUBLICATION
Sales No. E.16.I.11

ISBN: 978-92-1-101341-2
eISBN: 978-92-1-058277-3
ISSN: 0082-8084

# CONTENTS

# INTRODUCTION

The Economic and Social Council, under the authority of the General Assembly, is the United Nations organ which coordinates the economic and social work of the United Nations and its system of organizations. The Council has 54 members and until 1991 held the following sessions each year: a short organizational session in New York in January, the first regular session in New York in May, the second regular session in Geneva in July. The rules of procedure of the Council were amended by resolution 1992/2 and from 1992 on, the Council held an organizational session in February in New York and one substantive session, with one "high-level segment" a year; the substantive session took place in alternate years in New York and Geneva between May and July. The General Assembly, in its resolution 68/1, requested the Economic and Social Council to adjust its programme of work to a July-to-July cycle. The Council continues to have one substantive and one organizational session. From 2014, the Council holds a substantive session in New York and the humanitarian affairs segment alternates between New York and Geneva.

The *Index to Proceedings of the Economic and Social Council* is an annual bibliographic guide to the proceedings and documentation of the Economic and Social Council. This issue covers the 2015 session. The *Index* is prepared by the Dag Hammarskjöld Library, Department of Public Information, as one of the products of the United Nations Bibliographic Information System (UNBIS).

## ARRANGEMENT OF THE INDEX

The *Index* consists of the following parts:

**Sessional information**, listing member States and their terms of office as well as the officers of the Council and providing information on rules of procedure and resolutions and decisions;

**Check-list of meetings**, listing the meetings of the Economic and Social Council;

**Agenda**, listing matters considered by and brought before the Council and the subject headings under which these items appear in the Subject index;

**Subject index**, providing topical access to Economic and Social Council documentation arranged alphabetically by subject and listing documents considered under each item, meetings at which the items were considered and the action taken by the Council;

**Index to speeches**, providing access to speeches that were made before the Council. The Index is divided into three sections: corporate names/countries, speakers and subjects.

*Speakers' names are based on information found in United Nations documents. To submit a name correction, please send an e-mail to Library-NY@un.org*

**List of resolutions**, listing resolutions adopted by the Council and indicating for each session the resolution number, the subject and the meeting and date when the resolution was adopted;

**List of documents**, listing documents issued for the 2015 session and providing information on the republication of provisional documents in printed *Official Records*;

## SERIES SYMBOLS

In 1978 certain modifications were introduced in the citation and series symbols of the documents of the Economic and Social Council. They are as follows:

(a) The sessions of the Council are formally identified as the organizational and substantive sessions of a particular calendar year, as prescribed in rule 1 of the rules of procedure of the Council;

(b) Special sessions, including subject-oriented sessions, are numbered consecutively within each year, and are identified as the first special session (year), second special session (year), etc;

(c) Ad hoc sessional committees may be established as required and are described as ad hoc sessional committees on particular subjects;

(d) *Supplements* to the *Official Records* are numbered consecutively, with Supplements No. 1 and 1A containing the resolutions and decisions adopted during the year.

Symbols of documents of the Council and its ad hoc committees or other bodies consist of combinations as appropriate, of the following elements:

(a) The parent body (i.e. the Economic and Social Council): E/- ;

(b) The year of consideration.

## DOCUMENTATION OF THE ECONOMIC AND SOCIAL COUNCIL

Summary records of plenary meetings of the Economic and Social Council are first issued in provisional form for limited distribution. They are later combined in corrected form in a single printed volume of *Official Records* for the year.

All summary records may be identified by their symbol, which consists of the series symbol followed by SR. and then a number which corresponds to the number of the meeting. The 5th plenary meeting, for example, is cited as E/2015/SR.5.

Some documents may later be printed as *Supplements* to the *Official Records* (and are so indicated in this index); others are issued only in provisional form.

## HOW TO OBTAIN DOCUMENTS

Printed documentation of the Economic and Social Council for 2015 may be obtained or purchased from authorized sales agents by providing the following information:

***Official Records of the Economic and Social Council, 2015***:

**Meeting No.** (specify meeting number) for summary record fascicles;

**Supplement No.** (specify supplement number).

# ABBREVIATIONS

| | |
|---|---|
| Add. | addendum, addenda |
| A.I. | Agenda item |
| Corr. | corrigendum, corrigenda |
| ECA | Economic Commission for Africa |
| ECE | Economic Commission for Europe |
| ECLAC | Economic Commission for Latin America and the Caribbean |
| ECOSOC | Economic and Social Council |
| ESCAP | Economic and Social Commission for Asia and the Pacific |
| ESCOR | *Official Records of the Economic and Social Council* |
| ESCWA | Economic and Social Commission for Western Asia |
| FAO | Food and Agriculture Organization |
| GAOR | *Official Records of the General Assembly* |
| IBRD | International Bank for Reconstruction and Development |
| ILO | International Labour Organization |
| IMF | International Monetary Fund |
| ITU | International Telecommunication Union |
| No. | Number |
| OECD | Organisation for Economic Co-operation and Development |
| Rev. | Revision |
| sess. | session |
| Suppl. | Supplement |
| UN | United Nations |
| UNCTAD | United Nations Conference on Trade and Development |
| UNDP | United Nations Development Programme |
| Unesco | United Nations Educational, Scientific and Cultural Organization |
| UNFPA | United Nations Population Fund |
| UN-HABITAT | United Nations Settlement Programme |
| UNHCR | United Nations High Commissioner for Refugees |
| UNICEF | United Nations Children's Fund |
| UNIDO | United Nations Industrial Development Organization |
| UNITAR | United Nations Institute for Training and Research |

# ABBREVIATIONS

| | |
|---|---|
| UNOPS | United Nations Office for Project Services |
| UNRWA | United Nations Relief and Works Agency for Palestine Refugees in the Near East |
| WHO | World Health Organization |

# SESSIONAL INFORMATION

## MEMBERS AND TERM OF OFFICE

| Members | Date of election by the General Assembly | Term of office (1 Jan.-31 Dec.) | Members | Date of election by the General Assembly | Term of office (1 Jan.-31 Dec.) |
|---|---|---|---|---|---|
| Albania | 8 Nov. 2012 | 2013-2015 | Italy | 18 Nov. 2013 | 2015 |
| Antigua and Barbuda | 30 Oct. 2013 | 2014-2016 | Japan | 29 Oct. 2014 | 2015-2017 |
| Argentina | 29 Oct. 2014 | 2015-2017 | Kazakhstan | 30 Oct. 2013 | 2014-2016 |
| Australia | 10 Nov. 2014 | 2015 | Kuwait | 8 Nov. 2012 | 2013-2015 |
| Austria | 29 Oct. 2014 | 2015-2017 | Kyrgyzstan | 8 Nov. 2012 | 2013-2015 |
| Bangladesh | 30 Oct. 2013 | 2014-2016 | Mauritania | 29 Oct. 2014 | 2015-2017 |
| Benin | 8 Nov. 2012 | 2013-2015 | Mauritius | 8 Nov. 2012 | 2013-2015 |
| Bolivia (Plurinational State of) | 8 Nov. 2012 | 2013-2015 | Nepal | 8 Nov. 2012 | 2013-2015 |
| Botswana | 30 Oct. 2013 | 2014-2016 | Pakistan | 29 Oct. 2014 | 2015-2017 |
| Brazil | 29 Oct. 2014 | 2015-2017 | Panama | 30 Oct. 2013 | 2014-2016 |
| Burkina Faso | 29 Oct. 2014 | 2015-2017 | Portugal | 29 Oct. 2014 | 2015-2017 |
| China | 30 Oct. 2013 | 2014-2016 | Republic of Korea | 30 Oct. 2013 | 2014-2016 |
| Colombia | 8 Nov. 2012 | 2013-2015 | Russian Federation | 30 Oct. 2013 | 2014-2016 |
| Congo | 30 Oct. 2013 | 2014-2016 | San Marino | 8 Nov. 2012 | 2013-2015 |
| Croatia | 8 Nov. 2012 | 2013-2015 | Serbia | 30 Oct. 2013 | 2014-2016 |
| Democratic Republic of the Congo | 30 Oct. 2013 | 2014-2016 | South Africa | 8 Nov. 2012 | 2013-2015 |
| Estonia | 29 Oct. 2014 | 2015-2017 | Sudan | 8 Nov. 2012 | 2013-2015 |
| Finland | 10 Nov. 2014 | 2015-2016 | Sweden | 30 Oct. 2013 | 2014-2016 |
| France | 29 Oct. 2014 | 2015-2017 | Switzerland | 10 Nov. 2014 | 2015-2016 |
| Georgia | 30 Oct. 2013 | 2014-2016 | Togo | 30 Oct. 2013 | 2014-2016 |
| Germany | 29 Oct. 2014 | 2015-2017 | Trinidad and Tobago | 29 Oct. 2014 | 2015-2017 |
| Ghana | 29 Oct. 2014 | 2015-2017 | Tunisia | 8 Nov. 2012 | 2013-2015 |
| Greece | 29 Oct. 2014 | 2015-2017 | Turkmenistan | 8 Nov. 2012 | 2013-2015 |
| Guatemala | 30 Oct. 2013 | 2014-2016 | Uganda | 29 Oct. 2014 | 2015-2017 |
| Haiti | 8 Nov. 2012 | 2013-2015 | United Kingdom | 30 Oct. 2013 | 2014-2016 |
| Honduras | 29 Oct. 2014 | 2015-2017 | United States | 8 Nov. 2012 | 2013-2015 |
| India | 29 Oct. 2014 | 2015-2017 | Zimbabwe | 29 Oct. 2014 | 2015-2017 |

## OFFICERS

| | |
|---|---|
| President | Martin Sajdik (Austria) was elected by acclamation at the 1st plenary meeting, 2014 session (organizational session). |
| Vice-Presidents | Ibrahim Dabbashi (Libya), Oh Joon (Republic of Korea), Carlos Enrique García González (El Salvador) were elected by acclamation at the 1st plenary meeting, 2014 session (organizational session). Vladimir Drobnjak (Croatia) was elected by acclamation at the 2nd plenary meeting, 2014 session (organizational session). María Emma Mejía Vélez (Colombia) was elected by acclamation at the 30th meeting, 2014 session, to complete the term of office of Carlos Enrique García González (El Salvador) (resumed organizational session). Mohamed Khaled Khiari (Tunisia) was elected by acclamation at the 7th meeting, 2015 session, to complete the term of office of Ibrahim Dabbashi (Libya). |
| Secretary | Jennifer De Laurentis |

# RULES OF PROCEDURE

The rules of procedure of the Economic and Social Council contained in document E/5715/Rev.2 (Sales No. E.92.I.22) were in effect during the 2015 session of the Council.

# RESOLUTIONS AND DECISIONS

Resolutions and decisions of the 2015 session are collected in document E/2015/99 (ESCOR, 2015, Suppl. no. 1).

Resolutions are listed separately on pages 93-94 under the heading "List of resolutions".

# CHECK-LIST OF MEETINGS

(Symbol: E/2015/SR.-)

| Meeting | Date, 2014 | Meeting | Date, 2015 | Meeting | Date, 2015 |
|---------|-----------|---------|-----------|---------|-----------|
| 1 | 21 July | 18 | 31 Mar. | 38 | 18 June |
| 2 | 22 July | 19 | 1 Apr. | 39 | 19 June |
| 3 | 5 Dec. | 20 | 1 Apr. | 40 | 19 June |
| 4 | 8 Dec. | 21 | 8 Apr. | 41 | 29 June |
| 5 | 15 Dec. | 22 | 8 Apr. | 42 | 6 July |
| 6 | 15 Dec. | 23 | 9 Apr. | 43 | 7 July |
|   |          | 24 | 10 Apr. | 44 | 8 July |
|   | **Date, 2015** | 25 | 20 Apr. | 45 | 8 July |
|   |          | 26 | 20 Apr. | 46 | 9 July |
| 7 | 13 Jan. | 27 | 21 Apr. | 47 (A) | 9 July |
| 8 | 30 Jan. | 28 | 22 Apr. | 47 (B) | 9 July |
| 9 | 23 Feb. | 29 | 22 Apr. | 48 | 10 July |
| 10 | 23 Feb. | 30 | 15 May | 49 | 10 July |
| 11 | 24 Feb. | 31 | 8 June | 50 | 20 July |
| 12 | 24 Feb. | 32 | 8 June | 51 | 20 July |
| 13 | 25 Feb. | 33 | 9 June | 52 | 21 July |
| 14 | 4 Mar. | 34 | 9 June | 53 | 21 July |
| 15 | 30 Mar. | 35 | 10 June | 54 | 22 July |
| 16 | 30 Mar. | 36 | 10 June | 55 | 22 July |
| 17 | 31 Mar. | 37 | 17 June | 56 | 23 July |

# AGENDA

1. Election of the Bureau.
   *See:* UN. ECONOMIC AND SOCIAL COUNCIL (2014-2015 : NEW YORK AND GENEVA)–OFFICERS

2. Adoption of the agenda and other organizational matters.
   *See:* UN. ECONOMIC AND SOCIAL COUNCIL (2014-2015 : NEW YORK AND GENEVA)–AGENDA

3. Basic programme of work of the Council.
   *See:* UN. ECONOMIC AND SOCIAL COUNCIL–WORK PROGRAMME (2014-2015)

4. Elections, nominations, confirmations, and appointments.

   *See:* INTERNATIONAL NARCOTICS CONTROL BOARD–MEMBERS
   
   JOINT UNITED NATIONS PROGRAMME ON HIV/AIDS. PROGRAMME COORDINATION BOARD–MEMBERS
   
   UN. COMMISSION FOR SOCIAL DEVELOPMENT–MEMBERS
   
   UN. COMMISSION ON CRIME PREVENTION AND CRIMINAL JUSTICE–MEMBERS
   
   UN. COMMISSION ON NARCOTIC DRUGS–MEMBERS
   
   UN. COMMISSION ON POPULATION AND DEVELOPMENT–MEMBERS
   
   UN. COMMISSION ON SCIENCE AND TECHNOLOGY FOR DEVELOPMENT–MEMBERS
   
   UN. COMMISSION ON THE STATUS OF WOMEN–MEMBERS
   
   UN. COMMITTEE FOR DEVELOPMENT POLICY–MEMBERS
   
   UN. COMMITTEE FOR PROGRAMME AND COORDINATION–MEMBERS
   
   UN. COMMITTEE FOR THE UNITED NATIONS POPULATION AWARD—MEMBERS
   
   UN. EXECUTIVE COMMITTEE OF THE UNHCR PROGRAMME—MEMBERS
   
   UN. INTERGOVERNMENTAL WORKING GROUP OF EXPERTS ON INTERNATIONAL STANDARDS OF
        ACCOUNTING AND REPORTING–MEMBERS
   
   UN. PEACEBUILDING COMMISSION. ORGANIZATIONAL COMMITTEE—MEMBERS
   
   UN. PERMANENT FORUM ON INDIGENOUS ISSUES–MEMBERS
   
   UN. STATISTICAL COMMISSION–MEMBERS
   
   UN-HABITAT. GOVERNING COUNCIL–MEMBERS
   
   UN-WOMEN. EXECUTIVE BOARD–MEMBERS
   
   UNDP/UNFPA/UNOPS EXECUTIVE BOARD–MEMBERS
   
   UNICEF. EXECUTIVE BOARD–MEMBERS
   
   WORLD FOOD PROGRAMME. EXECUTIVE BOARD–MEMBERS

5. High-level segment.
   (a) Ministerial Meeting of the High-Level Political Forum on Sustainable Development, convened under the auspices of the Economic and Social Council.
       *See:* SUSTAINABLE DEVELOPMENT–MINISTERIAL MEETING
   (b) High-level policy dialogue with international financial and trade institutions.
       *See:* INTERNATIONAL FINANCIAL INSTITUTIONS
   (c) Annual ministerial review: managing the transition from the Millennium Development Goals to the Sustainable Development Goals: what it will take.
       *See:* SUSTAINABLE DEVELOPMENT GOALS
   (d) Thematic discussion: strengthening and building institutions for policy integration in the post-2015 era.
       *See:* INSTITUTION BUILDING

# AGENDA

6. High-Level Political Forum on Sustainable Development, convened under the auspices of the Economic and Social Council.
   *See:* SUSTAINABLE DEVELOPMENT–HIGH-LEVEL POLITICAL FORUM

7. Operational activities of the United Nations for international development cooperation.
   *See:* OPERATIONAL ACTIVITIES–UN
   (a) Follow-up to policy recommendations of the General Assembly and the Council.
       *See:* UN POLICY RECOMMENDATIONS
   (b) Reports of the Executive Boards of the United Nations Development Programme/United Nations Population Fund/United Nations Office for Project Services, the United Nations Children's Fund, the United Nations Entity for Gender Equality and the Empowerment of Women, and the World Food Programme.
       *See:* UNDP/UNFPA/UNOPS
             UNICEF
             UN-WOMEN
             WORLD FOOD PROGRAMME
   (c) South-South cooperation for development.
       *See:* SOUTH-SOUTH COOPERATION

8. Integration segment.
   *See:* INTEGRATION SEGMENT

9. Special economic, humanitarian and disaster relief assistance.
   *See:* HUMANITARIAN ASSISTANCE

10. The role of the United Nations System in implementing the ministerial declaration of the high-level segment of the substantive session of the Economic and Social Council.

11. Implementation of and follow-up to major United Nations conferences and summits.
    *See:* UN CONFERENCES
    (a) Follow-up to the International Conference on Financing for Development.
        *See:* DEVELOPMENT FINANCE–CONFERENCE (2002 : MONTERREY, MEXICO)
    (b) Review and coordination of the implementation of the Programme of Action for the Least Developed Countries for the Decade 2011-2020.
        *See:* LEAST DEVELOPED COUNTRIES–INTERNATIONAL DECADE (2011-2020)

12. Coordination, programme and other questions.
    *See:* COORDINATION AND PROGRAMMES
    (a) Reports of coordination bodies.
        *See:* COORDINATION-REPORTS
    (b) Proposed programme budget for the biennium 2016-2017.
        *See:* UN–BUDGET (2016-2017)
    (c) Mainstreaming a gender perspective into all policies and programmes in the United Nations System.
        *See:* GENDER MAINSTREAMING–UN SYSTEM
    (d) Long-term programme of support for Haiti.
        *See:* ECONOMIC ASSISTANCE–HAITI
    (e) African countries emerging from conflict.
        *See:* POST-CONFLICT RECONSTRUCTION–AFRICA
    (f) Prevention and control of non-communicable diseases.
        *See:* NON-COMMUNICABLE DISEASES
    (g) Joint United Nations Programme on HIV/AIDS.
        *See:* AIDS
    (h) Calendar of conferences and meetings in the economic, social and related fields.
        *See:* UN–CALENDAR OF MEETINGS

# AGENDA

13. Implementation of General Assembly resolutions 50/227, 52/12 B, 57/270 B, 60/265, 61/16, 67/290 and 68/1.
    *See:* RESOLUTIONS–UN. GENERAL ASSEMBLY–IMPLEMENTATION

14. Implementation of the Declaration on the Granting of Independence to Colonial Countries and Peoples by the specialized agencies and the international institutions associated with the United Nations.
    *See:* DECOLONIZATION

15. Regional cooperation.
    *See:* REGIONAL COOPERATION
    *See also:* REGIONAL COOPERATION–AFRICA
           REGIONAL COOPERATION–ASIA AND THE PACIFIC
           REGIONAL COOPERATION–EUROPE
           REGIONAL COOPERATION–LATIN AMERICA AND THE CARIBBEAN
           REGIONAL COOPERATION–WESTERN ASIA

16. Economic and social repercussions of the Israeli occupation on the living conditions of the Palestinian people in the Occupied Palestinian Territory, including East Jerusalem, and the Arab population in the occupied Syrian Golan.
    *See:* PALESTINIANS–TERRITORIES OCCUPIED BY ISRAEL–LIVING CONDITIONS

17. Non-governmental organizations.
    *See:* NON-GOVERNMENTAL ORGANIZATIONS

18. Economic and environmental questions.
    *See:* ENVIRONMENT–ECONOMIC ASPECTS
    (a) Sustainable development.
        *See:* SUSTAINABLE DEVELOPMENT
    (b) Science and technology for development.
        *See:* SCIENCE AND TECHNOLOGY–DEVELOPMENT
    (c) Statistics.
        *See:* STATISTICS
    (d) Human settlements.
        *See:* HUMAN SETTLEMENTS
    (e) Environment.
        *See:* ENVIRONMENT
    (f) Population and development.
        *See:* POPULATION–DEVELOPMENT
    (g) Public administration and development.
        *See:* PUBLIC ADMINISTRATION
    (h) International cooperation in tax matters.
        *See:* TAXATION
    (i) Cartography.
        *See:* CARTOGRAPHY
    (j) Women and development.
        *See:* WOMEN IN DEVELOPMENT
    (k) United Nations Forum on Forests.
        *See:* UN FORUM ON FORESTS
    (l) Transport of dangerous goods.
        *See:* DANGEROUS GOODS TRANSPORT
    (m) Assistance to 3rd States affected by the application of sanctions.
        *See:* SANCTIONS COMPLIANCE–ECONOMIC ASSISTANCE

# AGENDA

19.  Social and human rights questions.
     (a)  Advancement of women.
          *See:* WOMEN'S ADVANCEMENT
     (b)  Social development.
          *See:* SOCIAL DEVELOPMENT
     (c)  Crime prevention and criminal justice.
          *See:* CRIME PREVENTION
     (d)  Narcotic drugs.
          *See:* NARCOTIC DRUGS
     (e)  United Nations High Commissioner for Refugees.
          *See:* REFUGEES
     (f)  Comprehensive implementation of the Durban Declaration and Programme of Action.
          *See:* RACIAL DISCRIMINATION–PROGRAMME OF ACTION
     (g)  Human rights.
          *See:* HUMAN RIGHTS
          *See also:* ECONOMIC, SOCIAL AND CULTURAL RIGHTS–TREATY (1966)
     (h)  Permanent Forum on Indigenous Issues.
          *See:* UN. PERMANENT FORUM ON INDIGENOUS ISSUES

20.  United Nations research and training institutes.
     *See:* UN–TRAINING AND RESEARCH INSTITUTIONS

# OTHER MATTERS INCLUDED IN THE INDEX

## AIDS (Agenda item 12g)

### Reports

E/2015/8  Joint United Nations Programme on HIV/AIDS : note / by the Secretary-General.
Issued: 28 Jan. 2015. - Transmits report of the Executive Director of the Joint United Nations Programme on HIV/AIDS (UNAIDS), prepared pursuant to Economic and Social Council resolution 2013/11.

### Draft resolutions/decisions

E/2015/L.5  Joint United Nations Programme on HIV/AIDS : draft resolution / submitted by the President of the Council, Martin Sajdik (Austria), on the basis of informal consultations.

### Discussion in plenary

E/2015/SR.22  (8 Apr. 2015).
At the 22nd meeting, draft resolution E/2015/L.5 was adopted without vote: resolution 2015/2.

### Resolutions

E/RES/2015/2  Joint United Nations Programme on HIV/AIDS : resolution / adopted by the Economic and Social Council.
(Adopted without vote, 22nd plenary meeting, 8 Apr. 2015)

## BRETTON WOODS INSTITUTIONS

### General documents

E/2015/52  Coherence, coordination and cooperation in the context of financing for sustainable development and the post-2015 development agenda : note / by the Secretary-General.

### Discussion in plenary

E/2015/SR.25  (20 Apr. 2015).

E/2015/SR.26  (20 Apr. 2015).

E/2015/SR.27  (21 Apr. 2015).

## CARTOGRAPHY (Agenda item 18i)

### Reports

E/2015/46  (E/C.20/2015/17)  (ESCOR, 2015, Suppl. no. 26)  Committee of Experts on Global Geospatial Information Management : report on the 5th session (5-7 August 2015).
Issued: 2015.

### Discussion in plenary

E/2015/SR.55  (22 July 2015).

## COORDINATION AND PROGRAMMES (Agenda item 12)

### Discussion in plenary

E/2015/SR.6  (15 Dec. 2014).

## COORDINATION-REPORTS (Agenda item 12a)

### Reports

E/2015/71  Annual overview report of the United Nations System Chief Executives Board for Coordination for 2014.
Issued: 29 Apr. 2015.

### Discussion in plenary

E/2015/SR.35  (10 June 2015).

E/2015/SR.52  (21 July 2015).
At the 52nd meeting, the Council took note of the report of the Committee on its 55th session (A/70/16), the annual overview report of the United Nations System Chief Executive Board for Coordination for 2014 (E/2015/71) and the relevant sections of the proposed programme budget for the biennium 2016-2017 (A/70/6): decision 2015/232.

## CRIME PREVENTION (Agenda item 19c)

### Reports

E/2015/30  (E/CN.15/2015/19)  (ESCOR, 2015, Suppl. no. 10)  Commission on Crime Prevention and Criminal Justice : report on the 24th session (5 December 2014 and 18-22 May 2015).
Issued: 2015.

E/2015/30/Add.1  (E/CN.15/2015/19/Add.1)  (ESCOR, 2015, Suppl. no. 10A)  Commission on Crime Prevention and Criminal Justice : report on the reconvened 24th session (10-11 December 2015).
Issued: 2016.

E/2015/49  Capital punishment and implementation of the safeguards guaranteeing protection of the rights of those facing the death penalty : report of the Secretary-General.
Issued: 13 Apr. 2015.

E/2015/49/Corr.1  Capital punishment and implementation of the safeguards guaranteeing protection of the rights of those facing the death penalty : report of the Secretary-General : corrigendum.
Issued: 12 June 2015. - Corrects text.

E/2015/81  (A/70/90)  Thirteenth United Nations Congress on Crime Prevention and Criminal Justice : report of the Secretary-General.
Issued: 9 June 2015.

## CRIME PREVENTION (Agenda item 19c) (continued)

### Discussion in plenary

E/2015/SR.53 (21 July 2015).
At the 53rd meeting, draft decision in E/2014/30/Add.1 entitled "Report of the Commission on Crime Prevention and Criminal Justice on its reconvened 23rd session" was adopted without vote: decision 2015/233; action on draft resolutions in E/2015/30-E/CN.15/2015/19, Section A was as follows: draft resolution I entitled "Thirteenth United Nations Congress on Crime Prevention and Criminal Justice", adopted without vote: resolution 2015/19; draft resolution II entitled "United Nations Standard Minimum Rules for the Treatment of Prisoners (the Mandela Rules)", adopted without vote: resolution 2015/20; draft resolution III entitled "Taking action against gender-related killing of women and girls", adopted without vote: resolution 2015/21; draft resolution IV entitled "Technical assistance for implementing the international conventions and protocols related to counter-terrorism", adopted without vote: resolution 2015/22; action on draft resolutions in E/2015/30-E/CN.15/2015/19, Section B was as follows: draft resolution I entitled "Implementation of the United Nations Global Plan of Action to Combat Trafficking in Persons", adopted without vote: resolution 2015/23; draft resolution II entitled "Improving the quality and availability of statistics on crime and criminal justice for policy development", adopted without vote: resolution 2015/24; action on draft decisions in E/2015/30-E/CN.15/2015/19, Section C was as follows: draft decision I entitled "Improving the governance and financial situation of the United Nations Office on Drugs and Crime: extension of the mandate of the standing Open-ended Intergovernmental Working Group on Improving the Governance and Financial Situation of the United Nations Office on Drugs and Crime", adopted without vote: decision 2015/234; draft decision II entitled "Report of the Commission on Crime Prevention and Criminal Justice on its 24th session and provisional agenda for its 25th session", adopted without vote: decision 2015/235; draft decision III entitled "Appointment of a member of the Board of Trustees of the United Nations Interregional Crime and Justice Research Institute", adopted without vote: decision 2015/236; at the same meeting, the Council took note of the report of the Secretary-General on the 13th United Nations Congress on Crime Prevention and Criminal Justice (A/70/90-E/2015/81), the report of the Secretary-General on capital punishment and implementation of the safeguards guaranteeing protection of the rights of those facing the death penalty (E/2015/49 and E/2015/49/Corr.1): decision 2015/240.

### Resolutions

E/RES/2015/19 Thirteenth United Nations Congress on Crime Prevention and Criminal Justice : resolution / adopted by the Economic and Social Council.
(Adopted without vote, 53rd plenary meeting, 21 July 2015)

## CRIME PREVENTION (Agenda item 19c) (continued)

E/RES/2015/20 United Nations Standard Minimum Rules for the Treatment of Prisoners (the Mandela Rules) : resolution / adopted by the Economic and Social Council.
(Adopted without vote, 53rd plenary meeting, 21 July 2015)

E/RES/2015/21 Taking action against gender-related killing of women and girls : resolution / adopted by the Economic and Social Council.
(Adopted without vote, 53rd plenary meeting, 21 July 2015)

E/RES/2015/22 Technical assistance for implementing the international conventions and protocols related to counter-terrorism : resolution / adopted by the Economic and Social Council.
(Adopted without vote, 53rd plenary meeting, 21 July 2015)

E/RES/2015/23 Implementation of the United Nations Global Plan of Action to Combat Trafficking in Persons : resolution / adopted by the Economic and Social Council.
(Adopted without vote, 53rd plenary meeting, 21 July 2015)

E/RES/2015/24 Improving the quality and availability of statistics on crime and criminal justice for policy development : resolution / adopted by the Economic and Social Council.
(Adopted without vote, 53rd plenary meeting, 21 July 2015)

## DANGEROUS GOODS TRANSPORT (Agenda item 18l)

### Reports

E/2015/66 Work of the Committee of Experts on the Transport of Dangerous Goods and on the Globally Harmonized System of Classification and Labelling of Chemicals : report of the Secretary-General.
Issued: 20 Apr. 2015.

### Discussion in plenary

E/2015/SR.32 (8 June 2015).
At the 32nd meeting, draft resolution in E/2015/66 entitled "Work of the Committee of Experts on the Transport of Dangerous Goods and on the Globally Harmonized System of Classification and Labelling of Chemicals" was adopted without vote: resolution 2015/7.

### Resolutions

E/RES/2015/7 Work of the Committee of Experts on the Transport of Dangerous Goods and on the Globally Harmonized System of Classification and Labelling of Chemicals : resolution / adopted by the Economic and Social Council.
(Adopted without vote, 32nd plenary meeting, 8 June 2015)

## DECOLONIZATION (Agenda item 14)

### Reports

E/2015/57 (A/70/76) Assistance to the Palestinian people : report of the Secretary-General.
Issued: 1 Apr. 2015.

E/2015/65 Report of the President of the Council on consultations with the Special Committee on the Situation with Regard to the Implementation of the Declaration on the Granting of Independence to Colonial Countries and Peoples : information submitted by the specialized agencies and other organizations of the United Nations system on their activities with regard to the implementation of the Declaration.
Issued: 16 Apr. 2015.

### Draft resolutions/decisions

E/2015/L.24 Support to Non-Self-Governing Territories by the specialized agencies and international institutions associated with the United Nations : draft resolution'/ Bolivia (Plurinational State of), Cuba, Ecuador, Nicaragua and Venezuela (Bolivarian Republic of).

### Discussion in plenary

E/2015/SR.50 (20 July 2015).
At the 50th meeting, draft resolution E/2015/L.24 was adopted (19-0-25): resolution 2015/16.

### Resolutions

E/RES/2015/16 Support to Non-Self-Governing Territories by the specialized agencies and international institutions associated with the United Nations : resolution / adopted by the Economic and Social Council.
(Adopted 19-0-25, 50th plenary meeting, 20 July 2015)

## DEVELOPMENT FINANCE–CONFERENCE (2002 : MONTERREY, MEXICO) (Agenda item 11a)

### General documents

E/2015/77 (A/70/85) Summary by the President of the Economic and Social Council of the Special High-Level Meeting of the Council with the World Bank, the International Monetary Fund, the World Trade Organization and the United Nations Conference on Trade and Development (New York, 20 and 21 April 2015).

### Discussion in plenary

E/2015/SR.33 (9 June 2015).

## EBOLA VIRUS DISEASE

### Discussion in plenary

E/2015/SR.3 (5 Dec. 2014).

## ECONOMIC ASSISTANCE–HAITI (Agenda item 12d)

### Reports

E/2015/84 Report of the Ad Hoc Advisory Group on Haiti.
Issued: 30 June 2015.

## ECONOMIC ASSISTANCE–HAITI (Agenda item 12d) (continued)

### General documents

E/2015/87 Note verbale, 22 July 2015, from the Dominican Republic. Rejects alleged negative characterization of the Dominican Republic in some sections of the report presented on 21 July 2015 by the Ad Hoc Advisory Group on Haiti to the members of the Council (E/2015/84).

### Draft resolutions/decisions

E/2015/L.18 Ad Hoc Advisory Group on Haiti : draft resolution / Canada.

E/2015/L.18/Rev.1 Ad Hoc Advisory Group on Haiti : draft resolution / Argentina, Benin, Brazil, Canada, Chile, Colombia, Croatia, Cyprus, Czech Republic, Estonia, Finland, Georgia, Germany, Greece, Guatemala, Haiti, Israel, Italy, Japan, Luxembourg, Mali, Mexico, Morocco, Peru, Poland, Slovenia, Spain, Sweden, Trinidad and Tobago, United States of America and Uruguay.

### Discussion in plenary

E/2015/SR.52 (21 July 2015).
At the 52nd meeting, draft resolution E/2015/L.18/Rev.1 was adopted without vote: resolution 2015/18.

### Resolutions

E/RES/2015/18 Ad Hoc Advisory Group on Haiti : resolution / adopted by the Economic and Social Council.
(Adopted without vote, 52nd plenary meeting, 21 July 2015)

## ECONOMIC SURVEYS

### Reports

E/2015/50 World economic and social survey. 2014/2015, MDG lessons for post-2015 : overview.
Issued: 20 Apr. 2015.

E/2015/50/Rev.1 (ST/ESA/360) World economic and social survey. 2014/2015, Learning from national policies supporting MDG implementation.
Issued: 2016.

E/2015/73 World economic situation and prospects as of mid-2015.
Issued: 7 May 2015.

## ECONOMIC, SOCIAL AND CULTURAL RIGHTS–TREATY (1966) (Agenda item 19g)

### Reports

E/2015/22 (E/C.12/2014/3) (ESCOR, 2015, Suppl. no. 2) Committee on Economic, Social and Cultural Rights : report on the 52nd and 53rd sessions (28 April-23 May 2014, 10-28 November 2014).
Issued: 2015.

## GENDER MAINSTREAMING–UN SYSTEM (Agenda item 12c)

### Reports

E/2015/58  Mainstreaming a gender perspective into all policies and programmes in the United Nations system : report of the Secretary-General.
Issued: 1 Apr. 2015.

### Draft resolutions/decisions

E/2015/L.11  Mainstreaming a gender perspective into all policies and programmes in the United Nations system : draft resolution / submitted by the Vice-President of the Council, Oh Joon (Republic of Korea), on the basis of informal consultations.

### Discussion in plenary

E/2015/SR.32  (8 June 2015).

E/2015/SR.36  (10 June 2015).
At the 36th meeting, draft resolution E/2015/L.11, as orally amended, was adopted without vote: resolution 2015/12.

### Resolutions

E/RES/2015/12  Mainstreaming a gender perspective into all policies and programmes in the Untied Nations system : resolution / adopted by the Economic and Social Council.
(Adopted without vote, 36th plenary meeting, 10 June 2015)

## HUMAN RIGHTS (Agenda item 19g)

### Reports

E/2015/59  Report of the United Nations High Commissioner for Human Rights.
Issued: 19 May 2015.

### Discussion in plenary

E/2015/SR.53  (21 July 2015).
At the 53rd meeting, the Council took note of the report of the United Nations High Commissioner for Human Rights (E/2015/59), the report of the Committee on Economic, Social and Cultural Rights on its 52nd and 53rd sessions (E/2015/22) and the report of the Committee on the Rights of Persons with Disabilities on its 9th to 12th sessions (A/70/55): decision 2015/241.

## HUMAN SETTLEMENTS (Agenda item 18d)

### Reports

E/2015/72  Coordinated implementation of the Habitat Agenda : report of the Secretary-General.
Issued: 5 May 2015.

### Draft resolutions/decisions

E/2015/L.17  Human settlements : draft resolution / South Africa [on behalf of the Group of 77 and China].

### Discussion in plenary

E/2015/SR.50  (20 July 2015).

## HUMAN SETTLEMENTS (Agenda item 18d) (continued)

E/2015/SR.55  (22 July 2015).
At the 55th meeting, draft resolution E/2015/L.17, as orally revised, was adopted without vote: resolution 2015/34.

### Resolutions

E/RES/2015/34  Human settlements : resolution / adopted by the Economic and Social Council.
(Adopted without vote, 55th plenary meeting, 22 July 2015)

## HUMANITARIAN ASSISTANCE (Agenda item 9)

### Reports

E/2015/64  (A/70/77)  Strengthening of the coordination of emergency humanitarian assistance of the United Nations : report of the Secretary-General.
Issued: 17 Apr. 2015.

### Draft resolutions/decisions

E/2015/L.15  Strengthening of the coordination of emergency humanitarian assistance of the United Nations : draft resolution / submitted by the Vice-President of the Council, Mohamed Khaled Khiari (Tunisia), on the basis of informal consultations.

### Discussion in plenary

E/2015/SR.37  (17 June 2015).

E/2015/SR.38  (18 June 2015).

E/2015/SR.39  (19 June 2015).

E/2015/SR.40  (19 June 2015).
At the 40th meeting, draft resolution E/2015/L.15 was adopted without vote: resolution 2015/14.

### Resolutions

E/RES/2015/14  Strengthening of the coordination of emergency humanitarian assistance of the United Nations : resolution / adopted by the Economic and Social Council.
(Adopted without vote, 40th plenary meeting, 19 June 2015)

## INSTITUTION BUILDING (Agenda item 5d)

### Reports

E/2015/69  Strengthening and building institutions for policy integration in the post-2015 era : report of the Secretary-General.
Issued: 24 Apr. 2015.

### Discussion in plenary

E/2015/SR.43  (7 July 2015).

E/2015/SR.44  (8 July 2015).

E/2015/SR.49  (10 July 2015).

## INTERNATIONAL FINANCIAL INSTITUTIONS (Agenda item 5b)

### Discussion in plenary

E/2015/SR.46 (9 July 2015).

## INTERNATIONAL NARCOTICS CONTROL BOARD– MEMBERS (Agenda item 4)

### General documents

E/2015/1/Add.1 Agenda : Economic and Social Council, 2015 session, 21 July 2014-22 July 2015 : addendum.

E/2015/9/Add.1 Election of 1 member of the International Narcotics Control Board from among candidates nominated by the World Health Organization : note / by the Secretary-General.

### Discussion in plenary

E/2015/SR.21 (8 Apr. 2015).
At the 21st meeting, Richard P. Mattick (Australia) was elected as a member of the International Narcotics Control Board for a term beginning on the date of election and expiring on 1 Mar. 2017: decision 2015/201 B.

## JOINT UNITED NATIONS PROGRAMME ON HIV/AIDS. PROGRAMME COORDINATION BOARD–MEMBERS (Agenda item 4)

### General documents

E/2015/1/Add.1 Agenda : Economic and Social Council, 2015 session, 21 July 2014-22 July 2015 : addendum.

E/2015/9/Add.10 Election of 9 members of the Programme Coordinating Board of the Joint United Nations Programme on HIV/AIDS : note / by the Secretary-General.

### Discussion in plenary

E/2015/SR.21 (8 Apr. 2015).
At the 21st meeting, China, Ecuador, Ghana, Japan, Malawi and Russian Federation were elected as members of the Programme Coordinating Board of the Joint United Nations Programme on HIV/AIDS by acclamation for a 3-year term beginning on 1 Jan. 2016 and expiring on 31 Dec. 2018: decision 2015/201 B.

## LEAST DEVELOPED COUNTRIES– INTERNATIONAL DECADE (2011-2020) (Agenda item 11b)

### Reports

E/2015/75 (A/70/83) Implementation of the Programme of Action for the Least Developed Countries for the Decade 2011-2020 : report of the Secretary-General.
Issued: 11 May 2015.

### Draft resolutions/decisions

E/2015/L.23 Programme of Action for the Least Developed Countries for the Decade 2011-2020 : draft resolution / South Africa [on behalf of the Group of 77 and China].

## LEAST DEVELOPED COUNTRIES– INTERNATIONAL DECADE (2011-2020) (Agenda item 11b) (continued)

### Discussion in plenary

E/2015/SR.55 (22 July 2015).

E/2015/SR.56 (23 July 2015).
At the 56th meeting, draft resolution E/2015/L.23, as revised, was adopted without vote: resolution 2015/35.

### Resolutions

E/RES/2015/35 Programme of Action for the Least Developed Countries for the Decade 2011-2020 : resolution / adopted by the Economic and Social Council.
(Adopted without vote, 56th plenary meeting, 23 July 2015)

## MILLENNIUM DEVELOPMENT GOALS

### Reports

E/2015/50 World economic and social survey. 2014/2015, MDG lessons for post-2015 : overview.
Issued: 20 Apr. 2015.

E/2015/50/Rev.1 (ST/ESA/360) World economic and social survey. 2014/2015, Learning from national policies supporting MDG implementation.
Issued: 2016.

E/2015/60 Letter, 1 Apr. 2015, from the Philippines. Transmits national report of the Philippines on progress towards the achievement of the internationally agreed goals, including the Millennium Development Goals, for the annual ministerial review to be held during the high-level segment of the 2015 session of the Economic and Social Council.

E/2015/61 Letter, 9 Apr. 2015, from Mongolia. Transmits national report of Mongolia on progress towards the achievement of the internationally agreed goals, including the Millennium Development Goals, for the annual ministerial review to be held during the high-level segment of the 2015 session of the Economic and Social Council.

E/2015/62 Letter, 10 Apr. 2015, from Kyrgyzstan. Transmits national report of Kyrgyzstan on progress towards the achievement of the internationally agreed goals, including the Millennium Development Goals, for the annual ministerial review to be held during the high-level segment of the 2015 session of the Economic and Social Council.

E/2015/63 Letter, 1 Apr. 2015, from Zambia. Transmits national report of Zambia on progress towards the achievement of the internationally agreed goals, including the Millennium Development Goals, for the annual ministerial review to be held during the high-level segment of the 2015 session of the Economic and Social Council.

E/2015/68 Managing the transition from the Millennium Development Goals to the sustainable development goals : what it will take : report of the Secretary-General.
Issued: 24 Apr. 2015.

## MILLENNIUM DEVELOPMENT GOALS (continued)

### Discussion in plenary

E/2015/SR.44  (8 July 2015).

E/2015/SR.45  (8 July 2015).

E/2015/SR.46  (9 July 2015).

E/2015/SR.48  (10 July 2015).

## NARCOTIC DRUGS (Agenda item 19d)

### Reports

E/2015/28  (E/CN.7/2015/15) (ESCOR, 2015, Suppl. no. 8) Commission on Narcotic Drugs : report on the 58th session (5 December 2014 and 9-17 March 2015).
Issued: 2015.

E/2015/28/Add.1  (E/CN.7/2015/15/Add.1) (ESCOR, 2015, Suppl. no. 8A) Commission on Narcotic Drugs : report on the reconvened 58th session (9-11 December 2015).
Issued: 2016.

E/2015/79  (A/70/87) Report on the progress made by the Commission on Narcotic Drugs in preparation for the special session of the General Assembly on the world drug problem to be held in 2016 : note / by the Secretary-General.
Issued: 14 May 2015. - Transmits, pursuant to General Assembly resolution 69/200, the report of the Commission on Narcotic Drugs on the progress made in preparation for the special session of the General Assembly on the world drug problem to be held in 2016.

### Discussion in plenary

E/2015/SR.53  (21 July 2015).
At the 53rd meeting, action on draft resolution and draft decisions in E/2015/28-E/CN.7/2015/15 was as follows: draft resolution entitled "Special session of the General Assembly on the world drug problem to be held in 2016", adopted without vote: resolution 2015/25; draft decision I entitled "Improving the governance and financial situation of the United Nations Office on Drugs and Crime: extension of the mandate of the standing open-ended intergovernmental working group on improving the governance and financial situation of the United Nations Office on Drugs and Crime", adopted without vote: decision 2015/237; draft decision II entitled "Report of the Commission on Narcotic Drugs on its 58th session and provisional agenda for its 59th session", adopted without vote: decision 2015/238; draft decision III entitled "Report of the International Narcotics Control Board", adopted without vote: decision 2015/239; at the same meeting, the Council took note of the note by the Secretary-General transmitting the report on the progress made by the Commission on Narcotic Drugs in preparation for the special session of the General Assembly on the world drug problem to be held in 2016 (A/70/87-E/2015/79): decision 2015/240.

## NARCOTIC DRUGS (Agenda item 19d) (continued)

### Resolutions

E/RES/2015/25  Special session of the General Assembly on the world drug problem to be held in 2016 : resolution / adopted by the Economic and Social Council.
(Adopted without vote, 53rd plenary meeting, 21 July 2015)

## NON-COMMUNICABLE DISEASES (Agenda item 12f)

### Reports

E/2015/53  United Nations Inter-Agency Task Force on the Prevention and Control of Non-Communicable Diseases : note / by the Secretary-General.
Issued: 25 Mar. 2015. - Transmits report of the Director General of the World Health Organization on the UN Inter-Agency Task Force on the Prevention and Control of Non-Communicable Diseases, submitted pursuant to Economic and Social Council resolution 2014/10.

### Draft resolutions/decisions

E/2015/L.14  United Nations Inter-Agency Task Force on the Prevention and Control of Non-Communicable Diseases : draft resolution / Belarus, Russian Federation and Turkmenistan.

### Discussion in plenary

E/2015/SR.33  (9 June 2015).
At the 33rd meeting, draft resolution E/2015/L.14 was adopted without vote: resolution 2015/8.

E/2015/SR.47 (A)  (9 July 2015).

### Resolutions

E/RES/2015/8  United Nations Inter-Agency Task Force on the Prevention and Control of Non-Communicable Diseases : resolution / adopted by the Economic and Social Council.
(Adopted without vote, 33rd plenary meeting, 9 June 2015)

## NON-GOVERNMENTAL ORGANIZATIONS (Agenda item 17)

### Reports

E/2015/32 (Part I)  Report of the Committee on Non-Governmental Organizations on its 2015 regular session (New York, 26 January to 4 February and 6 and 13 February 2015).
Issued: 18 Feb. 2015.

E/2015/32 (Part II)  Report of the Committee on Non-Governmental Organizations on its 2015 resumed session (New York, 26 May-3 June and 12 June 2015).
Issued: 17 June 2015.

## NON-GOVERNMENTAL ORGANIZATIONS (Agenda item 17) (continued)

### General documents

E/2015/INF/5 List of non-governmental organizations in consultative status with the Economic and Social Council as of 1 September 2015 : note / by the Secretary-General.

### Draft resolutions/decisions

E/2015/L.21 Application of the non-governmental organization Freedom Now for consultative status with the Economic and Social Council : draft decision / Australia, France, Germany, Switzerland, United Kingdom of Great Britain and Northern Ireland, United States of America and Uruguay.

E/2015/L.25 Application of the non-governmental organization Palestinian Return Centre for consultative status with the Economic and Social Council : draft decision / Israel.

### Discussion in plenary

E/2015/SR.22 (8 Apr. 2015).
At the 22nd meeting, action on draft decisions in E/2015/32 (Part I) was as follows: draft decision I entitled "Applications for consultative status and requests for reclassification received from non-governmental organizations", adopted without vote: decision 2015/207; draft decision II entitled "Withdrawal of consultative status of non-governmental organizations", adopted without vote: decision 2015/208; draft decision III entitled "Report of the Committee on Non-Governmental Organizations on its 2015 regular session", adopted without vote: decision 2015/209.

E/2015/SR.47 (A) (9 July 2015).

## NON-GOVERNMENTAL ORGANIZATIONS (Agenda item 17) (continued)

E/2015/SR.51 (20 July 2015).
At the 51st meeting, action on draft decisions was as follows: draft decision E/2015/L.21, adopted (29-9-11): decision 2015/222; draft decision E/2015/L.25, rejected (16-13-18); at the same meeting, action on draft decisions in E/2015/32 (Part II) was as follows: draft decision I entitled "Applications for consultative status and requests for reclassification received from non-governmental organizations", adopted without vote: decision 2015/223; draft decision II entitled "Withdrawal of consultative status of the non-governmental organization African Technical Association", adopted without vote: decision 2015/224; draft decision III entitled "Withdrawal of consultative status of the non-governmental organization African Technology Development Link", adopted without vote: decision 2015/225; draft decision IV entitled "Suspension of consultative status of non-governmental organizations with outstanding quadrennial reports, pursuant to Council resolution 2008/4", adopted without vote: decision 2015/226; draft decision V entitled "Reinstatement of consultative status of non-governmental organizations that submitted outstanding quadrennial reports, pursuant to Council resolution 2008/4", adopted without vote: decision 2015/227; draft decision VI entitled "Withdrawal of consultative status of non-governmental organizations in accordance with Council resolution 2008/4", adopted without vote: decision 2015/228; draft decision VII entitled "Dates and provisional agenda of the 2016 session of the Committee on Non-Governmental Organizations", adopted without vote: decision 2015/229; draft decision VIII entitled "Report of the Committee on Non-Governmental Organizations on its 2015 resumed session", adopted without vote: decision 2015/230.

## OPERATIONAL ACTIVITIES–UN (Agenda item 7)

### Draft resolutions/decisions

E/2015/L.3 Progress in the implementation of General Assembly resolution 67/226 on the quadrennial comprehensive policy review of operational activities for development of the United Nations system : draft resolution / South Africa [on behalf of the Group of 77 and China].
The draft resolution was withdrawn by its sponsors in the light of the adoption of draft resolution E/2015/L.16 (E/2015/SR.41).

E/2015/L.16 Progress in the implementation of General Assembly resolution 67/226 on the quadrennial comprehensive policy review of operational activities for development of the United Nations system : draft resolution / submitted by the Vice-President of the Council, María Emma Mejía Vélez (Colombia), on the basis of informal consultations on draft resolution E/2015/L.3.

### Discussion in plenary

E/2015/SR.5 (15 Dec. 2014).

E/2015/SR.6 (15 Dec. 2014).

E/2015/SR.8 (30 Jan. 2015).

E/2015/SR.9 (23 Feb. 2015).

## OPERATIONAL ACTIVITIES–UN (Agenda item 7) (continued)

E/2015/SR.10  (23 Feb. 2015).

E/2015/SR.34  (9 June 2015).

E/2015/SR.41  (29 June 2015).
At the 41st meeting, draft resolution E/2015/L.16 was adopted without vote: resolution 2015/15; draft resolution E/2015/L.3 was withdrawn.

### Resolutions

E/RES/2015/15  Progress in the implementation of General Assembly resolution 67/226 on the quadrennial comprehensive policy review of operational activities for development of the United Nations system : resolution / adopted by the Economic and Social Council.
(Adopted without vote, 41st plenary meeting, 29 June 2015)

## PALESTINIANS–TERRITORIES OCCUPIED BY ISRAEL–LIVING CONDITIONS (Agenda item 16)

### Reports

E/2015/13  (A/70/82)  Economic and social repercussions of the Israeli occupation on the living conditions of the Palestinian people in the Occupied Palestinian Territory, including East Jerusalem, and the Arab population in the occupied Syrian Golan : note / by the Secretary-General.
Issued: 8 May 2015. - Transmits report prepared by the Economic and Social Commission for Western Asia, submitted in response to the Economic and Social Council resolution 2014/26 and General Assembly resolution 69/241.

### Draft resolutions/decisions

E/2015/L.22  Economic and social repercussions of the Israeli occupation on the living conditions of the Palestinian people in the Occupied Palestinian Territory, including East Jerusalem, and the Arab population in the occupied Syrian Golan : draft resolution / South Africa [on behalf the Group of 77 and China].

### Discussion in plenary

E/2015/SR.50  (20 July 2015).
At the 50th meeting, draft resolution E/2015/L.22 was adopted (42-2-2): resolution 2015/17.

### Resolutions

E/RES/2015/17  Economic and social repercussions of the Israeli occupation on the living conditions of the Palestinian people in the Occupied Palestinian Territory, including East Jerusalem, and the Arab population in the occupied Syrian Golan : resolution / adopted by the Economic and Social Council.
(Adopted 42-2-2, 50th plenary meeting, 20 July 2015)

## POPULATION–DEVELOPMENT (Agenda item 18f)

### Reports

E/2015/25  (E/CN.9/2015/7)  (ESCOR, 2015, Suppl. no. 5)  Commission on Population and Development : report on the 48th session (11 April 2014 and 13-17 April 2015).
Issued: 2015.

### Discussion in plenary

E/2015/SR.55  (22 July 2015).
At the 55th meeting, action on draft decisions in E/2015/25 was as follows: draft decision entitled "Report of the Commission on Population and Development on its 48th session and provisional agenda for its 49th session", adopted without vote: decision 2015/253; draft decision entitled "Future organization and methods of work of the Commission on Population and Development", adopted without vote: decision 2015/252.

## POST-CONFLICT RECONSTRUCTION–AFRICA (Agenda item 12e)

### Reports

E/2015/74  Implementation of integrated, coherent and coordinated support to South Sudan by the United Nations system : report of the Secretary-General.
Issued: 11 May 2015.

### Draft resolutions/decisions

E/2015/L.20  African countries emerging from conflict : draft decision / submitted by the Vice-President of the Council, Oh Joon (Republic of Korea).

### Discussion in plenary

E/2015/SR.52  (21 July 2015).
At the 52nd meeting, draft decision E/2015/L.20 was adopted without vote: decision 2015/231.

## PUBLIC ADMINISTRATION (Agenda item 18g)

### Reports

E/2015/44  (E/C.16/2015/7)  (ESCOR, 2015, Suppl. no. 24)  Committee of Experts on Public Administration : report on the 14th session (20-24 April 2015).
Issued: 2015.

### Discussion in plenary

E/2015/SR.54  (22 July 2015).
At the 54th meeting, action on draft resolution and draft decision in E/2015/44 was as follows: draft resolution entitled "Report of the Committee of Experts on Public Administration on its 14th session", adopted without vote: resolution 2015/28; draft decision entitled "Venue, dates and provisional agenda of the 15th session of Committee of Experts on Public Administration", adopted without vote: decision 2015/247.

### Resolutions

E/RES/2015/28  Report of the Committee of Experts on Public Administration on its 14th session : resolution / adopted by the Economic and Social Council.
(Adopted without vote, 54th plenary meeting, 22 July 2015)

## RACIAL DISCRIMINATION–PROGRAMME OF ACTION (Agenda item 19f)

### Discussion in plenary

E/2015/SR.53 (21 July 2015).

## REFUGEES (Agenda item 19e)

### Discussion in plenary

E/2015/SR.53 (21 July 2015).

## REGIONAL COOPERATION (Agenda item 15)

### Reports

E/2015/15 Regional cooperation in the economic, social and related fields : report of the Secretary-General.
Issued: 11 May 2015.

E/2015/15/Add.1 Regional cooperation in the economic, social and related fields : report of the Secretary-General : addendum.
Issued: 11 May 2015.

E/2015/15/Add.2 Regional cooperation in the economic, social and related fields : report of the Secretary-General : addendum.
Issued: 11 June 2015.

E/2015/16 Economic situation in the Economic Commission for Europe region (Europe, North America and the Commonwealth of Independent States), 2014-2015 : note / by the Secretary-General.
Issued: 20 Apr. 2015. - Transmits report on the economic situation in the Economic Commission for Europe region (Europe, North America and the Commonwealth of Independent States) for the period 2014-2015.

E/2015/17 Overview of economic and social conditions in Africa, 2014-2015 : note / by the Secretary-General.
Issued: 29 Apr. 2015. - Transmits an overview report of the economic and social conditions in Africa for the period 2014-2015.

E/2015/19 Situation and outlook for Latin America and the Caribbean 2014-2015 : note / by the Secretary-General.
Issued: 8 May 2015. - Transmits report on the situation and outlook for Latin America and the Caribbean for the period 2014-2015.

E/2015/21 Project for a Europe-Africa fixed link through the Strait of Gibraltar : note / by the Secretary-General.
Issued: 20 Apr. 2015. - Transmits report prepared in accordance with the Economic and Social Council resolution 2009/11 by the Executive Secretaries of the Economic Commission for Europe and the Economic Commission for Africa on the activities carried out within the framework of the project for a Europe-Africa fixed link through the Strait of Gibraltar.

### General documents

E/2015/18 Summary of the Economic and Social Survey of Asia and the Pacific 2015 : note / by the Secretary-General.

## REGIONAL COOPERATION (Agenda item 15) (continued)

E/2015/20 Summary of the survey of economic and social developments in the Economic and Social Commission for Western Asia region, 2014-2015 : note / by the Secretary-General.

### Discussion in plenary

E/2015/SR.47 (B) (9 July 2015).

E/2015/SR.54 (22 July 2015).
At the 54th meeting, the Council took note of the reports contained in documents E/2015/15, E/2015/15/Add.1, E/2015/15/Add.2, E/2015/16, E/2015/17, E/2015/18, E/2015/19, E/2015/20 and E/2015/21: decision 2015/251; at the same meeting, draft resolution in E/2015/15/Add.1, Section B entitled "Admission of Norway as a member of the Economic Commission for Latin America and the Caribbean" was adopted without vote: resolution 2015/29; at the same meeting, action on draft resolutions in E/2015/15/Add.2, chap. 1, section A was as follows: draft resolution I entitled "Restructuring the conference structure of the Commission to be fit for the evolving post-2015 development agenda", adopted without vote: resolution 2015/30; draft resolution II entitled "Establishment of the Asian and Pacific Centre for the Development of Disaster Information Management", adopted without vote: resolution 2015/31; at the same meeting, draft resolution in E/2015/15/Add.2, chap. 2, Section B entitled "Admission of Mauritania as a member of the Economic and Social Commission for Western Asia" was adopted without vote: resolution 2015/32.

### Resolutions

E/RES/2015/29 Admission of Norway to membership in the Economic Commission for Latin America and the Caribbean : resolution / adopted by the Economic and Social Council.
(Adopted without vote, 54th plenary meeting, 22 July 2015)

E/RES/2015/30 Restructuring the conference structure of the Economic and Social Commission for Asia and the Pacific to be fit for the evolving post-2015 development agenda : resolution / adopted by the Economic and Social Council.
(Adopted without vote, 54th plenary meeting, 22 July 2015)

E/RES/2015/31 Establishment of the Asian and Pacific Centre for the Development of Disaster Information Management : resolution / adopted by the Economic and Social Council.
(Adopted without vote, 54th plenary meeting, 22 July 2015)

E/RES/2015/32 Admission of Mauritania to membership in the Economic and Social Commission for Western Asia : resolution / adopted by the Economic and Social Council.
(Adopted without vote, 54th plenary meeting, 22 July 2015)

## REGIONAL COOPERATION–AFRICA (Agenda item 15)

### Reports

E/2015/15/Add.1 Regional cooperation in the economic, social and related fields : report of the Secretary-General : addendum.
Issued: 11 May 2015.

E/2015/17 Overview of economic and social conditions in Africa, 2014-2015 : note / by the Secretary-General.
Issued: 29 Apr. 2015. - Transmits an overview report of the economic and social conditions in Africa for the period 2014-2015.

E/2015/21 Project for a Europe-Africa fixed link through the Strait of Gibraltar : note / by the Secretary-General.
Issued: 20 Apr. 2015. - Transmits report prepared in accordance with the Economic and Social Council resolution 2009/11 by the Executive Secretaries of the Economic Commission for Europe and the Economic Commission for Africa on the activities carried out within the framework of the project for a Europe-Africa fixed link through the Strait of Gibraltar.

## REGIONAL COOPERATION–ASIA AND THE PACIFIC (Agenda item 15)

### Reports

E/2015/15/Add.2 Regional cooperation in the economic, social and related fields : report of the Secretary-General : addendum.
Issued: 11 June 2015.

E/2015/39 (E/ESCAP/71/42) (ESCOR, 2015, Suppl. no. 19) Economic and Social Commission for Asia and the Pacific : annual report (9 August 2014-29 May 2015).
Issued: 2015.

### General documents

E/2015/18 Summary of the Economic and Social Survey of Asia and the Pacific 2015 : note / by the Secretary-General.

### Discussion in plenary

E/2015/SR.54 (22 July 2015).
At the 54th meeting, action on draft resolutions in E/2015/15/Add.2, chap. 1, section A was as follows: draft resolution I entitled "Restructuring the conference structure of the Commission to be fit for the evolving post-2015 development agenda", adopted without vote: resolution 2015/30; draft resolution II entitled "Establishment of the Asian and Pacific Centre for the Development of Disaster Information Management", adopted without vote: resolution 2015/31.

### Resolutions

E/RES/2015/30 Restructuring the conference structure of the Economic and Social Commission for Asia and the Pacific to be fit for the evolving post-2015 development agenda : resolution / adopted by the Economic and Social Council.
(Adopted without vote, 54th plenary meeting, 22 July 2015)

## REGIONAL COOPERATION–ASIA AND THE PACIFIC (Agenda item 15) (continued)

E/RES/2015/31 Establishment of the Asian and Pacific Centre for the Development of Disaster Information Management : resolution / adopted by the Economic and Social Council.
(Adopted without vote, 54th plenary meeting, 22 July 2015)

## REGIONAL COOPERATION–EUROPE (Agenda item 15)

### Reports

E/2015/15/Add.1 Regional cooperation in the economic, social and related fields : report of the Secretary-General : addendum.
Issued: 11 May 2015.

E/2015/16 Economic situation in the Economic Commission for Europe region (Europe, North America and the Commonwealth of Independent States), 2014-2015 : note / by the Secretary-General.
Issued: 20 Apr. 2015. - Transmits report on the economic situation in the Economic Commission for Europe region (Europe, North America and the Commonwealth of Independent States) for the period 2014-2015.

E/2015/21 Project for a Europe-Africa fixed link through the Strait of Gibraltar : note / by the Secretary-General.
Issued: 20 Apr. 2015. - Transmits report prepared in accordance with the Economic and Social Council resolution 2009/11 by the Executive Secretaries of the Economic Commission for Europe and the Economic Commission for Africa on the activities carried out within the framework of the project for a Europe-Africa fixed link through the Strait of Gibraltar.

E/2015/37 (E/ECE/1472) (ESCOR, 2015, Suppl. no. 17) Economic Commission for Europe : biennial report (12 April 2013-16 April 2015).
Issued: 2015.

## REGIONAL COOPERATION–LATIN AMERICA AND THE CARIBBEAN (Agenda item 15)

### Reports

E/2015/15/Add.1 Regional cooperation in the economic, social and related fields : report of the Secretary-General : addendum.
Issued: 11 May 2015.

E/2015/19 Situation and outlook for Latin America and the Caribbean 2014-2015 : note / by the Secretary-General.
Issued: 8 May 2015. - Transmits report on the situation and outlook for Latin America and the Caribbean for the period 2014-2015.

### Discussion in plenary

E/2015/SR.54 (22 July 2015).
At the 54th meeting, draft resolution in E/2015/15/Add.1, Section B entitled "Admission of Norway as a member of the Economic Commission for Latin America and the Caribbean" was adopted without vote: resolution 2015/29.

## REGIONAL COOPERATION–LATIN AMERICA AND THE CARIBBEAN (Agenda item 15) (continued)

### Resolutions

E/RES/2015/29  Admission of Norway to membership in the Economic Commission for Latin America and the Caribbean : resolution / adopted by the Economic and Social Council.
(Adopted without vote, 54th plenary meeting, 22 July 2015)

## REGIONAL COOPERATION–WESTERN ASIA (Agenda item 15)

### Reports

E/2015/15/Add.2  Regional cooperation in the economic, social and related fields : report of the Secretary-General : addendum.
Issued: 11 June 2015.

### General documents

E/2015/20  Summary of the survey of economic and social developments in the Economic and Social Commission for Western Asia region, 2014-2015 : note / by the Secretary-General.

### Discussion in plenary

E/2015/SR.54  (22 July 2015).
At the 54th meeting, draft resolution in E/2015/15/Add.2, chap. 2, Section B entitled "Admission of Mauritania as a member of the Economic and Social Commission for Western Asia" was adopted without vote: resolution 2015/32.

### Resolutions

E/RES/2015/32  Admission of Mauritania to membership in the Economic and Social Commission for Western Asia : resolution / adopted by the Economic and Social Council.
(Adopted without vote, 54th plenary meeting, 22 July 2015)

## SANCTIONS COMPLIANCE–ECONOMIC ASSISTANCE (Agenda item 18m)

### Discussion in plenary

E/2015/SR.33  (9 June 2015).

## SCIENCE AND TECHNOLOGY–DEVELOPMENT (Agenda item 18b)

### Reports

E/2015/10  (A/70/63) Progress made in the implementation of and follow-up to the outcomes of the World Summit on the Information Society at the regional and international levels : report of the Secretary General.
Issued: 23 Feb. 2015.

E/2015/31  (E/CN.16/2015/4) (ESCOR, 2015, Suppl. no. 11) Commission on Science and Technology for Development : report on the 18th session (4-8 May 2015).
Issued: 2015.

## SCIENCE AND TECHNOLOGY–DEVELOPMENT (Agenda item 18b) (continued)

### General documents

E/2015/78  Discussions on the theme of the 18th session of the Commission on Science and Technology for Development, "Managing the transition from the Millennium Development Goals to the sustainable development goals : the role of science, technology and innovation" : note / by the Secretary-General.

### Discussion in plenary

E/2015/SR.47 (A)  (9 July 2015).

E/2015/SR.54  (22 July 2015).
At the 54th meeting, action on draft resolutions in E/2015/31, Section A was as follows: draft resolution I entitled "Assessment of the progress made in the implementation of and follow-up to the outcomes of the World Summit on the Information Society", adopted without vote: resolution 2015/26; draft resolution II entitled "Science, technology and innovation for development", adopted without vote: resolution 2015/27; action on draft decisions in E/2015/31, Section B was as follows: draft decision I entitled "Extension of the mandate of the Gender Advisory Board of the Commission on Science and Technology for Development", adopted without vote: decision 2015/242; draft decision II entitled "Participation of non-governmental organizations and civil society entities in the work of the Commission on Science and Technology for Development", adopted without vote: decision 2015/243; draft decision III entitled "Participation of academic and technical entities in the work of the Commission on Science and Technology for Development", adopted without vote: decision 2015/244; draft decision IV entitled "Participation of business sector entities, including the private sector, in the work of the Commission on Science and Technology for Development", adopted without vote: decision 2015/245; draft decision V entitled "Report of the Commission on Science and Technology for Development on its 18th session and provisional agenda and documentation for the 19th session of the Commission", adopted without vote: decision 2015/246.

### Resolutions

E/RES/2015/26  Assessment of the progress made in the implementation of and follow-up to the outcomes of the World Summit on the Information Society : resolution / adopted by the Economic and Social Council.
(Adopted without vote, 54th plenary meeting, 22 July 2015)

E/RES/2015/27  Science, technology and innovation for development : resolution / adopted by the Economic and Social Council.
(Adopted without vote, 54th plenary meeting, 22 July 2015)

## SOCIAL DEVELOPMENT (Agenda item 19b)

### Reports

E/2015/3 (A/70/61) Celebration of the 20th anniversary of the International Year of the Family in 2014 : report of the Secretary-General.
Issued: 18 Nov. 2014.

E/2015/26 (E/CN.5/2015/9) (ESCOR, 2015, Suppl. no. 6) Commission for Social Development : report on the 53rd session (21 February 2014 and 4-13 February 2015).
Issued: 2015.

E/2015/26/Corr.1 (ESCOR, 2015, Suppl. no. 6) Commission for Social Development : report on the 53rd session (21 February 2014 and 4-13 February 2015) : corrigendum.
Issued: 3 Nov. 2015. - Corrects text.

### Discussion in plenary

E/2015/SR.31 (8 June 2015).

E/2015/SR.32 (8 June 2015).
At the 32nd meeting, action on draft resolutions and draft decisions in E/2015/26-E/N.5/2015/9 was as follows: draft resolution I entitled "Social dimensions of the New Partnership for Africa's Development", adopted without vote: resolution 2015/3; draft resolution II entitled "Promoting the rights of persons with disabilities and strengthening the mainstreaming of disability in the post-2015 development agenda", adopted without vote: resolution 2015/4; draft resolution III entitled "Modalities for the 3rd review and appraisal of the Madrid International Plan of Action on Ageing, 2002", adopted without vote: resolution 2015/5; draft decision entitled "Report of the Commission for Social Development on its 53rd session and provisional agenda and documentation for the 54th session", adopted without vote: decision 2015/212; draft decision entitled "Nomination of members of the Board of the United Nations Research Institute for Social Development", adopted without vote: decision 2015/213.

### Resolutions

E/RES/2015/3 Social dimensions of the New Partnership for Africa's Development : resolution / adopted by the Economic and Social Council.
(Adopted without vote, 32nd plenary meeting, 8 June 2015)

E/RES/2015/4 Promoting the rights of persons with disabilities and strengthening the mainstreaming of disability in the post-2015 development agenda : resolution / adopted by the Economic and Social Council.
(Adopted without vote, 32nd plenary meeting, 8 June 2015)

E/RES/2015/5 Modalities for the 3rd review and appraisal of the Madrid International Plan of Action on Ageing, 2002 : resolution / adopted by the Economic and Social Council.
(Adopted without vote, 32nd plenary meeting, 8 June 2015)

## SOUTH-SOUTH COOPERATION (Agenda item 7c)

### Discussion in plenary

E/2015/SR.12 (24 Feb. 2015).

E/2015/SR.13 (25 Feb. 2015).

## STATISTICS (Agenda item 18c)

### Reports

E/2015/24 (E/CN.3/2015/40) (ESCOR, 2015, Suppl. no. 24) Statistical Commission : report on the 46th session (3-6 March 2015).
Issued: 2015.

### Discussion in plenary

E/2015/SR.35 (10 June 2015).
At the 35th meeting, action on draft resolution and draft decision in E/2015/24 was as follows: draft resolution entitled "2020 World Population and Housing Census Programme", adopted without vote: resolution 2015/10; draft decision entitled "Report of the Statistical Commission on its 46th session and the provisional agenda and dates for the 47th session of the Commission", adopted without vote: decision 2015/216.

### Resolutions

E/RES/2015/10 2020 World Population and Housing Census Programme : resolution / adopted by the Economic and Social Council.
(Adopted without vote, 35th plenary meeting, 10 June 2015)

## SUSTAINABLE DEVELOPMENT (Agenda item 18a)

### Reports

E/2015/33 (ESCOR, 2015, Suppl. no. 13) Committee for Development Policy : report on the 17th session (23-27 March 2015).
Issued: 2015.

E/2015/82 (A/70/92) Report on the main decisions and policy recommendations of the Committee on World Food Security : note / by the Secretary-General.
Issued: 9 June 2015. - Transmits report on the main decisions and policy recommendations of the Committee on World Food Security.

E/2015/82/Corr.1 (A/70/92/Corr.1) Report on the main decisions and policy recommendations of the Committee on World Food Security : note : corrigendum / by the Secretary-General.
Issued: 25 June 2015. - Corrects text.

### Draft resolutions/decisions

E/2015/L.13 Report of the Committee for Development Policy on its 17th session : draft resolution / submitted by the Vice-President of the Council, Oh Joon (Republic of Korea), on the basis of informal consultations.

### Discussion in plenary

E/2015/SR.3 (5 Dec. 2014).

E/2015/SR.4 (8 Dec. 2014).

E/2015/SR.15 (30 Mar. 2015).

E/2015/SR.16 (30 Mar. 2015).

## SUSTAINABLE DEVELOPMENT (Agenda item 18a) (continued)

E/2015/SR.17  (31 Mar. 2015).

E/2015/SR.18  (31 Mar. 2015).

E/2015/SR.19  (1 Apr. 2015).

E/2015/SR.20  (1 Apr. 2015).

E/2015/SR.35  (10 June 2015).
At the 35th meeting, draft resolution E/2015/L.13 was adopted without vote: resolution 2015/11.

E/2015/SR.43  (7 July 2015).

E/2015/SR.44  (8 July 2015).

E/2015/SR.47 (A)  (9 July 2015).

E/2015/SR.50  (20 July 2015).
At the 50th meeting, the Council took note of the report of the Secretary-General on the mainstreaming of the three dimensions of sustainable development throughout the United Nations system (A/70/75-E/2015/55) and the report on the main decisions and policy recommendations of the Committee on World Food Security (A/70/92-E/2015/82 and A/70/92/Corr.1-E/2015/82/Corr.1): decision 2015/220.

### Resolutions

E/RES/2015/11  Report of the Committee for Development Policy on its 17th session : resolution / adopted by the Economic and Social Council.
(Adopted without vote, 35th plenary meeting, 10 June 2015)

## SUSTAINABLE DEVELOPMENT–HIGH-LEVEL POLITICAL FORUM (Agenda item 6)

### Reports

E/2015/56  Progress report on the 10-Year Framework of Programmes on Sustainable Consumption and Production Patterns : note / by the Secretary-General.
Issued: 31 Mar. 2015. - Transmits progress report on the Ten-Year Framework of Programmes on Sustainable Consumption and Production Patterns, prepared by UNEP, pursuant to General Assembly resolutions 67/203, 68/210 and 69/214.

### General documents

E/2015/86  (A/70/137)  Summary report of the 2014 parliamentary hearing : note / by the President of the General Assembly.

E/HLS/2015/1  Ministerial Declaration of the High-Level Segment of the 2015 session of the Economic and Social Council on the theme "Managing the Transition from the Millennium Development Goals to the Sustainable Development Goals : What It Will Take" : Ministerial Declaration of the High-Level Political Forum on Sustainable Development Convened under the Auspices of the Economic and Social Council on the Theme "Strengthening Integration, Implementation and Review : the High-Level Political Forum on Sustainable Development after 2015".

## SUSTAINABLE DEVELOPMENT–HIGH-LEVEL POLITICAL FORUM (Agenda item 6)

### Discussion in plenary

E/2015/SR.43  (7 July 2015).

E/2015/SR.44  (8 July 2015).

E/2015/SR.47 (A)  (9 July 2015).

## SUSTAINABLE DEVELOPMENT–MINISTERIAL MEETING (Agenda item 5a)

### Reports

E/2015/56  Progress report on the 10-Year Framework of Programmes on Sustainable Consumption and Production Patterns : note / by the Secretary-General.
Issued: 31 Mar. 2015. - Transmits progress report on the Ten-Year Framework of Programmes on Sustainable Consumption and Production Patterns, prepared by UNEP, pursuant to General Assembly resolutions 67/203, 68/210 and 69/214.

### General documents

E/HLS/2015/1  Ministerial Declaration of the High-Level Segment of the 2015 session of the Economic and Social Council on the theme "Managing the Transition from the Millennium Development Goals to the Sustainable Development Goals : What It Will Take" : Ministerial Declaration of the High-Level Political Forum on Sustainable Development Convened under the Auspices of the Economic and Social Council on the Theme "Strengthening Integration, Implementation and Review : the High-Level Political Forum on Sustainable Development after 2015".

### Draft resolutions/decisions

E/2015/L.19  (E/HLPF/2015/L.2)  Draft Ministerial Declaration of the High-Level Segment of the 2015 session of the Economic and Social Council and the High-Level Political Forum on Sustainable Development convened under the auspices of the Council / submitted by the President of the Council, Martin Sajdik (Austria).

### Discussion in plenary

E/2015/SR.42  (6 July 2015).

E/2015/SR.45  (8 July 2015).

## SUSTAINABLE DEVELOPMENT GOALS (Agenda item 5c)

### Reports

E/2015/60  Letter, 1 Apr. 2015, from the Philippines. Transmits national report of the Philippines on progress towards the achievement of the internationally agreed goals, including the Millennium Development Goals, for the annual ministerial review to be held during the high-level segment of the 2015 session of the Economic and Social Council.

## SUSTAINABLE DEVELOPMENT GOALS (Agenda item 5c) (continued)

E/2015/61  Letter, 9 Apr. 2015, from Mongolia. Transmits national report of Mongolia on progress towards the achievement of the internationally agreed goals, including the Millennium Development Goals, for the annual ministerial review to be held during the high-level segment of the 2015 session of the Economic and Social Council.

E/2015/62  Letter, 10 Apr. 2015, from Kyrgyzstan. Transmits national report of Kyrgyzstan on progress towards the achievement of the internationally agreed goals, including the Millennium Development Goals, for the annual ministerial review to be held during the high-level segment of the 2015 session of the Economic and Social Council.

E/2015/63  Letter, 1 Apr. 2015, from Zambia. Transmits national report of Zambia on progress towards the achievement of the internationally agreed goals, including the Millennium Development Goals, for the annual ministerial review to be held during the high-level segment of the 2015 session of the Economic and Social Council.

E/2015/68  Managing the transition from the Millennium Development Goals to the sustainable development goals : what it will take : report of the Secretary-General. Issued: 24 Apr. 2015.

### General documents

E/2015/78  Discussions on the theme of the 18th session of the Commission on Science and Technology for Development, "Managing the transition from the Millennium Development Goals to the sustainable development goals : the role of science, technology and innovation" : note / by the Secretary-General.

E/2015/NGO/1  Statement / submitted by Child Aid Development Foundation International.

E/2015/NGO/2  Statement / submitted by Women's Health and Education Organization.

E/2015/NGO/3  Statement / submitted by Association mauritanienne pour la promotion du droit.

E/2015/NGO/4  Statement / submitted by Amis des étrangers au Togo.

E/2015/NGO/5  Statement / submitted by Center for Global Nonkilling.

E/2015/NGO/6  Statement / submitted by Ecoforum of Non-Governmental Organizations of Uzbekistan.

E/2015/NGO/7  Statement / submitted by Modern Advocacy, Humanitarian, Social and Rehabilitation Association.

E/2015/NGO/8  Statement / submitted by Foundation for Human Horizon.

E/2015/NGO/9  Statement / submitted by International Federation of Psoriasis Associations.

E/2015/NGO/10  Statement / submitted by Krityanand UNESCO Club Jamshedpur.

## SUSTAINABLE DEVELOPMENT GOALS (Agenda item 5c) (continued)

E/2015/NGO/11  Statement / submitted by African-British Returnees International.

E/2015/NGO/12  Statement / submitted by Aube nouvelle pour la femme et le développement.

E/2015/NGO/13  Statement / submitted by Gede Foundation.

E/2015/NGO/14  Statement / submitted by Society for Upliftment of Masses.

E/2015/NGO/15  Statement / submitted by International Federation of University Women.

E/2015/NGO/16  Statement / submitted by World for World Organization.

E/2015/NGO/17  Statement / submitted by Centre africain de recherche industrielle (CARI).

E/2015/NGO/18  Statement / submitted by Fondation d'entreprise Sanofi espoir.

E/2015/NGO/19  Statement / submitted by WaterLex.

E/2015/NGO/20  Statement / submitted by Confédération des organisations familiales de l'Union européene.

E/2015/NGO/21  Statement / submitted by Educational Foundation for African Women.

E/2015/NGO/22  Statement / submitted by Priests for Life.

E/2015/NGO/23  Statement / submitted by Fundación Global Democracia y Desarrollo and Global Foundation for Democracy and Development.

E/2015/NGO/24  Statement / submitted by New Progressive Alliance.

E/2015/NGO/25  Statement / submitted by CLIPSAS.

E/2015/NGO/26  Statement / submitted by International Presentation Association.

E/2015/NGO/27  Statement / submitted by Legião da Boa Vontade.

E/2015/NGO/28  Statement / submitted by All India Women's Conference.

E/2015/NGO/29  Statement / submitted by Children's Project International.

E/2015/NGO/30  Statement / submitted by Korean Association for Supporting the Sustainable Development Goals.

E/2015/NGO/31  Statement / submitted by Convention of Independent Financial Advisors.

E/2015/NGO/32  Statement / submitted by Comité français pour l'Afrique du Sud.

E/2015/NGO/33  Statement / submitted by International Federation for Home Economics.

E/2015/NGO/34  Statement / submitted by World Federation of Societies of Anaesthesiologists.

E/2015/NGO/35  Statement / submitted by Center for Africa Development and Progress.

## SUSTAINABLE DEVELOPMENT GOALS (Agenda item 5c) (continued)

E/2015/NGO/36  Statement / submitted by Maryknoll Sisters of St. Dominic.

E/2015/NGO/37  Statement / submitted by World Family Organization.

E/2015/NGO/38  Statement / submitted by OceanCare.

E/2015/NGO/39  Statement / submitted by Roshd Foundation.

E/2015/NGO/40  Statement / submitted by Islamic Research and Information Artistic and Cultural Institute.

E/2015/NGO/41  Statement / submitted by International Council of Nurses.

E/2015/NGO/42  Statement / submitted by Fairtrade Labelling Organizations International.

E/2015/NGO/43  Statement / submitted by Smile Foundation.

E/2015/NGO/44  Statement / submitted by Catholic Health Association of India.

E/2015/NGO/45  Statement / submitted by Roundtable on Sustainable Palm Oil.

E/2015/NGO/46  Statement / submitted by High Atlas Foundation.

E/2015/NGO/47  Statement / submitted by Soroptimist International.

E/2015/NGO/48  Statement / submitted by Foundation for Responsible Media.

E/2015/NGO/49  Statement / submitted by Federación Española de Mujeres Directivas, Ejecutivas, Profesionales y Empresarias.

E/2015/NGO/50  Statement / submitted by Pacific Rim Institute for Development and Education.

E/2015/NGO/51  Statement / submitted by Marangopoulos Foundation for Human Rights.

E/2015/NGO/52  Statement / submitted by International Council of AIDS Service Organizations.

E/2015/NGO/53  Statement / submitted by Women's Board Educational Cooperation Society.

E/2015/NGO/54  Statement / submitted by Manavata.

E/2015/NGO/55  Statement / submitted by Commonwealth Association of Surveying and Land Economy.

E/2015/NGO/56  Statement / submitted by Stat-View Association.

E/2015/NGO/57  Statement / submitted by Global Forum on Human Settlements.

E/2015/NGO/58  Statement / submitted by United Cities and Local Governments.

E/2015/NGO/59  Statement / submitted by Society to Support Children Suffering from Cancer.

E/2015/NGO/60  Statement / submitted by Make Mothers Matter.

## SUSTAINABLE DEVELOPMENT GOALS (Agenda item 5c) (continued)

E/2015/NGO/61  Statement / submitted by Christian Blind Mission.

E/2015/NGO/62  Statement / submitted by Albert B. Sabin Vaccine Institute.

E/2015/NGO/63  Statement / submitted by International Federation for Family Development.

E/2015/NGO/64  Statement / submitted by Association démocratique des femmes du Maroc.

E/2015/NGO/65  Statement / submitted by Gazeteciler ve Yazarlar Vakfi.

E/2015/NGO/66  Statement / submitted by Licht für die Welt - Christoffel Entwicklungszusammenarbeit.

E/2015/NGO/67  Statement / submitted by Corporativa de Fundaciones.

E/2015/NGO/68  Statement / submitted by International Council for Education of People with Visual Impairment.

E/2015/NGO/69  Statement / submitted by Population Institute.

E/2015/NGO/70  Statement / submitted by World Federation for Mental Health.

E/2015/NGO/71  Statement / submitted by Fundación para Estudio e Investigación de la Mujer.

### Discussion in plenary

E/2015/SR.43  (7 July 2015).

E/2015/SR.44  (8 July 2015).

E/2015/SR.45  (8 July 2015).

E/2015/SR.46  (9 July 2015).

E/2015/SR.48  (10 July 2015).

## TAXATION (Agenda item 18h)
### Reports

E/2015/45  (E/C.18/2015/6)  (ESCOR, 2015, Suppl. no. 25)  Committee of Experts on International Cooperation in Tax Matters : report on the 11th session (19-23 October 2015).
    Issued: 2015.

E/2015/51  Further strengthening the work of the Committee of Experts on International Cooperation in Tax Matters : report of the Secretary-General.
    Issued: 11 Mar. 2015.

### Draft resolutions/decisions

E/2015/L.9  Committee of Experts on International Cooperation in Tax Matters : draft resolution / South Africa [on behalf of the Group of 77 and China].
    The draft resolution was withdrawn (E/2015/SR.56).

E/2015/L.12  Venue and dates of and provisional agenda for the 11th session of the Committee of Experts on International Cooperation in Tax Matters : draft decision / submitted by the Vice-President of the Council, Oh Joon (Republic of Korea).

## TAXATION (Agenda item 18h) (continued)

### Discussion in plenary

E/2015/SR.28 (22 Apr. 2015).

E/2015/SR.29 (22 Apr. 2015).

E/2015/SR.33 (9 June 2015).
At the 33rd meeting, draft decision E/2015/L.12 was adopted without vote: decision 2015/214.

E/2015/SR.55 (22 July 2015).

E/2015/SR.56 (23 July 2015).
At the 56th meeting, draft resolution E/2015/L.9 was withdrawn.

## UN–BUDGET (2016-2017) (Agenda item 12b)

### Discussion in plenary

E/2015/SR.52 (21 July 2015).
At the 52nd meeting, the Council took note of the report of the Committee on its 55th session (A/70/16), the annual overview report of the United Nations System Chief Executive Board for Coordination for 2014 (E/2015/71) and the relevant sections of the proposed programme budget for the biennium 2016-2017 (A/70/6): decision 2015/232.

## UN–CALENDAR OF MEETINGS (Agenda item 12h)

### General documents

E/2015/85 Letter, 1 July 2015, from the Chair of the Committee on Conferences. Refers to para. 11 of General Assembly resolution 53/208 A and paras. 5 to 9 of Assembly resolution 69/250; decides to avoid holding meetings on Orthodox Good Friday, Yom Kippur, the Day of Vesak, Diwali, Gurpurab and Orthodox Christmas and that these arrangements should be taken into account when drafting future calendars of conferences and meetings and recommends adoption of the provisional calendar of conferences and meetings of the Council and its subsidiary organs for 2016-2017.

E/2015/L.8 Provisional calendar of conferences and meetings in the economic, social and related fields for 2016 and 2017 : note / by the Secretariat.

### Discussion in plenary

E/2015/SR.55 (22 July 2015).
At the 55th meeting, the Council approved the provisional calendar of conferences and meetings in the economic, social and related fields for 2016 and 2017 (E/2015/L.8): decision 2015/256.

## UN–TRAINING AND RESEARCH INSTITUTIONS (Agenda item 20)

### Reports

E/2015/7 Report of the Council of the United Nations University on the work of the University.
Issued: 22 Jan. 2015.

E/2015/12 United Nations Institute for Training and Research : report of the Secretary-General.
Issued: 10 Feb. 2015.

## UN–TRAINING AND RESEARCH INSTITUTIONS (Agenda item 20) (continued)

E/2015/54 United Nations System Staff College : report of the Secretary-General.
Issued: 26 Mar. 2015.

E/2015/70 (A/70/79) Consultations on research, training and library services : report of the Secretary-General.
Issued: 27 Apr. 2015.

### Draft resolutions/decisions

E/2015/L.10 United Nations System Staff College in Turin, Italy : draft resolution / submitted by the Vice-President of the Council, Oh Joon (Republic of Korea), on the basis of informal consultations.

### Discussion in plenary

E/2015/SR.33 (9 June 2015).
At the 33rd meeting, draft resolution E/2015/L.10 was adopted without vote: resolution 2015/9.

### Resolutions

E/RES/2015/9 United Nations System Staff College in Turin, Italy : resolution / adopted by the Economic and Social Council.
(Adopted without vote, 33rd plenary meeting, 9 June 2015)

## UN. COMMISSION FOR SOCIAL DEVELOPMENT–MEMBERS (Agenda item 4)

### General documents

E/2015/1/Add.1 Agenda : Economic and Social Council, 2015 session, 21 July 2014-22 July 2015 : addendum.

E/2015/9 Election of members of the functional commissions of the Economic and Social Council : note / by the Secretary-General.

### Discussion in plenary

E/2015/SR.21 (8 Apr. 2015).
At the 21st meeting, Bangladesh, El Salvador, Ghana, Japan, Paraguay, Peru, Republic of Korea, Republic of Moldova, Russian Federation, Rwanda were elected as members of the Commission for Social Development by acclamation for a 4-year term beginning at the 1st meeting of the Commission's 55th session in 2016 and expiring at the close of the Commission's 58th session in 2020; Austria was elected as a member by acclamation for a term beginning on the date of election and expiring at the close of the Commission's 57th session in 2019: decision 2015/201 B.

## UN. COMMISSION ON CRIME PREVENTION AND CRIMINAL JUSTICE–MEMBERS (Agenda item 4)

### General documents

E/2015/1/Add.1 Agenda : Economic and Social Council, 2015 session, 21 July 2014-22 July 2015 : addendum.

E/2015/9 Election of members of the functional commissions of the Economic and Social Council : note / by the Secretary-General.

## UN. COMMISSION ON CRIME PREVENTION AND CRIMINAL JUSTICE–MEMBERS (Agenda item 4) (continued)

### Discussion in plenary

E/2015/SR.21  (8 Apr. 2015).

At the 21st meeting, Austria, Belarus, Benin, Brazil, Cameroon, Chile, Côte d'Ivoire, Cuba, France, Guatemala, India, Iran (Islamic Republic of), Mexico, Pakistan, Republic of Korea, Saudi Arabia, Serbia, South Africa, Sweden and United States were elected as members of the Commission on Crime Prevention and Criminal Justice by acclamation for a 3-year term beginning on 1 Jan. 2016 and expiring on 31 Dec. 2018: decision 2015/201 B.

## UN. COMMISSION ON NARCOTIC DRUGS–MEMBERS (Agenda item 4)

### General documents

E/2015/1/Add.1  Agenda : Economic and Social Council, 2015 session, 21 July 2014-22 July 2015 : addendum.

E/2015/9  Election of members of the functional commissions of the Economic and Social Council : note / by the Secretary-General.

### Discussion in plenary

E/2015/SR.21  (8 Apr. 2015).

At the 21st meeting, Argentina, Austria, Belarus, Cameroon, Democratic Republic of the Congo, Ecuador, El Salvador, Germany, Guatemala, Israel, Italy, Kenya, Mauritania, Mexico, Netherlands, Norway, Pakistan, Peru, Qatar, South Africa, Spain, Sudan, Turkey, Uganda, United States and Uruguay were elected as members of the Commission on Narcotic Drugs by acclamation for a 4-year term beginning on 1 Jan. 2016; China, Iran (Islamic Republic of), Japan, Pakistan, Qatar, Republic of Korea and Thailand were elected by vote as members of the Commission for a 4-year term beginning on 1 Jan. 2016: decision 2015/201 B.

## UN. COMMISSION ON POPULATION AND DEVELOPMENT–MEMBERS (Agenda item 4)

### General documents

E/2015/1/Add.1  Agenda : Economic and Social Council, 2015 session, 21 July 2014-22 July 2015 : addendum.

E/2015/9  Election of members of the functional commissions of the Economic and Social Council : note / by the Secretary-General.

## UN. COMMISSION ON POPULATION AND DEVELOPMENT–MEMBERS (Agenda item 4) (continued)

### Discussion in plenary

E/2015/SR.21  (8 Apr. 2015).

At the 21st meeting, Chile, Morocco, Qatar, Republic of Moldova, Sudan, Turkmenistan and Uganda were elected as members of the Commission on Population and Development by acclamation for a 4-year term beginning at the 1st meeting of the Commission's 50th session in 2016 and expiring at the close of its 53rd session in 2020; Iraq was elected as a member for a term beginning on the date of election and expiring at the close of the Commission's 50th session in 2017; Jamaica was elected as a member for a term beginning on the 1st meeting of the Commission's 49th session in 2015 and expiring at the close of the Commission's 52nd session in 2019: decision 2015/201 B.

## UN. COMMISSION ON SCIENCE AND TECHNOLOGY FOR DEVELOPMENT–MEMBERS (Agenda item 4)

### General documents

E/2015/9  Election of members of the functional commissions of the Economic and Social Council : note / by the Secretary-General.

## UN. COMMISSION ON THE STATUS OF WOMEN–MEMBERS (Agenda item 4)

### General documents

E/2015/1/Add.1  Agenda : Economic and Social Council, 2015 session, 21 July 2014-22 July 2015 : addendum.

E/2015/9  Election of members of the functional commissions of the Economic and Social Council : note / by the Secretary-General.

### Discussion in plenary

E/2015/SR.21  (8 Apr. 2015).

At the 21st meeting, Brazil, Eritrea, Guatemala, Kuwait, Nigeria, Norway, Qatar, Russian Federation, Trinidad and Tobago and United Kingdom were elected as members of the Commission on the Status of Women by acclamation for a 4-year term beginning at the 1st meeting of the Commission's 61st session in 2016 and expiring at the close of the Commission's 64th session in 2020: decision 2015/201 B.

## UN. COMMITTEE FOR DEVELOPMENT POLICY–MEMBERS (Agenda item 4)

### General documents

E/2015/1/Add.1  Agenda : Economic and Social Council, 2015 session, 21 July 2014-22 July 2015 : addendum.

E/2015/9/Add.4  Appointment of 24 members of the Committee for Development Policy : note / by the Secretary-General.

## UN. COMMITTEE FOR DEVELOPMENT POLICY– MEMBERS (Agenda item 4) (continued)

### Discussion in plenary

E/2015/SR.21  (8 Apr. 2015).
At the 21st meeting, the Council approved the nomination by the Secretary-General of the 24 experts (E/2015/9/Add.4) for a 3-year term beginning on 1 Jan. 2016: decision 2015/201 B.

## UN. COMMITTEE FOR PROGRAMME AND COORDINATION–MEMBERS (Agenda item 4)

### General documents

E/2015/1/Add.1  Agenda : Economic and Social Council, 2015 session, 21 July 2014-22 July 2015 : addendum.

E/2015/9/Add.2  Nomination of 7 members of the Committee for Programme and Coordination : note / by the Secretary-General.

### Discussion in plenary

E/2015/SR.21  (8 Apr. 2015).
At the 21st meeting, Argentina, France, Peru, Russian Federation, United Republic of Tanzania and Zimbabwe were nominated for election by the General Assembly to the Committee for Programme and Coordination for a 3-year term beginning on 1 Jan. 2016 and expiring on 31 Dec. 2018; Portugal was nominated for election by the General Assembly to the Committee for a term beginning on the date of election and expiring on 31 Dec. 2017: decision 2015/201 B.

E/2015/SR.30  (15 May 2015).
At the 30th meeting, United Kingdom was elected as a member of the Committee for Programme and Coordination by acclamation for a term beginning on the date of election by the General Assembly and expiring on 31 Dec. 2017: decision 2015/201 D.

## UN. COMMITTEE FOR THE UNITED NATIONS POPULATION AWARD–MEMBERS (Agenda item 4)

### General documents

E/2015/1/Add.1  Agenda : Economic and Social Council, 2015 session, 21 July 2014-22 July 2015 : addendum.

E/2015/9/Add.9  Election of 10 members of the Committee for the United Nations Population Award : note / by the Secretary-General.

### Discussion in plenary

E/2015/SR.21  (8 Apr. 2015).
At the 21st meeting, Bangladesh and Islamic Republic of Iran were elected as members of the Committee for the United Nations Population Award by acclamation for a 3-year term beginning on 1 Jan. 2016: decision 2015/201 B.

## UN. ECONOMIC AND SOCIAL COUNCIL (2014- 2015 : NEW YORK AND GENEVA)–AGENDA (Agenda item 2)

### General documents

E/2015/1  Provisional agenda : Economic and Social Council, 2015 session, 21 July 2014-22 July 2015.

E/2015/2  Letter, 17 July 2014, from the President of the Economic and Social Council. Request for revisions to the provisional agenda of the 2015 session of the Economic and Social Council.

E/2015/80  Requests from non-governmental organizations to be heard by the Economic and Social Council.

E/2015/100  Annotated provisional agenda for the 2015 session of the Economic and Social Council.

### Draft resolutions/decisions

E/2014/L.23  Theme for the integration segment of the 2015 session of the Economic and Social Council : draft decision / submitted by the President of the Council, Martin Sajdik (Austria).

E/2014/L.24  Themes for the 2015 and 2016 sessions of the Economic and Social Council : draft decision / submitted by the President of the Council, Martin Sajdik (Austria).

E/2015/L.1  Working arrangements for the 2015 session of the Economic and Social Council : draft decision / submitted by the President of the Council, Martin Sajdik (Austria).

E/2015/L.1/Rev.1  Working arrangements for the 2015 session of the Economic and Social Council : [revised] draft decision / submitted by the President of the Council, Martin Sajdik (Austria).

E/2015/L.2  2015 thematic discussion of the Economic and Social Council : draft decision / submitted by the President of the Council, Martin Sajdik (Austria).

E/2015/L.4  Membership of the Economic and Social Council in the Organizational Committee of the Peacebuilding Commission : draft resolution / submitted by the President of the Council, Martin Sajdik (Austria).

E/2015/L.6  Theme for the humanitarian affairs segment of the 2015 session of the Economic and Social Council : draft decision / submitted by the Vice-President of the Council, Mohamed Khaled Khiari (Tunisia), on the basis of informal consultations.

E/2015/L.7  Economic and Social Council event to discuss the transition from relief to development : draft decision / submitted by the Vice-Presidents of the Council, María Emma Mejía Vélez (Colombia) and Mohamed Khaled Khiari (Tunisia), on the basis of informal consultations.

### Discussion in plenary

E/2014/SR.53  (18 Nov. 2014).
At the 53rd meeting, draft decision E/2015/L.2 was adopted without vote: decision 2015/206.

## UN. ECONOMIC AND SOCIAL COUNCIL (2014-2015 : NEW YORK AND GENEVA)–AGENDA (Agenda item 2) (continued)

E/2015/SR.1  (21 July 2014).
At the 1st meeting, draft decision E/2014/L.24 was adopted without vote: decision 2015/203; draft decision E/2014/L.23 was adopted without vote: decision 2015/204.

E/2015/SR.2  (22 July 2014).
At the 2nd meeting, draft decision E/2015/L.1, as orally amended, was adopted without vote: decision 2015/205.

E/2015/SR.14  (4 Mar. 2015).
At the 14th meeting, draft resolution E/2015/L.4 was adopted without vote: resolution 2015/1.

E/2015/SR.30  (15 May 2015).
At the 30th meeting, action on draft decisions was as follows: draft decision E/2015/L.6, adopted without vote: decision 2015/210; draft decision E/2015/L.7, adopted without vote: decision 2015/211.

E/2015/SR.36  (10 June 2015).
At the 36th meeting, the Council adopted the recommendation of the Committee on Non-Governmental Organizations that the organizations listed in document E/2015/80 be heard by the Council during the high-level segment of its 2015 session: decision 2015/217.

### Resolutions

E/RES/2015/1  Membership of the Economic and Social Council in the Organizational Committee of the Peacebuilding Commission : resolution / adopted by the Economic and Social Council.
(Adopted without vote, 14th plenary meeting, 4 Mar. 2015)

## UN. ECONOMIC AND SOCIAL COUNCIL (2014-2015 : NEW YORK AND GENEVA)–OFFICERS (Agenda item 1)

### Discussion in plenary

E/2015/SR.7  (13 Jan. 2015).
At the 7th meeting, Mohamed Khaled Khiari (Tunisia) was elected Vice-President of the Council for the remainder of its 2015 session by acclamation.

## UN. ECONOMIC AND SOCIAL COUNCIL (2014-2015 : NEW YORK AND GENEVA)–PARTICIPANTS

### General documents

E/2015/INF/4  List of participants : Economic and Social Council, 2015 session.

## UN. ECONOMIC AND SOCIAL COUNCIL (2014-2015 : NEW YORK AND GENEVA)–RESOLUTIONS AND DECISIONS

### General documents

E/2015/99  (ESCOR, 2015, Suppl. no. 1)  Resolutions and decisions of the Economic and Social Council : 2015 session, New York and Geneva [New York: 21 and 22 July and 18 November 2014; and 13 January, 25 February, 4 March, 30 March to 1 April, 8 to 10 April, 15 May, 8 to 10 and 29 June, 6 to 10 July and 20 to 23 July 2015; Geneva: 17 to 19 June 2015].

E/2015/INF/2  (To be issued in ESCOR, 2015, Suppl. no. 1 (E/2015/99))  Action taken by the Economic and Social Council at its 2015 session : note / by the Secretariat.

E/2015/INF/2/Corr.1  Action taken by the Economic and Social Council at its 2015 session : note : corrigendum / by the Secretary-General [i.e. Secretariat].

## UN. EXECUTIVE COMMITTEE OF THE UNHCR PROGRAMME–MEMBERS (Agenda item 4)

### General documents

E/2015/1/Add.1  Agenda : Economic and Social Council, 2015 session, 21 July 2014-22 July 2015 : addendum.

### Discussion in plenary

E/2015/SR.21  (8 Apr. 2015).
At the 21st meeting, Armenia, Chad, Georgia and Uruguay were elected as members of the Executive Committee of the Programme of the United Nations High Commissioner for Refugees by acclamation: decision 2015/201 B.

## UN. INTERGOVERNMENTAL WORKING GROUP OF EXPERTS ON INTERNATIONAL STANDARDS OF ACCOUNTING AND REPORTING–MEMBERS (Agenda item 4)

### General documents

E/2015/1/Add.1  Agenda : Economic and Social Council, 2015 session, 21 July 2014-22 July 2015 : addendum.

E/2015/9/Add.3  Election of 13 members of the Intergovernmental Working Group of Experts on International Standards of Accounting and Reporting : note / by the Secretary-General.

### Discussion in plenary

E/2015/SR.21  (8 Apr. 2015).
At the 21st meeting, Benin, Brazil, Cameroon, Kenya and Uganda were elected as members of the Intergovernmental Working Group of Experts on International Standards of Accounting and Reporting by acclamation for a 3-year term beginning on 1 Jan. 2016 and expiring on 31 Dec. 2018: decision 2015/201 B.

## UN. PEACEBUILDING COMMISSION. ORGANIZATIONAL COMMITTEE–MEMBERS (Agenda item 4)

### Discussion in plenary

E/2015/SR.14 (4 Mar. 2015).
At the 14th meeting, the following States members were elected as members of the Organizational Committee of the Peacebuilding Commission by acclamation for a term of office ending on 31 Dec. 2016: Brazil, Croatia, Italy, Nepal, Republic of Korea, South Africa and Trinidad and Tobago: decision 2015/201 A.

## UN. PERMANENT FORUM ON INDIGENOUS ISSUES (Agenda item 19h)

### Reports

E/2015/43 (E/CN.19/2015/10) (ESCOR, 2015, Suppl. no. 23) Permanent Forum on Indigenous Issues : report on the 14th session (20 April-1 May 2015).
Issued: 2015.

E/2015/76 (A/70/84) Progress made in the implementation of the outcome document of the high-level plenary meeting of the General Assembly known as the World Conference on Indigenous Peoples : report of the Secretary-General.
Issued: 18 May 2015.

### Discussion in plenary

E/2015/SR.54 (22 July 2015).
At the 54th meeting, action on draft decisions in E/2015/43 was follows: draft decision I entitled "International expert group meeting on the theme "Indigenous languages: preservation and revitalization (articles 13, 14 and 16 of the United Nations Declaration on the Rights of Indigenous Peoples)"", adopted without vote: decision 2015/248; draft decision II entitled "Venue and dates for the 15th session of the Permanent Forum on Indigenous Issues", adopted without vote: decision 2015/249; draft decision III entitled "Report of the Permanent Forum on Indigenous Issues on its 14th session and provisional agenda for its 15th sessions", adopted without vote: decision 2015/250.

## UN. PERMANENT FORUM ON INDIGENOUS ISSUES–MEMBERS (Agenda item 4)

### Discussion in plenary

E/2015/SR.21 (8 Apr. 2015).

## UN. STATISTICAL COMMISSION–MEMBERS (Agenda item 4)

### General documents

E/2015/1/Add.1 Agenda : Economic and Social Council, 2015 session, 21 July 2014-22 July 2015 : addendum.

E/2015/9 Election of members of the functional commissions of the Economic and Social Council : note / by the Secretary-General.

## UN. STATISTICAL COMMISSION–MEMBERS (Agenda item 4) (continued)

### Discussion in plenary

E/2015/SR.21 (8 Apr. 2015).
At the 21st meeting, Cuba, Kenya, Latvia, Qatar, Republic of Korea, Romania and Togo were elected as members of the Statistical Commission by acclamation for a 4-year term beginning on 1 Jan. 2016: decision 2015/201 B.

E/2015/SR.30 (15 May 2015).
At the 30th meeting, United States was elected as a member of the Statistical Commission by acclamation for a term beginning on 1 Jan. 2016 and expiring on 31 Dec. 2019: decision 2015/201 D.

## UN CONFERENCES (Agenda item 11)

### Reports

E/2015/55 (A/70/75) Mainstreaming of the three dimensions of sustainable development throughout the United Nations system : report of the Secretary-General.
Issued: 30 Mar. 2015.

### Discussion in plenary

E/2015/SR.36 (10 June 2015).

E/2015/SR.50 (20 July 2015).
At the 50th meeting, the Council took note of the report of the Secretary-General on the mainstreaming of the three dimensions of sustainable development throughout the United Nations system (A/70/75-E/2015/55) and the report on the main decisions and policy recommendations of the Committee on World Food Security (A/70/92-E/2015/82 and A/70/92/Corr.1-E/2015/82/Corr.1): decision 2015/220.

## UN FORUM ON FORESTS (Agenda item 18k)

### Reports

E/2015/42 (E/CN.18/2015/14) (ESCOR, 2015, Suppl. no. 22) United Nations Forum on Forests : report on the 11th session (19 April 2013 and 4 to 15 May 2015).
Issued: 2015.

E/2015/42/Corr.1 (E/CN.18/2015/14/Corr.1) (ESCOR, 2015, Suppl. no. 22) United Nations Forum on Forests : report on the 11th session (19 April 2013 and 4 to 15 May 2015) : corrigendum.
Issued: 24 July 2015. - Corrects text.

### Discussion in plenary

E/2015/SR.55 (22 July 2015).
At the 55th meeting, draft resolution and draft decision in E/2015/42 was as follows: draft resolution entitled "International arrangement on forests beyond 2015", adopted without vote: resolution 2015/33; draft decision entitled "Ministerial declaration of the high-level segment of the 11th session of the United Nations Forum on Forests on the international arrangement on 'The forests we want: beyond 2015'", adopted without vote: decision 2015/254; at the same meeting, the Council took note of the report of the United Nations Forum on Forests on its 11th session (E/2015/42): decision 2015/255.

## UN FORUM ON FORESTS (Agenda item 18k) (continued)

### Resolutions

E/RES/2015/33  International arrangement on forests beyond 2015 : resolution / adopted by the Economic and Social Council.
(Adopted without vote, 55th plenary meeting, 22 July 2015)

## UN POLICY RECOMMENDATIONS (Agenda item 7a)

### Reports

E/2015/4  (A/70/62)  Implementation of General Assembly resolution 67/226 on the quadrennial comprehensive policy review of operational activities for development of the United Nations system : report of the Secretary-General.
Issued: 13 Jan. 2015.

### Discussion in plenary

E/2015/SR.9  (23 Feb. 2015).

E/2015/SR.10  (23 Feb. 2015).

E/2015/SR.12  (24 Feb. 2015).

E/2015/SR.13  (25 Feb. 2015).

## UN-HABITAT. GOVERNING COUNCIL–MEMBERS (Agenda item 4)

### General documents

E/2015/1/Add.1  Agenda : Economic and Social Council, 2015 session, 21 July 2014-22 July 2015 : addendum.

E/2015/9/Add.11  Election of 19 members of the Governing Council of the United Nations Human Settlements Programme : note / by the Secretary-General.

### Discussion in plenary

E/2015/SR.21  (8 Apr. 2015).
At the 21st meeting, Angola, Bahrain, Brazil, Chad, Chile, Georgia, Germany, India, Kenya, Mexico, Nigeria, Serbia, Sweden and Turkmenistan were elected as members of the Governing Council of the United Nations Human Settlements Programme by acclamation for a 4-year term beginning on 1 Jan. 2016 and expiring on 31 Dec. 2019; Georgia and Serbia were elected as members of the Governing Council by acclamation for a term of office beginning on the date of election and expiring on 31 Dec. 2015: decision 2015/201 B.

E/2015/SR.24  (10 Apr. 2015).
At the 24th meeting, Sweden was elected as a member of the Governing Council of the UN Human Settlements Programme by acclamation for a term beginning on the date of election and expiring on 31 Dec. 2015: decision 2015/201 C.

E/2015/SR.30  (15 May 2015).
At the 30th meeting, Israel was elected as a member of the Governing Council of the UN Human Settlements by acclamation for a term beginning on 1 Jan. 2016 and expiring on 31 Dec. 2019: decision 2015/201 D.

## UN-WOMEN (Agenda item 7b)

### General documents

E/2015/47  Reports of the Executive Board of the United Nations Entity for Gender Equality and the Empowerment of Women on its 1st and 2nd regular sessions and its annual session of 2014 : note / by the Secretariat.
Note of transmittal only.

### Discussion in plenary

E/2015/SR.11  (24 Feb. 2015).

E/2015/SR.41  (29 June 2015).
At the 41st meeting, the Council took note of the following documents: Report of the Executive Board of the United Nations Children's Fund on its 1st and 2nd regular sessions and annual session of 2014 (E/2014/34/Rev.1); the Report of the Executive Board of the United Nations Development Programme, the United Nations Population Fund and the United Nations Office for Project Services on its work during 2014 (E/2015/35); the Report of the Executive Board of the World Food Programme on the 1st and 2nd regular sessions and annual session of 2014 (E/2015/36); and the reports of the Executive Board of the United Nations Entity for Gender Equality and the Empowerment of Women on its 1st and 2nd regular sessions and its annual session of 2014 (E/2015/47): decision 2015/219.

## UN-WOMEN. EXECUTIVE BOARD–MEMBERS (Agenda item 4)

### General documents

E/2015/1/Add.1  Agenda : Economic and Social Council, 2015 session, 21 July 2014-22 July 2015 : addendum.

E/2015/9/Add.7  Election of 17 members of the Executive Board of the United Nations Entity for Gender Equality and the Empowerment of Women : note / by the Secretary-General.

### Discussion in plenary

E/2015/SR.23  (9 Apr. 2015).

E/2015/SR.24  (10 Apr. 2015).
At the 24th meeting, the following States were elected as members of the Executive Board of the United Nations Entity for Gender Equality and the Empowerment of Women: Antigua and Barbuda, Comoros, Croatia, Gabon, Germany, Guyana, Iran (Islamic Republic of), Liberia, Luxembourg, Namibia, Panama, Pakistan, Russian Federation, Samoa, Tunisia, Turkmenistan, United Arab Emirates for a 3-year term beginning on 1 Jan. 2016 and expiring 31 Dec. 2018; Canada, Denmark, Spain, Netherlands, Norway and Sweden for a term beginning on 1 Jan. 2016 and expiring on 31 Dec. 2016: decision 2015/201 C.

## UNDP/UNFPA/UNOPS (Agenda item 7b)

### Reports

E/2015/35 (ESCOR, 2015, Suppl. no. 15) Executive Board of the United Nations Development Programme, the United Nations Population Fund and the United Nations Office for Project Services : report of the Executive Board on its work during 2015.
Issued: 2015.

### Discussion in plenary

E/2015/SR.11 (24 Feb. 2015).

E/2015/SR.41 (29 June 2015).
At the 41st meeting, the Council took note of the following documents: Report of the Executive Board of the United Nations Children's Fund on its 1st and 2nd regular sessions and annual session of 2014 (E/2014/34/Rev.1); the Report of the Executive Board of the United Nations Development Programme, the United Nations Population Fund and the United Nations Office for Project Services on its work during 2014 (E/2015/35); the Report of the Executive Board of the World Food Programme on the 1st and 2nd regular sessions and annual session of 2014 (E/2015/36); and the reports of the Executive Board of the United Nations Entity for Gender Equality and the Empowerment of Women on its 1st and 2nd regular sessions and its annual session of 2014 (E/2015/47): decision 2015/219.

## UNDP/UNFPA/UNOPS EXECUTIVE BOARD– MEMBERS (Agenda item 4)

### General documents

E/2015/1/Add.1 Agenda : Economic and Social Council, 2015 session, 21 July 2014-22 July 2015 : addendum.

E/2015/9/Add.6 Election of 14 members of the Executive Board of the United Nations Development Programme/United Nations Population Fund/United Nations Office for Project Services : note / by the Secretary-General.

### Discussion in plenary

E/2015/SR.21 (8 Apr. 2015).
At the 21st meeting, Austria, Belarus, Benin, Cameroon, Chad, France, Haiti, Japan, Lao People's Republic, Malawi, Republic of Korea, Samoa, Spain and Uganda were elected as members of the Executive Board of the United Nations Development Programme/United Nations Population Fund/United Nations Office for Project Services by acclamation for a 3-year term beginning on 1 Jan. 2016 and expiring on 31 Dec. 2018; Belgium, Canada, Switzerland and Turkey were elected as members of the Executive Board: Belgium, Canada and Turkey beginning on 1 Jan. 2016 and expiring on 31 Dec. 2017 and Switzerland beginning on 1 Jan. 2016 and expiring on 31 Dec. 2016: decision 2015/201 B.

## UNICEF (Agenda item 7b)

### Reports

E/2015/34 (Part I) (E/ICEF/2015/7 (Part I)) Report of the Executive Board of the United Nations Children's Fund on the work of its 1st regular session of 2015 (3-5 February 2015).
Issued: 20 Mar. 2015.

E/2015/34 (Part II) (E/ICEF/2015/7 (Part II)) (To be issued as ESCOR, 2015, Suppl. no. 14 (E/2015/34/Rev.1-E/ICEF/2015/7/Rev.1)) Report of the Executive Board of the United Nations Children's Fund on the work of its annual session of 2015 (16-18 June 2015).
Issued: 14 July 2015.

E/2015/34/Rev.1 (E/ICEF/2015/7/Rev.1) (ESCOR, 2015, Suppl. no. 14) Executive Board of the United Nations Children's Fund : report on the 1st and 2nd regular sessions and annual session of 2015.
Issued: 2015.

### Discussion in plenary

E/2015/SR.11 (24 Feb. 2015).

E/2015/SR.41 (29 June 2015).
At the 41st meeting, the Council took note of the following documents: Report of the Executive Board of the United Nations Children's Fund on its 1st and 2nd regular sessions and annual session of 2014 (E/2014/34/Rev.1); the Report of the Executive Board of the United Nations Development Programme, the United Nations Population Fund and the United Nations Office for Project Services on its work during 2014 (E/2015/35); the Report of the Executive Board of the World Food Programme on the 1st and 2nd regular sessions and annual session of 2014 (E/2015/36); and the reports of the Executive Board of the United Nations Entity for Gender Equality and the Empowerment of Women on its 1st and 2nd regular sessions and its annual session of 2014 (E/2015/47): decision 2015/219.

## UNICEF. EXECUTIVE BOARD–MEMBERS (Agenda item 4)

### General documents

E/2015/1/Add.1 Agenda : Economic and Social Council, 2015 session, 21 July 2014-22 July 2015 : addendum.

E/2015/9/Add.5 Election of 14 members of the Executive Board of the United Nations Children's Fund : note / by the Secretary-General.

## UNICEF. EXECUTIVE BOARD–MEMBERS (Agenda item 4) (continued)

### Discussion in plenary

E/2015/SR.21  (8 Apr. 2015).

At the 21st meeting, Australia, Bosnia and Herzegovina, Botswana, Cameroon, Denmark, El Salvador, Ethiopia, India, Iran (Islamic Republic of), Libya, Nepal, Sierra Leone, Sweden and Switzerland were elected as members of the Executive Board of the United Nations Children's Fund by acclamation for a 3-year term beginning on 1 Jan. 2016 and expiring on 31 Dec. 2018; Andorra, Luxembourg and United Kingdom were elected as members of the Executive Board: Andorra for a term of office beginning on 1 Jan. 2016 and expiring on 31 Dec. 2016, Luxembourg beginning on 1 Jan. 2016 and expiring on 31 Dec. 2017 and United Kingdom beginning on 1 Jan. 2016 and expiring on 31 Dec. 2016: decision 2015/201 B.

## WOMEN IN DEVELOPMENT (Agenda item 18j)

### Reports

E/2015/27  (E/CN.6/2015/10)  (ESCOR, 2015, Suppl. no. 7)  Commission on the Status of Women : report on the 59th session (21 March 2014 and 9-20 March 2015). Issued: 2015.

### Discussion in plenary

E/2015/SR.47 (A)  (9 July 2015).

## WOMEN'S ADVANCEMENT (Agenda item 19a)

### Reports

E/2015/27  (E/CN.6/2015/10)  (ESCOR, 2015, Suppl. no. 7)  Commission on the Status of Women : report on the 59th session (21 March 2014 and 9-20 March 2015). Issued: 2015.

### General documents

E/2015/67  Results of the 57th, 58th and 59th sessions of the Committee on the Elimination of Discrimination against Women : note / by the Secretariat.

### Discussion in plenary

E/2015/SR.32  (8 June 2015).

At the 32nd meeting, action on draft resolution and draft decision in E/2015/27-E/N.6/2015/10 was as follows: draft resolution II entitled "Future organization and methods of work of the Commission on the Status of Women", adopted without vote: resolution 2015/6; draft decision entitled "Report of the Commission on the Status of Women on its 59th session and provisional agenda and documentation for the 60th session of the Commission", adopted without vote: decision 2015/218.

E/2015/SR.36  (10 June 2015).

At the 36th meeting, action on draft resolution and draft decision in E/2015/27 was as follows: draft resolution I entitled "Situation of and assistance to Palestinian women", adopted (16-2-20): resolution 2015/13; draft decision entitled "Report of the Commission on the Status of Women on its 59th session and provisional agenda and documentation for the 60th session of the Commission", adopted without vote: decision 2015/218.

## WOMEN'S ADVANCEMENT (Agenda item 19a) (continued)

### Resolutions

E/RES/2015/6  Future organization and methods of work of the Commission on the Status of Women : resolution / adopted by the Economic and Social Council.

(Adopted without vote, 32nd plenary meeting, 8 June 2015)

E/RES/2015/13  Situation of and assistance to Palestinian women : resolution / adopted by the Economic and Social Council.

(Adopted 16-2-20, 36th plenary meeting, 10 June 2015)

## WORLD FOOD PROGRAMME (Agenda item 7b)

### Reports

E/2015/14  Annual performance report of the World Food Programme for 2014 : note / by the Secretary-General. Issued: 23 Nov. 2015.

E/2015/36  (ESCOR, 2015, Suppl. no. 16)  Executive Board of the World Food Programme : report on the 1st and 2nd regular sessions and annual session of 2014. Issued: 2015.

### Discussion in plenary

E/2015/SR.11  (24 Feb. 2015).

E/2015/SR.41  (29 June 2015).

At the 41st meeting, the Council took note of the following documents: Report of the Executive Board of the United Nations Children's Fund on its 1st and 2nd regular sessions and annual session of 2014 (E/2014/34/Rev.1); the Report of the Executive Board of the United Nations Development Programme, the United Nations Population Fund and the United Nations Office for Project Services on its work during 2014 (E/2015/35); the Report of the Executive Board of the World Food Programme on the 1st and 2nd regular sessions and annual session of 2014 (E/2015/36); and the reports of the Executive Board of the United Nations Entity for Gender Equality and the Empowerment of Women on its 1st and 2nd regular sessions and its annual session of 2014 (E/2015/47): decision 2015/219.

## WORLD FOOD PROGRAMME. EXECUTIVE BOARD–MEMBERS (Agenda item 4)

### General documents

E/2015/1/Add.1  Agenda : Economic and Social Council, 2015 session, 21 July 2014-22 July 2015 : addendum.

E/2015/9/Add.8  Election of 6 members of the Executive Board of the World Food Programme : note / by the Secretary-General.

### Discussion in plenary

E/2015/SR.14  (4 Mar. 2015).

At the 14th meeting, Guatemala was elected as a member of the Executive Board of the World Food Programme by acclamation to complete the term of office of Panama, which would expire on 31 Dec. 2017: decision 2015/201 A.

## WORLD FOOD PROGRAMME. EXECUTIVE BOARD–MEMBERS (Agenda item 4) (continued)

E/2015/SR.21  (8 Apr. 2015).

At the 21st meeting, India, France, Liberia, Netherlands and Russian Federation were elected as members of the Executive Board of the World Food Programme by acclamation for a 3-year term beginning on 1 Jan. 2016 and expiring on 31 Dec. 2018; China was elected as a member of the Executive Board by acclamation for a term of office beginning on 1 Jan. 2016 and expiring on 31 Dec. 2017: decision 2015/201 B.

# INDEX TO SPEECHES

## EXPLANATORY NOTE

Certain speakers are permitted to address the
*Economic and Social* Council in their personal capacity.
In such cases, a triple asterisk (***) appears in place of
the corporate name/country affiliation in each section
of the Index to speeches.

***

HUMANITARIAN ASSISTANCE (Agenda item 9)
Izam, Fatime Abdoulaye – E/2015/SR.37
Saleh, Idriss Moussa – E/2015/SR.37;
E/2015/SR.39
INSTITUTION BUILDING (Agenda item 5d)
El-Keib, Abdurrahim – E/2015/SR.49
MILLENNIUM DEVELOPMENT GOALS
Lagumdzija, Zlatko – E/2015/SR.46
Nanxi, Liu – E/2015/SR.45
Onano, Vivian – E/2015/SR.46
Shank, Michael – E/2015/SR.48
SOCIAL DEVELOPMENT (Agenda item 19b)
Frei Montalva, Eduardo – E/2015/SR.31
SUSTAINABLE DEVELOPMENT GOALS (Agenda item 5c)
Lagumdzija, Zlatko – E/2015/SR.46
Nanxi, Liu – E/2015/SR.45
Onano, Vivian – E/2015/SR.46
Shank, Michael – E/2015/SR.48

## Academia Diplomática de Chile

REGIONAL COOPERATION (Agenda item 15)
Somavía, Juan – E/2015/SR.47(B)

## Action aide aux familles démunies (Mali)

SUSTAINABLE DEVELOPMENT (Agenda item 18a)
Touré, Ténin – E/2015/SR.47(A)
WOMEN IN DEVELOPMENT (Agenda item 18j)
Touré, Ténin – E/2015/SR.47(A)

## Afghanistan. Human Rights Commission

HUMANITARIAN ASSISTANCE (Agenda item 9)
Samar, Sima – E/2015/SR.39

## African Tax Administration Forum

TAXATION (Agenda item 18h)
Marais, Lincoln – E/2015/SR.28

## African Union. African Risk Capacity. Insurance Company Limited

HUMANITARIAN ASSISTANCE (Agenda item 9)
Wilcox, Richard – E/2015/SR.38

## African Union. Commission

EBOLA VIRUS DISEASE
Potgieter-Gqubule, Febe – E/2015/SR.3
SUSTAINABLE DEVELOPMENT (Agenda item 18a)
Potgieter-Gqubule, Febe – E/2015/SR.3

## Al Jazeera America (Television network)

SUSTAINABLE DEVELOPMENT (Agenda item 18a)
Velshi, Ali – E/2015/SR.20

## Albania

NON-GOVERNMENTAL ORGANIZATIONS (Agenda item 17)
Hoxha, Ferit – E/2015/SR.51
OPERATIONAL ACTIVITIES–UN (Agenda item 7)
Hoxha, Ferit – E/2015/SR.8

## Albania (continued)

SUSTAINABLE DEVELOPMENT (Agenda item 18a)
Prizreni, Ingrit – E/2015/SR.19

## Algeria

HUMANITARIAN ASSISTANCE (Agenda item 9)
Chir, Kamel – E/2015/SR.38
Khelif, Hamza – E/2015/SR.37; E/2015/SR.39
UN–TRAINING AND RESEARCH INSTITUTIONS (Agenda item 20)
Djacta, Larbi – E/2015/SR.33

## Alliance of Small Island States

SUSTAINABLE DEVELOPMENT (Agenda item 18a)
Sareer, Ahmed (Maldives) – E/2015/SR.43
SUSTAINABLE DEVELOPMENT–HIGH-LEVEL POLITICAL FORUM (Agenda item 6)
Sareer, Ahmed (Maldives) – E/2015/SR.43

## Angola

HUMANITARIAN ASSISTANCE (Agenda item 9)
Dos Santos, Patricia Fatima B. – E/2015/SR.39

## ArcelorMittal (Firm)

EBOLA VIRUS DISEASE
Knight, Alan – E/2015/SR.3
SUSTAINABLE DEVELOPMENT (Agenda item 18a)
Knight, Alan – E/2015/SR.3

## Argentina

DECOLONIZATION (Agenda item 14)
Mazzeo, Gonzalo Sebastián – E/2015/SR.50
HUMANITARIAN ASSISTANCE (Agenda item 9)
Mercado, Julio César – E/2015/SR.40
Vilas, Paula – E/2015/SR.39
OPERATIONAL ACTIVITIES–UN (Agenda item 7)
Crilchuk, Guido – E/2015/SR.34
Perceval, María Cristina – E/2015/SR.8
SOCIAL DEVELOPMENT (Agenda item 19b)
Perceval, María Cristina – E/2015/SR.31
SOUTH-SOUTH COOPERATION (Agenda item 7c)
Perceval, María Cristina – E/2015/SR.13
SUSTAINABLE DEVELOPMENT (Agenda item 18a)
Di Luca, Sebastián – E/2015/SR.19
Oporto, Mario Néstor – E/2015/SR.47(A)
Perceval, María Cristina – E/2015/SR.15
SUSTAINABLE DEVELOPMENT–HIGH-LEVEL POLITICAL FORUM (Agenda item 6)
Oporto, Mario Néstor – E/2015/SR.47(A)
UN POLICY RECOMMENDATIONS (Agenda item 7a)
Perceval, María Cristina – E/2015/SR.13

## Armenia

BRETTON WOODS INSTITUTIONS
Gabrielyan, Vache – E/2015/SR.25
Simonyan, Sofya – E/2015/SR.26; E/2015/SR.27

## Australia

HUMANITARIAN ASSISTANCE (Agenda item 9)
Isbister, Jamie – E/2015/SR.37

## Australia (continued)

OPERATIONAL ACTIVITIES–UN (Agenda item 7)
Stokes, Christopher John – E/2015/SR.8;
E/2015/SR.34
REGIONAL COOPERATION–ASIA AND THE PACIFIC
(Agenda item 15)
Henderson, Nathan – E/2015/SR.54
SUSTAINABLE DEVELOPMENT (Agenda item 18a)
Haddad, Amy – E/2015/SR.19
SUSTAINABLE DEVELOPMENT–HIGH-LEVEL
POLITICAL FORUM (Agenda item 6)
Donaldson, Kirstin – E/2015/SR.44
UN FORUM ON FORESTS (Agenda item 18k)
Henderson, Nathan – E/2015/SR.55
UN POLICY RECOMMENDATIONS (Agenda item 7a)
Versegi, Peter Lloyd – E/2015/SR.12
UN-WOMEN (Agenda item 7b)
Stokes, Christopher John – E/2015/SR.11
UNDP/UNFPA/UNOPS (Agenda item 7b)
Stokes, Christopher John – E/2015/SR.11
Versegi, Peter Lloyd – E/2015/SR.12
UNICEF (Agenda item 7b)
Stokes, Christopher John – E/2015/SR.11
WORLD FOOD PROGRAMME (Agenda item 7b)
Stokes, Christopher John – E/2015/SR.11

## Austria

MILLENNIUM DEVELOPMENT GOALS
Stessl, Sonja – E/2015/SR.45
SUSTAINABLE DEVELOPMENT GOALS (Agenda item
5c)
Stessl, Sonja – E/2015/SR.45

## Azerbaijan

BRETTON WOODS INSTITUTIONS
Ibrahimova, Khanim – E/2015/SR.26

## Bahamas

MILLENNIUM DEVELOPMENT GOALS
Virgill-Rolle, Nicola – E/2015/SR.48
SUSTAINABLE DEVELOPMENT GOALS (Agenda item
5c)
Virgill-Rolle, Nicola – E/2015/SR.48

## Bahamas. National Insurance Board

INSTITUTION BUILDING (Agenda item 5d)
Bethel, Rowena G. – E/2015/SR.49

## Bahrain

SUSTAINABLE DEVELOPMENT (Agenda item 18a)
Alsaleh, Faeqa Saeed – E/2015/SR.43

## Bangladesh

BRETTON WOODS INSTITUTIONS
Mitra, Barun Dev – E/2015/SR.26
HUMANITARIAN ASSISTANCE (Agenda item 9)
Ahsan, M. Shameem – E/2015/SR.40
Faizunnesa, Sadia – E/2015/SR.38
REGIONAL COOPERATION–ASIA AND THE PACIFIC
(Agenda item 15)
Elias, Andalib – E/2015/SR.54

## Bangladesh (continued)

SUSTAINABLE DEVELOPMENT (Agenda item 18a)
Momen, Abulkalam Abdul – E/2015/SR.44
TAXATION (Agenda item 18h)
Rahman, Mustafizur – E/2015/SR.28; E/2015/SR.29

## Belgium

OPERATIONAL ACTIVITIES–UN (Agenda item 7)
Frankinet, Bénédicte – E/2015/SR.6
SUSTAINABLE DEVELOPMENT (Agenda item 18a)
Frankinet, Bénédicte – E/2015/SR.18

## Benin

BRETTON WOODS INSTITUTIONS
Zinsou, Eric Jean-Marie – E/2015/SR.26

## Beyond 2015 (Organization : Brussels)

SUSTAINABLE DEVELOPMENT (Agenda item 18a)
Badenoch, Charles (World Vision) –
E/2015/SR.47(A)

## Botswana

SUSTAINABLE DEVELOPMENT (Agenda item 18a)
Ntwaagae, Charles – E/2015/SR.44
SUSTAINABLE DEVELOPMENT–HIGH-LEVEL
POLITICAL FORUM (Agenda item 6)
Ntwaagae, Charles – E/2015/SR.44

## Brazil

EBOLA VIRUS DISEASE
Patriota, Antonio de Aguiar – E/2015/SR.3
HUMANITARIAN ASSISTANCE (Agenda item 9)
Dalcero, Pedro Luiz – E/2015/SR.40
INSTITUTION BUILDING (Agenda item 5d)
Patriota, Antonio de Aguiar – E/2015/SR.44
OPERATIONAL ACTIVITIES–UN (Agenda item 7)
Favero, Mauricio Fernando Dias – E/2015/SR.5;
E/2015/SR.6; E/2015/SR.8
Patriota, Antonio de Aguiar – E/2015/SR.34
POPULATION–DEVELOPMENT (Agenda item 18f)
Patriota, Erika Almeida Watanabe – E/2015/SR.55
SOUTH-SOUTH COOPERATION (Agenda item 7c)
Patriota, Guilherme de Aguiar – E/2015/SR.12;
E/2015/SR.13
SUSTAINABLE DEVELOPMENT (Agenda item 18a)
Patriota, Antonio de Aguiar – E/2015/SR.3;
E/2015/SR.19
UN. ECONOMIC AND SOCIAL COUNCIL (2014-2015 :
NEW YORK AND GENEVA)–AGENDA (Agenda item 2)
Favero, Mauricio Fernando Dias – E/2015/SR.1;
E/2015/SR.2
UN. PERMANENT FORUM ON INDIGENOUS ISSUES
(Agenda item 19h)
Yassine, Amena Martins – E/2015/SR.54
UN FORUM ON FORESTS (Agenda item 18k)
Santos, Sérgio Rodrigues dos – E/2015/SR.55
UN POLICY RECOMMENDATIONS (Agenda item 7a)
Patriota, Guilherme de Aguiar – E/2015/SR.13
UN-WOMEN (Agenda item 7b)
Ribeiro, Adriana Telles – E/2015/SR.11
UNDP/UNFPA/UNOPS (Agenda item 7b)
Ribeiro, Adriana Telles – E/2015/SR.11

**Brazil (continued)**

UNICEF (Agenda item 7b)
Ribeiro, Adriana Telles – E/2015/SR.11
WORLD FOOD PROGRAMME (Agenda item 7b)
Ribeiro, Adriana Telles – E/2015/SR.11

**Bread for the World (Organization)**

BRETTON WOODS INSTITUTIONS
Hanfstaengl, Eva – E/2015/SR.27

**Brookings Institution (Washington, D.C.)**

MILLENNIUM DEVELOPMENT GOALS
McArthur, John W. – E/2015/SR.46
SUSTAINABLE DEVELOPMENT GOALS (Agenda item 5c)
McArthur, John W. – E/2015/SR.46

**Burkina Faso**

SUSTAINABLE DEVELOPMENT (Agenda item 18a)
Ouedraogo-Boni, Bibiane – E/2015/SR.43

**Cable News Network (United States)**

SUSTAINABLE DEVELOPMENT (Agenda item 18a)
Quest, Richard – E/2015/SR.15

**Canada**

BRETTON WOODS INSTITUTIONS
Grant, Michael Douglas – E/2015/SR.26
HUMANITARIAN ASSISTANCE (Agenda item 9)
Godin, Catherine – E/2015/SR.37
Tabah, Joshua – E/2015/SR.39
OPERATIONAL ACTIVITIES–UN (Agenda item 7)
Hentic, Isabelle – E/2015/SR.6
SUSTAINABLE DEVELOPMENT (Agenda item 18a)
Grant, Michael Douglas – E/2015/SR.19

**Caribbean Community**

OPERATIONAL ACTIVITIES–UN (Agenda item 7)
Haynes, Rueanna (Trinidad and Tobago) –
E/2015/SR.9
SUSTAINABLE DEVELOPMENT (Agenda item 18a)
Alamilla, Lisel (Belize) – E/2015/SR.43
Christie, Perry G. (Bahamas) – E/2015/SR.15
SUSTAINABLE DEVELOPMENT–HIGH-LEVEL
POLITICAL FORUM (Agenda item 6)
Alamilla, Lisel (Belize) – E/2015/SR.43
TAXATION (Agenda item 18h)
Francis, Tishka H. (Bahamas) – E/2015/SR.28
UN POLICY RECOMMENDATIONS (Agenda item 7a)
Haynes, Rueanna (Trinidad and Tobago) –
E/2015/SR.9

**Center for Global Development (Washington, D.C.)**

EBOLA VIRUS DISEASE
Over, A. Mead – E/2015/SR.3
SUSTAINABLE DEVELOPMENT (Agenda item 18a)
Over, A. Mead – E/2015/SR.3

**Centre for International Forestry Research**

OPERATIONAL ACTIVITIES–UN (Agenda item 7)
Aklilu, Bisrat – E/2015/SR.5

**Channel 4 News (London)**

HUMANITARIAN ASSISTANCE (Agenda item 9)
Snow, Jon – E/2015/SR.39

**Chile**

ECONOMIC ASSISTANCE–HAITI (Agenda item 12d)
Cabezas, Fernando Arturo – E/2015/SR.52
HUMANITARIAN ASSISTANCE (Agenda item 9)
Guesalaga, Patricio – E/2015/SR.40
UN. ECONOMIC AND SOCIAL COUNCIL (2014-2015 :
NEW YORK AND GENEVA)–AGENDA (Agenda item 2)
Aguirre, Patricio – E/2015/SR.1

**China**

EBOLA VIRUS DISEASE
Yao, Shaojun – E/2015/SR.3
HUMANITARIAN ASSISTANCE (Agenda item 9)
Wang, Dazhong – E/2015/SR.37
MILLENNIUM DEVELOPMENT GOALS
Wang, Min – E/2015/SR.44
OPERATIONAL ACTIVITIES–UN (Agenda item 7)
Wang, Dazhong – E/2015/SR.9
Wang, Hongbo – E/2015/SR.5; E/2015/SR.8;
E/2015/SR.34
SOCIAL DEVELOPMENT (Agenda item 19b)
Yao, Shaojun – E/2015/SR.31
SOUTH-SOUTH COOPERATION (Agenda item 7c)
Wang, Hongbo – E/2015/SR.12
SUSTAINABLE DEVELOPMENT (Agenda item 18a)
Yao, Shaojun – E/2015/SR.3
SUSTAINABLE DEVELOPMENT GOALS (Agenda item 5c)
Wang, Min – E/2015/SR.44
UN POLICY RECOMMENDATIONS (Agenda item 7a)
Wang, Dazhong – E/2015/SR.9
Wang, Hongbo – E/2015/SR.12
UN-WOMEN. EXECUTIVE BOARD–MEMBERS
(Agenda item 4)
Chu, Guang – E/2015/SR.23
UNDP/UNFPA/UNOPS (Agenda item 7b)
Wang, Hongbo – E/2015/SR.12

**Christian Aid (Organization)**

BRETTON WOODS INSTITUTIONS
Kohonen, Matti – E/2015/SR.27

**CIVICUS**

NON-GOVERNMENTAL ORGANIZATIONS (Agenda item 17)
Huffines, Jeffery – E/2015/SR.47(A)
SUSTAINABLE DEVELOPMENT (Agenda item 18a)
Huffines, Jeffery – E/2015/SR.47(A)
SUSTAINABLE DEVELOPMENT–HIGH-LEVEL
POLITICAL FORUM (Agenda item 6)
Huffines, Jeffery – E/2015/SR.47(A)

**CLIPSAS (Organization)**

SUSTAINABLE DEVELOPMENT (Agenda item 18a)
Daly, Louis A. – E/2015/SR.47(A)

## Colombia

BRETTON WOODS INSTITUTIONS
Cardenas Santamaria, Mauricio – E/2015/SR.25
Mejía Vélez, María Emma – E/2015/SR.27
HUMANITARIAN ASSISTANCE (Agenda item 9)
Londoño Soto, Beatriz – E/2015/SR.40
INSTITUTION BUILDING (Agenda item 5d)
Mejía Vélez, María Emma – E/2015/SR.44
NARCOTIC DRUGS (Agenda item 19d)
Morales López, Carlos Arturo – E/2015/SR.53
SOCIAL DEVELOPMENT (Agenda item 19b)
Mejía Vélez, María Emma – E/2015/SR.31
SOUTH-SOUTH COOPERATION (Agenda item 7c)
Ruíz Blanco, Miguel Camilo – E/2015/SR.12
SUSTAINABLE DEVELOPMENT (Agenda item 18a)
Mejía Vélez, María Emma – E/2015/SR.16
UN. ECONOMIC AND SOCIAL COUNCIL (2014-2015 :
NEW YORK AND GENEVA)–AGENDA (Agenda item 2)
Ruíz Blanco, Miguel Camilo – E/2015/SR.1
UN-WOMEN (Agenda item 7b)
Dávila, María Paulina – E/2015/SR.11
UNDP/UNFPA/UNOPS (Agenda item 7b)
Dávila, María Paulina – E/2015/SR.11
UNICEF (Agenda item 7b)
Dávila, María Paulina – E/2015/SR.11
WORLD FOOD PROGRAMME (Agenda item 7b)
Dávila, María Paulina – E/2015/SR.11

## Columbia University (New York)

SUSTAINABLE DEVELOPMENT (Agenda item 18a)
Stiglitz, Joseph E. – E/2015/SR.15

## Community of Latin American and Caribbean States

BRETTON WOODS INSTITUTIONS
Lasso Mendoza, Xavier (Ecuador) – E/2015/SR.25

## Coordinating Bureau of the Least Developed Countries. Chairman

LEAST DEVELOPED COUNTRIES–INTERNATIONAL
DECADE (2011-2020) (Agenda item 11b)
Zinsou, Jean-Francis Régis (Benin) – E/2015/SR.56

## Corporativa de Fundaciones (Organization : Mexico)

NON-GOVERNMENTAL ORGANIZATIONS (Agenda
item 17)
Pérez Rulfo Torres, David – E/2015/SR.47(A)
SUSTAINABLE DEVELOPMENT (Agenda item 18a)
Pérez Rulfo Torres, David – E/2015/SR.47(A)

## Costa Rica

OPERATIONAL ACTIVITIES–UN (Agenda item 7)
Calvo Calvo, William José – E/2015/SR.5
SUSTAINABLE DEVELOPMENT (Agenda item 18a)
Mora Delgado, Alexander – E/2015/SR.20

## Côte d'Ivoire

OPERATIONAL ACTIVITIES–UN (Agenda item 7)
Mabri Toikeusse, Albert – E/2015/SR.9

## Côte d'Ivoire (continued)

UN POLICY RECOMMENDATIONS (Agenda item 7a)
Mabri Toikeusse, Albert – E/2015/SR.9

## Croatia

BRETTON WOODS INSTITUTIONS
Drobnjak, Vladimir – E/2015/SR.27
SUSTAINABLE DEVELOPMENT (Agenda item 18a)
Klisovic, Josko – E/2015/SR.43
SUSTAINABLE DEVELOPMENT–HIGH-LEVEL
POLITICAL FORUM (Agenda item 6)
Klisovic, Josko – E/2015/SR.43

## Cuba

EBOLA VIRUS DISEASE
Guerra Rodríguez, Yolanda – E/2015/SR.3
HUMANITARIAN ASSISTANCE (Agenda item 9)
Pérez Alvarez, Claudia – E/2015/SR.39;
E/2015/SR.40
SUSTAINABLE DEVELOPMENT (Agenda item 18a)
Guerra Rodríguez, Yolanda – E/2015/SR.3
UN. ECONOMIC AND SOCIAL COUNCIL (2014-2015 :
NEW YORK AND GENEVA)–AGENDA (Agenda item 2)
Rodríguez Abascal, Ana Silvia – E/2015/SR.1

## Cyprus

SUSTAINABLE DEVELOPMENT (Agenda item 18a)
Kouyialis, Nicos – E/2015/SR.43
SUSTAINABLE DEVELOPMENT–HIGH-LEVEL
POLITICAL FORUM (Agenda item 6)
Kouyialis, Nicos – E/2015/SR.43

## Czech Republic

SUSTAINABLE DEVELOPMENT (Agenda item 18a)
Tlapa, Martin – E/2015/SR.43
SUSTAINABLE DEVELOPMENT–HIGH-LEVEL
POLITICAL FORUM (Agenda item 6)
Tlapa, Martin – E/2015/SR.43

## Dag Hammarskjöld Foundation (Uppsala, Sweden)

OPERATIONAL ACTIVITIES–UN (Agenda item 7)
Jenks, Bruce – E/2015/SR.5

## Denmark

SUSTAINABLE DEVELOPMENT–HIGH-LEVEL
POLITICAL FORUM (Agenda item 6)
Petersen, Ib – E/2015/SR.44

## Ebola Survival Fund

EBOLA VIRUS DISEASE
Wright, Jeffrey – E/2015/SR.3
SUSTAINABLE DEVELOPMENT (Agenda item 18a)
Wright, Jeffrey – E/2015/SR.3

## Ecuador

HUMANITARIAN ASSISTANCE (Agenda item 9)
Espinosa Garcés, María Fernanda – E/2015/SR.40

## Egypt

MILLENNIUM DEVELOPMENT GOALS
Aboulatta, Amr Abdellatif – E/2015/SR.44

## Egypt (continued)

SUSTAINABLE DEVELOPMENT–HIGH-LEVEL
POLITICAL FORUM (Agenda item 6)
    Aboulatta, Amr Abdellatif – E/2015/SR.44
SUSTAINABLE DEVELOPMENT GOALS (Agenda item
5c)
    Aboulatta, Amr Abdellatif – E/2015/SR.44
UN. ECONOMIC AND SOCIAL COUNCIL (2014-2015 :
NEW YORK AND GENEVA)–AGENDA (Agenda item 2)
    Khalil, Mootaz Ahmadein – E/2015/SR.1

## Equidad de Género : Ciudadanía, Trabajo y Familia, A.C. (Mexico)

BRETTON WOODS INSTITUTIONS
    Reyes Zúñiga, Luisa Emilia – E/2015/SR.27

## Estonia

HUMANITARIAN ASSISTANCE (Agenda item 9)
    Seilenthal, Jüri – E/2015/SR.37
SUSTAINABLE DEVELOPMENT (Agenda item 18a)
    Sarapuu, Margus – E/2015/SR.43
SUSTAINABLE DEVELOPMENT–HIGH-LEVEL
POLITICAL FORUM (Agenda item 6)
    Sarapuu, Margus – E/2015/SR.43

## Ethiopia

BRETTON WOODS INSTITUTIONS
    Tekeste Meskel, Abraham – E/2015/SR.25
HUMANITARIAN ASSISTANCE (Agenda item 9)
    Habtemariam, Yanit – E/2015/SR.38
    Kebret, Negash – E/2015/SR.40
OPERATIONAL ACTIVITIES–UN (Agenda item 7)
    Gedamu, Admasu Nebebe – E/2015/SR.8
    Gutulo, Belachew Gujubo – E/2015/SR.34

## Eurasian Economic Club of Scientists Association (Kazakhstan)

BRETTON WOODS INSTITUTIONS
    Karimsakov, Murat – E/2015/SR.25

## European Commission. Commissioner for Employment, Social Affairs, Skills and Labour Mobility

SUSTAINABLE DEVELOPMENT (Agenda item 18a)
    Thyssen, Marianne – E/2015/SR.15

## European Disability Forum

SUSTAINABLE DEVELOPMENT (Agenda item 18a)
    Cuk, Vladimir – E/2015/SR.47(A)

## European Union

BRETTON WOODS INSTITUTIONS
    Mimica, Neven – E/2015/SR.25
EBOLA VIRUS DISEASE
    Poulsen, Jan Pirouz – E/2015/SR.3
GENDER MAINSTREAMING–UN SYSTEM (Agenda
item 12c)
    Holtz, Aaron (United Kingdom) – E/2015/SR.36
HUMANITARIAN ASSISTANCE (Agenda item 9)
    Fink-Hooijer, Florika – E/2015/SR.38; E/2015/SR.39
    Jansons, Raimonds (Latvia) – E/2015/SR.37

## European Union (continued)

NON-GOVERNMENTAL ORGANIZATIONS (Agenda
item 17)
    Lucas, Sylvie (Luxembourg) – E/2015/SR.51
OPERATIONAL ACTIVITIES–UN (Agenda item 7)
    Bargawi, Omar – E/2015/SR.5; E/2015/SR.8
PALESTINIANS–TERRITORIES OCCUPIED BY
ISRAEL–LIVING CONDITIONS (Agenda item 16)
    Carroll, Erica (United Kingdom) – E/2015/SR.50
REGIONAL COOPERATION–ASIA AND THE PACIFIC
(Agenda item 15)
    Klausa, Agnieszka – E/2015/SR.54
SOCIAL DEVELOPMENT (Agenda item 19b)
    Köhler, Pit – E/2015/SR.31
SUSTAINABLE DEVELOPMENT (Agenda item 18a)
    Poulsen, Jan Pirouz – E/2015/SR.3
    Vella, Karmenu – E/2015/SR.43
SUSTAINABLE DEVELOPMENT–HIGH-LEVEL
POLITICAL FORUM (Agenda item 6)
    Vella, Karmenu – E/2015/SR.43
TAXATION (Agenda item 18h)
    Busuttil, John – E/2015/SR.28; E/2015/SR.56
UN. ECONOMIC AND SOCIAL COUNCIL (2014-2015 :
NEW YORK AND GENEVA)–AGENDA (Agenda item 2)
    Bargawi, Omar – E/2015/SR.1; E/2015/SR.2
UN FORUM ON FORESTS (Agenda item 18k)
    Beviglia Zampetti, Americo – E/2015/SR.55
UN POLICY RECOMMENDATIONS (Agenda item 7a)
    Beviglia Zampetti, Americo – E/2015/SR.13

## Fairtrade International

SUSTAINABLE DEVELOPMENT (Agenda item 18a)
    Theyer, Hans – E/2015/SR.47(A)

## FAO. Committee on World Food Security. Chair

SUSTAINABLE DEVELOPMENT (Agenda item 18a)
    Verburg, Gerda (Netherlands) – E/2015/SR.50

## Financial Transparency Coalition

TAXATION (Agenda item 18h)
    Fossard, Renaud – E/2015/SR.28

## Finland

EBOLA VIRUS DISEASE
    Taipale, Pilvi – E/2015/SR.3
HUMANITARIAN ASSISTANCE (Agenda item 9)
    Gebremedhin, Anna – E/2015/SR.37
SUSTAINABLE DEVELOPMENT (Agenda item 18a)
    Laatu, Riikka – E/2015/SR.43
    Taipale, Pilvi – E/2015/SR.3
    Wallin, Markku – E/2015/SR.15
    Wallin, Stefan – E/2015/SR.18
SUSTAINABLE DEVELOPMENT–HIGH-LEVEL
POLITICAL FORUM (Agenda item 6)
    Laatu, Riikka – E/2015/SR.43

## France

EBOLA VIRUS DISEASE
    Bartoli, Fabienne – E/2015/SR.3
HUMANITARIAN ASSISTANCE (Agenda item 9)
    Wagner, Thomas – E/2015/SR.40

## France (continued)

OPERATIONAL ACTIVITIES–UN (Agenda item 7)
    Gave, François – E/2015/SR.34
SUSTAINABLE DEVELOPMENT (Agenda item 18a)
    Bartoli, Fabienne – E/2015/SR.3
    Bedas, Bernard – E/2015/SR.18
SUSTAINABLE DEVELOPMENT–HIGH-LEVEL
POLITICAL FORUM (Agenda item 6)
    Delattre, François – E/2015/SR.44
UN. PERMANENT FORUM ON INDIGENOUS ISSUES
(Agenda item 19h)
    Selk, Vanessa – E/2015/SR.54

## Gabon

UN FORUM ON FORESTS (Agenda item 18k)
    Bibalou, Marianne Odette – E/2015/SR.55

## Germany

EBOLA VIRUS DISEASE
    Nell, Christian – E/2015/SR.3
HUMANITARIAN ASSISTANCE (Agenda item 9)
    Reiffenstuel, Anke – E/2015/SR.37; E/2015/SR.38
INSTITUTION BUILDING (Agenda item 5d)
    Kage, Stephanie – E/2015/SR.49
MILLENNIUM DEVELOPMENT GOALS
    Gies, Andreas – E/2015/SR.48
NON-GOVERNMENTAL ORGANIZATIONS (Agenda
item 17)
    Hullman, Christiane – E/2015/SR.51
OPERATIONAL ACTIVITIES–UN (Agenda item 7)
    Kern, Ursula Caroline – E/2015/SR.34
    Pfeil, Andreas – E/2015/SR.5
    Silberhorn, Thomas – E/2015/SR.9
SOUTH-SOUTH COOPERATION (Agenda item 7c)
    Krapp, Reinhard – E/2015/SR.13
SUSTAINABLE DEVELOPMENT (Agenda item 18a)
    Kage, Stephanie – E/2015/SR.15; E/2015/SR.20
    Nell, Christian – E/2015/SR.3
SUSTAINABLE DEVELOPMENT–HIGH-LEVEL
POLITICAL FORUM (Agenda item 6)
    Schwarzelühr-Sutter, Rita – E/2015/SR.44
SUSTAINABLE DEVELOPMENT GOALS (Agenda item
5c)
    Gies, Andreas – E/2015/SR.48
TAXATION (Agenda item 18h)
    Kage, Stephanie – E/2015/SR.28
UN POLICY RECOMMENDATIONS (Agenda item 7a)
    Krapp, Reinhard – E/2015/SR.13
    Silberhorn, Thomas – E/2015/SR.9

## Ghana

OPERATIONAL ACTIVITIES–UN (Agenda item 7)
    Tara, Mahama Samuel – E/2015/SR.8
TAXATION (Agenda item 18h)
    Dzadzra, Anthony – E/2015/SR.29

## Global Clearinghouse for Development Finance

BRETTON WOODS INSTITUTIONS
    Samuels, Barbara – E/2015/SR.26

## Global Foundation for Democracy and Development

SUSTAINABLE DEVELOPMENT (Agenda item 18a)
    Jourdan, Marc – E/2015/SR.47(A)

## Global Policy Forum

OPERATIONAL ACTIVITIES–UN (Agenda item 7)
    Adams, Barbara – E/2015/SR.6

## Gray Panthers (Organization)

SUSTAINABLE DEVELOPMENT (Agenda item 18a)
    Davis, Joan – E/2015/SR.15

## Group of 77

BRETTON WOODS INSTITUTIONS
    Mamabolo, Jeremiah Nyamane Kingsley (South
        Africa) – E/2015/SR.25
    Marobe, Simon Poni (South Africa) – E/2015/SR.26
HUMANITARIAN ASSISTANCE (Agenda item 9)
    Notutela, Ncumisa (South Africa) – E/2015/SR.37
OPERATIONAL ACTIVITIES–UN (Agenda item 7)
    Marobe, Simon Poni (South Africa) – E/2015/SR.34
    Mminele, Mahlatse (South Africa) – E/2015/SR.8
    Mollinedo Claros, Julio Lázaro (Bolivia (Plurinational
        State of)) – E/2015/SR.5
    Nyembe, Raymond Thulane (South Africa) –
        E/2015/SR.41
PALESTINIANS–TERRITORIES OCCUPIED BY
ISRAEL–LIVING CONDITIONS (Agenda item 16)
    Marobe, Simon Poni (South Africa) – E/2015/SR.50
SOUTH-SOUTH COOPERATION (Agenda item 7c)
    Mamabolo, Jeremiah Nyamane Kingsley (South
        Africa) – E/2015/SR.12
SUSTAINABLE DEVELOPMENT (Agenda item 18a)
    Mamabolo, Jeremiah Nyamane Kingsley (South
        Africa) – E/2015/SR.43
    Patel, Ebrahim (South Africa) – E/2015/SR.18
SUSTAINABLE DEVELOPMENT–HIGH-LEVEL
POLITICAL FORUM (Agenda item 6)
    Mamabolo, Jeremiah Nyamane Kingsley (South
        Africa) – E/2015/SR.43
TAXATION (Agenda item 18h)
    Marobe, Simon Poni (South Africa) – E/2015/SR.56
    Mminele, Mahlatse (South Africa) – E/2015/SR.28;
        E/2015/SR.33
UN–TRAINING AND RESEARCH INSTITUTIONS
(Agenda item 20)
    Mminele, Mahlatse (South Africa) – E/2015/SR.33
UN. ECONOMIC AND SOCIAL COUNCIL (2014-2015 :
NEW YORK AND GENEVA)–AGENDA (Agenda item 2)
    Mollinedo Claros, Julio Lázaro (Bolivia (Plurinational
        State of)) – E/2015/SR.1; E/2015/SR.2
UN FORUM ON FORESTS (Agenda item 18k)
    Malawana, Lawrence Xolani (South Africa) –
        E/2015/SR.55
UN POLICY RECOMMENDATIONS (Agenda item 7a)
    Mamabolo, Jeremiah Nyamane Kingsley (South
        Africa) – E/2015/SR.12
UNDP/UNFPA/UNOPS (Agenda item 7b)
    Mamabolo, Jeremiah Nyamane Kingsley (South
        Africa) – E/2015/SR.12

**Group of Friends of the World Conference on Indigenous Peoples**

UN. PERMANENT FORUM ON INDIGENOUS ISSUES (Agenda item 19h)
Montaño, Jorge (Mexico) – E/2015/SR.54

**Group of Least Developed Countries**

BRETTON WOODS INSTITUTIONS
Zinsou, Jean-Francis Régis (Benin) – E/2015/SR.25
LEAST DEVELOPED COUNTRIES–INTERNATIONAL DECADE (2011-2020) (Agenda item 11b)
Zinsou, Jean-Francis Régis (Benin) – E/2015/SR.50

**Guatemala**

ECONOMIC ASSISTANCE–HAITI (Agenda item 12d)
Carrera Castro, Fernando – E/2015/SR.52
NARCOTIC DRUGS (Agenda item 19d)
Carrera Castro, Fernando – E/2015/SR.53
OPERATIONAL ACTIVITIES–UN (Agenda item 7)
Carrera Castro, Fernando – E/2015/SR.5;
E/2015/SR.6; E/2015/SR.8; E/2015/SR.34
REGIONAL COOPERATION (Agenda item 15)
Carrera Castro, Fernando – E/2015/SR.47(B)

**Guinea**

EBOLA VIRUS DISEASE
Diare, Mohamed – E/2015/SR.3
SUSTAINABLE DEVELOPMENT (Agenda item 18a)
Diare, Mohamed – E/2015/SR.3

**Guyana**

BRETTON WOODS INSTITUTIONS
Talbot, George Wilfred – E/2015/SR.26
OPERATIONAL ACTIVITIES–UN (Agenda item 7)
Talbot, George Wilfred – E/2015/SR.10
UN POLICY RECOMMENDATIONS (Agenda item 7a)
Talbot, George Wilfred – E/2015/SR.10

**Holy See**

HUMANITARIAN ASSISTANCE (Agenda item 9)
Gyhra, Richard – E/2015/SR.40

**Honduras**

HUMANITARIAN ASSISTANCE (Agenda item 9)
Gómez Guifarro, Gilliam Noemi – E/2015/SR.40
OPERATIONAL ACTIVITIES–UN (Agenda item 7)
Suazo, Marco Antonio – E/2015/SR.8
SUSTAINABLE DEVELOPMENT (Agenda item 18a)
Cardona, Ricardo – E/2015/SR.43
Suazo, Marco Antonio – E/2015/SR.19

**IBRD**

BRETTON WOODS INSTITUTIONS
Eun, Sung-soo – E/2015/SR.26
Guindos Talavera, Beatriz de – E/2015/SR.27
Kostzer, Daniel – E/2015/SR.27
Mohieldin, Mahmoud – E/2015/SR.25;
E/2015/SR.27
Qureshi, Zia – E/2015/SR.26
Santala, Satu – E/2015/SR.27

**IBRD (continued)**

EBOLA VIRUS DISEASE
Thomas, Mark R. (Mark Roland) – E/2015/SR.3
HUMANITARIAN ASSISTANCE (Agenda item 9)
Kull, Daniel – E/2015/SR.38
INTERNATIONAL FINANCIAL INSTITUTIONS (Agenda item 5b)
Panzer, John – E/2015/SR.46
SUSTAINABLE DEVELOPMENT (Agenda item 18a)
Thomas, Mark R. (Mark Roland) – E/2015/SR.3
TAXATION (Agenda item 18h)
Verhoeven, Marijn – E/2015/SR.28

**ILO**

BRETTON WOODS INSTITUTIONS
Mahmood, Moazam – E/2015/SR.26
INTERNATIONAL FINANCIAL INSTITUTIONS (Agenda item 5b)
Torres, Raymond – E/2015/SR.46
SOCIAL DEVELOPMENT (Agenda item 19b)
Pinheiro, Vinícius Carvalho – E/2015/SR.31

**ILO. Director-General**

SUSTAINABLE DEVELOPMENT (Agenda item 18a)
Ryder, Guy – E/2015/SR.15; E/2015/SR.17;
E/2015/SR.20

**IMF**

BRETTON WOODS INSTITUTIONS
Helbling, Thomas – E/2015/SR.27
McDonald, Calvin A. – E/2015/SR.25

**IMF. Deputy Managing Director**

INTERNATIONAL FINANCIAL INSTITUTIONS (Agenda item 5b)
Zhu, Min – E/2015/SR.46
SUSTAINABLE DEVELOPMENT (Agenda item 18a)
Zhu, Min – E/2015/SR.15

**IMF. Fiscal Affairs Department**

TAXATION (Agenda item 18h)
Perry, Victoria J. – E/2015/SR.28; E/2015/SR.29

**India**

EBOLA VIRUS DISEASE
Joshi, Mayank – E/2015/SR.3
HUMANITARIAN ASSISTANCE (Agenda item 9)
Kumar, Ajit – E/2015/SR.40
SOUTH-SOUTH COOPERATION (Agenda item 7c)
Bishnoi, Bhagwant Singh – E/2015/SR.12
SUSTAINABLE DEVELOPMENT (Agenda item 18a)
Joshi, Mayank – E/2015/SR.3
Mukerji, Asoke Kumar – E/2015/SR.19
Sukhdev, Pavan – E/2015/SR.20
SUSTAINABLE DEVELOPMENT–HIGH-LEVEL POLITICAL FORUM (Agenda item 6)
Mukerji, Asoke Kumar – E/2015/SR.44
UN POLICY RECOMMENDATIONS (Agenda item 7a)
Bishnoi, Bhagwant Singh – E/2015/SR.12
UNDP/UNFPA/UNOPS (Agenda item 7b)
Bishnoi, Bhagwant Singh – E/2015/SR.12

## Indonesia

HUMANITARIAN ASSISTANCE (Agenda item 9)
Wibowo, Triyono – E/2015/SR.40
MILLENNIUM DEVELOPMENT GOALS
Percaya, Desra – E/2015/SR.48
OPERATIONAL ACTIVITIES–UN (Agenda item 7)
Chandra, Purnomo Ahmad – E/2015/SR.34
REGIONAL COOPERATION–ASIA AND THE PACIFIC
(Agenda item 15)
Rakhmatia, Nara Masista – E/2015/SR.54
SOUTH-SOUTH COOPERATION (Agenda item 7c)
Choesni, Tubagus A. – E/2015/SR.12; E/2015/SR.13
SUSTAINABLE DEVELOPMENT (Agenda item 18a)
Dhakiri, Hanif – E/2015/SR.16
Murniningtyas, Endah – E/2015/SR.43
Roostiavati, Agus Prihono – E/2015/SR.18
SUSTAINABLE DEVELOPMENT–HIGH-LEVEL
POLITICAL FORUM (Agenda item 6)
Murniningtyas, Endah – E/2015/SR.43
SUSTAINABLE DEVELOPMENT GOALS (Agenda item
5c)
Percaya, Desra – E/2015/SR.48
UN POLICY RECOMMENDATIONS (Agenda item 7a)
Choesni, Tubagus A. – E/2015/SR.13

## Inter-Agency Secretariat of the ISDR

HUMANITARIAN ASSISTANCE (Agenda item 9)
Wannous, Chadia – E/2015/SR.40

## Inter-American Center of Tax Administrations

TAXATION (Agenda item 18h)
Verdi, Marco – E/2015/SR.28; E/2015/SR.29

## Inter-Parliamentary Union

INSTITUTION BUILDING (Agenda item 5d)
Chowdhury, Saber – E/2015/SR.49
MILLENNIUM DEVELOPMENT GOALS
Chowdhury, Saber – E/2015/SR.46
SUSTAINABLE DEVELOPMENT GOALS (Agenda item
5c)
Chowdhury, Saber – E/2015/SR.46

## International Association of Economic and Social Councils and Similar Institutions

INSTITUTION BUILDING (Agenda item 5d)
Velikhov, E.P. – E/2015/SR.44
MILLENNIUM DEVELOPMENT GOALS
Velikhov, E.P. – E/2015/SR.44
SUSTAINABLE DEVELOPMENT GOALS (Agenda item
5c)
Velikhov, E.P. – E/2015/SR.44

## International Chamber of Commerce

BRETTON WOODS INSTITUTIONS
Kantrow, Louise – E/2015/SR.25

## International Committee for Arab-Israeli Reconciliation

SUSTAINABLE DEVELOPMENT (Agenda item 18a)
Karmakar, Sudhangshu – E/2015/SR.47(A)

## International Committee of the Red Cross

HUMANITARIAN ASSISTANCE (Agenda item 9)
Alderson, Helen – E/2015/SR.38
Colassis, Laurent – E/2015/SR.39
Martin, Christophe – E/2015/SR.40

## International Council for Education of People with Visual Impairment

SUSTAINABLE DEVELOPMENT (Agenda item 18a)
Ferrell, Kay Alicyn – E/2015/SR.47(A)

## International Criminal Court. Prosecutor

HUMANITARIAN ASSISTANCE (Agenda item 9)
Bensouda, Fatou – E/2015/SR.39

## International Disability Alliance

SUSTAINABLE DEVELOPMENT–MINISTERIAL
MEETING (Agenda item 5a)
Cuk, Vladimir – E/2015/SR.42

## International Federation for Family Development

SUSTAINABLE DEVELOPMENT (Agenda item 18a)
Richards, Mercedes – E/2015/SR.47(A)

## International Federation for Home Economics

SUSTAINABLE DEVELOPMENT (Agenda item 18a)
Minard, Margaret – E/2015/SR.47(A)

## International Federation of Red Cross and Red Crescent Societies

HUMANITARIAN ASSISTANCE (Agenda item 9)
Cotte, Walter – E/2015/SR.40

## International Narcotics Control Board. President

NARCOTIC DRUGS (Agenda item 19d)
Sipp, Werner – E/2015/SR.53

## International Organisation of Employers

SUSTAINABLE DEVELOPMENT (Agenda item 18a)
Funes de Rioja, Daniel – E/2015/SR.15

## International Organization for Migration

HUMANITARIAN ASSISTANCE (Agenda item 9)
Maze, Kerry – E/2015/SR.40

## International Trade Union Confederation

SUSTAINABLE DEVELOPMENT (Agenda item 18a)
Burrow, Sharan – E/2015/SR.15

## Iran (Islamic Republic of)

MILLENNIUM DEVELOPMENT GOALS
Saadat, Peiman – E/2015/SR.44
NON-GOVERNMENTAL ORGANIZATIONS (Agenda
item 17)
Vadiati, Forouzandeh – E/2015/SR.51
SUSTAINABLE DEVELOPMENT–HIGH-LEVEL
POLITICAL FORUM (Agenda item 6)
Saadat, Peiman – E/2015/SR.44

ECONOMIC AND SOCIAL COUNCIL – 2015 SESSION
INDEX TO SPEECHES – CORPORATE NAMES/COUNTRIES

## Iran (Islamic Republic of) (continued)

SUSTAINABLE DEVELOPMENT GOALS (Agenda item 5c)
 Saadat, Peiman – E/2015/SR.44
UN. COMMISSION ON NARCOTIC DRUGS–
MEMBERS (Agenda item 4)
 Dehghani, Gholamhossein – E/2015/SR.21
UN. ECONOMIC AND SOCIAL COUNCIL (2014-2015 :
NEW YORK AND GENEVA)–AGENDA (Agenda item 2)
 Momeni, Javad – E/2015/SR.1
UN FORUM ON FORESTS (Agenda item 18k)
 Momeni, Javad – E/2015/SR.55

## Ireland

HUMANITARIAN ASSISTANCE (Agenda item 9)
 O'Brien, Patricia – E/2015/SR.40
SOCIAL DEVELOPMENT (Agenda item 19b)
 Donoghue, David – E/2015/SR.31
SUSTAINABLE DEVELOPMENT (Agenda item 18a)
 Kelly, Alan – E/2015/SR.43
SUSTAINABLE DEVELOPMENT–HIGH-LEVEL
POLITICAL FORUM (Agenda item 6)
 Kelly, Alan – E/2015/SR.43

## Israel

INSTITUTION BUILDING (Agenda item 5d)
 Prosor, Ron – E/2015/SR.44
NON-GOVERNMENTAL ORGANIZATIONS (Agenda item 17)
 Roet, David Yitshak – E/2015/SR.51
PALESTINIANS–TERRITORIES OCCUPIED BY
ISRAEL–LIVING CONDITIONS (Agenda item 16)
 Meitzad, Hadas Ester – E/2015/SR.50
SUSTAINABLE DEVELOPMENT (Agenda item 18a)
 Prosor, Ron – E/2015/SR.44
 Roet, David Yitshak – E/2015/SR.19

## Italy

HUMANITARIAN ASSISTANCE (Agenda item 9)
 Serra, Maurizio – E/2015/SR.37
SUSTAINABLE DEVELOPMENT (Agenda item 18a)
 Cardi, Sebastiano – E/2015/SR.19
 Velo, Silvia – E/2015/SR.43
SUSTAINABLE DEVELOPMENT–HIGH-LEVEL
POLITICAL FORUM (Agenda item 6)
 Velo, Silvia – E/2015/SR.43
UN–TRAINING AND RESEARCH INSTITUTIONS
(Agenda item 20)
 Lambertini, Inigo – E/2015/SR.33

## Italy. Revenue Agency

TAXATION (Agenda item 18h)
 Cottani, Giammarco – E/2015/SR.29

## ITU

SUSTAINABLE DEVELOPMENT (Agenda item 18a)
 Bogdan-Martin, Doreen – E/2015/SR.47(A)
 Fowlie, Gary – E/2015/SR.19

## Jamaica

OPERATIONAL ACTIVITIES–UN (Agenda item 7)
 Rattray, Courtenay – E/2015/SR.9
SUSTAINABLE DEVELOPMENT–MINISTERIAL
MEETING (Agenda item 5a)
 Rattray, Courtenay – E/2015/SR.42
UN POLICY RECOMMENDATIONS (Agenda item 7a)
 Rattray, Courtenay – E/2015/SR.9

## Japan

GENDER MAINSTREAMING–UN SYSTEM (Agenda item 12c)
 Sumi, Junichi – E/2015/SR.36
HUMANITARIAN ASSISTANCE (Agenda item 9)
 Kaji, Misako – E/2015/SR.37
MILLENNIUM DEVELOPMENT GOALS
 Nakane, Kazuyuki – E/2015/SR.44; E/2015/SR.48
OPERATIONAL ACTIVITIES–UN (Agenda item 7)
 Minami, Hiroshi – E/2015/SR.34
 Usui, Masato – E/2015/SR.8
PALESTINIANS–TERRITORIES OCCUPIED BY
ISRAEL–LIVING CONDITIONS (Agenda item 16)
 Mikami, Yoshiyuki – E/2015/SR.50
REGIONAL COOPERATION–ASIA AND THE PACIFIC
(Agenda item 15)
 Onishi, Tomoko – E/2015/SR.54
SOUTH-SOUTH COOPERATION (Agenda item 7c)
 Momita, Yasuaki – E/2015/SR.12
SUSTAINABLE DEVELOPMENT (Agenda item 18a)
 Minami, Hiroshi – E/2015/SR.15
SUSTAINABLE DEVELOPMENT GOALS (Agenda item 5c)
 Nakane, Kazuyuki – E/2015/SR.44; E/2015/SR.48
UN. ECONOMIC AND SOCIAL COUNCIL (2014-2015 :
NEW YORK AND GENEVA)–AGENDA (Agenda item 2)
 Usui, Masato – E/2015/SR.1
UN FORUM ON FORESTS (Agenda item 18k)
 Mikami, Yoshiyuki – E/2015/SR.55
UN-WOMEN (Agenda item 7b)
 Minami, Hiroshi – E/2015/SR.11
UNDP/UNFPA/UNOPS (Agenda item 7b)
 Minami, Hiroshi – E/2015/SR.11
UNICEF (Agenda item 7b)
 Minami, Hiroshi – E/2015/SR.11
WORLD FOOD PROGRAMME (Agenda item 7b)
 Minami, Hiroshi – E/2015/SR.11

## Joint United Nations Programme on HIV/AIDS. Deputy Executive Director

AIDS (Agenda item 12g)
 Beagle, Jan – E/2015/SR.22
OPERATIONAL ACTIVITIES–UN (Agenda item 7)
 Beagle, Jan – E/2015/SR.5

## Jordan

HUMANITARIAN ASSISTANCE (Agenda item 9)
 Majali, Saja Sattam Habes – E/2015/SR.40

- 34 -

## Journalists and Writers Foundation (Turkey)

SUSTAINABLE DEVELOPMENT (Agenda item 18a)
    Ülker, Cemre – E/2015/SR.47(A)
WOMEN IN DEVELOPMENT (Agenda item 18j)
    Ülker, Cemre – E/2015/SR.47(A)

## Kazakhstan

BRETTON WOODS INSTITUTIONS
    Karimsakov, Murat – E/2015/SR.25
EBOLA VIRUS DISEASE
    Seksenbay, Tleuzhan S. – E/2015/SR.3
INSTITUTION BUILDING (Agenda item 5d)
    Abdrakhmanov, Kairat – E/2015/SR.44
OPERATIONAL ACTIVITIES–UN (Agenda item 7)
    Seksenbay, Tleuzhan S. – E/2015/SR.8
SUSTAINABLE DEVELOPMENT (Agenda item 18a)
    Abdrakhmanov, Kairat – E/2015/SR.18;
      E/2015/SR.44
    Seksenbay, Tleuzhan S. – E/2015/SR.3
SUSTAINABLE DEVELOPMENT–HIGH-LEVEL
POLITICAL FORUM (Agenda item 6)
    Abdrakhmanov, Kairat – E/2015/SR.44

## Kenya

HUMANITARIAN ASSISTANCE (Agenda item 9)
    Karau, Stephen Ndungu – E/2015/SR.40
OPERATIONAL ACTIVITIES–UN (Agenda item 7)
    Grignon, Koki Muli – E/2015/SR.9
SOUTH-SOUTH COOPERATION (Agenda item 7c)
    Grignon, Koki Muli – E/2015/SR.12
UN POLICY RECOMMENDATIONS (Agenda item 7a)
    Grignon, Koki Muli – E/2015/SR.9

## Kuwait

UN–TRAINING AND RESEARCH INSTITUTIONS
(Agenda item 20)
    Al-Sharrah, Abdullah Ahmad – E/2015/SR.33

## Kyrgyzstan

MILLENNIUM DEVELOPMENT GOALS
    Niyazalieva, Damira – E/2015/SR.48
OPERATIONAL ACTIVITIES–UN (Agenda item 7)
    Karybaeva, Mira – E/2015/SR.8
REGIONAL COOPERATION (Agenda item 15)
    Kabaev, Kuban – E/2015/SR.47(B)
SUSTAINABLE DEVELOPMENT (Agenda item 18a)
    Kydyrov, Talaibek – E/2015/SR.18
SUSTAINABLE DEVELOPMENT–HIGH-LEVEL
POLITICAL FORUM (Agenda item 6)
    Niyazalieva, Damira – E/2015/SR.44
SUSTAINABLE DEVELOPMENT GOALS (Agenda item
5c)
    Niyazalieva, Damira – E/2015/SR.48

## Lao People's Democratic Republic

OPERATIONAL ACTIVITIES–UN (Agenda item 7)
    Chanthaboury, Kikeo – E/2015/SR.10
UN POLICY RECOMMENDATIONS (Agenda item 7a)
    Chanthaboury, Kikeo – E/2015/SR.10; E/2015/SR.13

## League of Arab States

SUSTAINABLE DEVELOPMENT (Agenda item 18a)
    Nabulsi, Tarek – E/2015/SR.47(A)

## Legion of Good Will

SUSTAINABLE DEVELOPMENT (Agenda item 18a)
    Parmegiani, Danilo – E/2015/SR.47(A)

## Lesotho

INSTITUTION BUILDING (Agenda item 5d)
    Maope, Kelebone – E/2015/SR.44
SUSTAINABLE DEVELOPMENT–HIGH-LEVEL
POLITICAL FORUM (Agenda item 6)
    Maope, Kelebone – E/2015/SR.44

## Liberia

EBOLA VIRUS DISEASE
    Siaplay, Mounir – E/2015/SR.3
SUSTAINABLE DEVELOPMENT (Agenda item 18a)
    Siaplay, Mounir – E/2015/SR.3

## Libya

SUSTAINABLE DEVELOPMENT–HIGH-LEVEL
POLITICAL FORUM (Agenda item 6)
    Dabbashi, Ibrahim O.A. – E/2015/SR.44
UN–TRAINING AND RESEARCH INSTITUTIONS
(Agenda item 20)
    Eshanta, Abdulmonem A.H. – E/2015/SR.33

## Luxembourg

HUMANITARIAN ASSISTANCE (Agenda item 9)
    Hoscheit, Jean-Marc – E/2015/SR.40
OPERATIONAL ACTIVITIES–UN (Agenda item 7)
    Schneider, Romain – E/2015/SR.9
UN POLICY RECOMMENDATIONS (Agenda item 7a)
    Schneider, Romain – E/2015/SR.9

## Malaysia

CRIME PREVENTION (Agenda item 19c)
    Rosdi, Mustapha Kamal – E/2015/SR.53
MILLENNIUM DEVELOPMENT GOALS
    Raja Zaib Shah, Raja Reza bin – E/2015/SR.48
SUSTAINABLE DEVELOPMENT GOALS (Agenda item
5c)
    Raja Zaib Shah, Raja Reza bin – E/2015/SR.48

## Mali

EBOLA VIRUS DISEASE
    Doucouré, Dianguina dit Yaya – E/2015/SR.3
SUSTAINABLE DEVELOPMENT (Agenda item 18a)
    Doucouré, Dianguina dit Yaya – E/2015/SR.3

## Mexican Agency for International Development Cooperation

BRETTON WOODS INSTITUTIONS
    Valle Pereña, Juan Manuel – E/2015/SR.26

## Mexico

CRIME PREVENTION (Agenda item 19c)
Alba Góngora, Luis Alfonso de – E/2015/SR.53
HUMANITARIAN ASSISTANCE (Agenda item 9)
Lomónaco Tonda, Jorge – E/2015/SR.37
LEAST DEVELOPED COUNTRIES–INTERNATIONAL
DECADE (2011-2020) (Agenda item 11b)
Lara Rangel, Salvador de – E/2015/SR.50
NARCOTIC DRUGS (Agenda item 19d)
Alba Góngora, Luis Alfonso de – E/2015/SR.53
NON-GOVERNMENTAL ORGANIZATIONS (Agenda
item 17)
Ríos Sánchez, Bruno – E/2015/SR.51
OPERATIONAL ACTIVITIES–UN (Agenda item 7)
Colín Ortega, Gabriela – E/2015/SR.9
REGIONAL COOPERATION (Agenda item 15)
Camacho, Sara Luna – E/2015/SR.47(B)
SOCIAL DEVELOPMENT (Agenda item 19b)
Ríos Sánchez, Bruno – E/2015/SR.32
SOUTH-SOUTH COOPERATION (Agenda item 7c)
Colín Ortega, Gabriela – E/2015/SR.12
UN. ECONOMIC AND SOCIAL COUNCIL (2014-2015 :
NEW YORK AND GENEVA)–AGENDA (Agenda item 2)
Camacho, Sara Luna – E/2015/SR.1
UN POLICY RECOMMENDATIONS (Agenda item 7a)
Colín Ortega, Gabriela – E/2015/SR.9;
E/2015/SR.12
UNDP/UNFPA/UNOPS (Agenda item 7b)
Colín Ortega, Gabriela – E/2015/SR.12

## Monaco

MILLENNIUM DEVELOPMENT GOALS
Picco, Isabelle F. – E/2015/SR.44
SUSTAINABLE DEVELOPMENT–HIGH-LEVEL
POLITICAL FORUM (Agenda item 6)
Picco, Isabelle F. – E/2015/SR.44
SUSTAINABLE DEVELOPMENT GOALS (Agenda item
5c)
Picco, Isabelle F. – E/2015/SR.44

## Mongolia

MILLENNIUM DEVELOPMENT GOALS
Khurelbaatar, Gantsogt – E/2015/SR.48
SUSTAINABLE DEVELOPMENT GOALS (Agenda item
5c)
Khurelbaatar, Gantsogt – E/2015/SR.48

## Morocco

HUMANITARIAN ASSISTANCE (Agenda item 9)
Auajjar, Mohamed – E/2015/SR.37
El Mkhantar, Hassan – E/2015/SR.39
REGIONAL COOPERATION (Agenda item 15)
Hilale, Omar – E/2015/SR.54

## Mozambique

OPERATIONAL ACTIVITIES–UN (Agenda item 7)
Gumende, António – E/2015/SR.6

## Myanmar

SUSTAINABLE DEVELOPMENT (Agenda item 18a)
Lynn, Htin – E/2015/SR.35

## National Congress of American Indians (United States)

UN. PERMANENT FORUM ON INDIGENOUS ISSUES
(Agenda item 19h)
Crippa, Leonardo A. – E/2015/SR.54

## Nepal

BRETTON WOODS INSTITUTIONS
Pokharel, Shatrudhwan P.S. – E/2015/SR.26
HUMANITARIAN ASSISTANCE (Agenda item 9)
Dhital, Deepak – E/2015/SR.40
INSTITUTION BUILDING (Agenda item 5d)
Adhikari, Sewa Lamsal – E/2015/SR.44

## Netherlands

BRETTON WOODS INSTITUTIONS
Ploumen, Lilianne – E/2015/SR.26

## New Future Foundation (New York)

EBOLA VIRUS DISEASE
Blakely, Delois – E/2015/SR.3
SUSTAINABLE DEVELOPMENT (Agenda item 18a)
Blakely, Delois – E/2015/SR.3

## New York University

TAXATION (Agenda item 18h)
Kane, Mitchell – E/2015/SR.29

## New York University. Center on International Cooperation

OPERATIONAL ACTIVITIES–UN (Agenda item 7)
Steven, David – E/2015/SR.9
UN POLICY RECOMMENDATIONS (Agenda item 7a)
Steven, David – E/2015/SR.9

## New Zealand

HUMANITARIAN ASSISTANCE (Agenda item 9)
Reaich, Carl Allan – E/2015/SR.37; E/2015/SR.39

## Nigeria

SCIENCE AND TECHNOLOGY–DEVELOPMENT
(Agenda item 18b)
Johnson, Omobola – E/2015/SR.54

## Norway

BRETTON WOODS INSTITUTIONS
Pedersen, Geir O. – E/2015/SR.26
HUMANITARIAN ASSISTANCE (Agenda item 9)
Pedersen, Bard Glad – E/2015/SR.38
OPERATIONAL ACTIVITIES–UN (Agenda item 7)
Eckey, Susan – E/2015/SR.5; E/2015/SR.6
Fladby, Berit – E/2015/SR.10
Vestrheim, Alf Havard – E/2015/SR.34
SUSTAINABLE DEVELOPMENT (Agenda item 18a)
Kvalsoren, Anne Heidi – E/2015/SR.15
UN POLICY RECOMMENDATIONS (Agenda item 7a)
Fladby, Berit – E/2015/SR.10; E/2015/SR.12;
E/2015/SR.13

## Norway. Prime Minister

SUSTAINABLE DEVELOPMENT–MINISTERIAL
MEETING (Agenda item 5a)
Solberg, Erna – E/2015/SR.42

## OECD. Centre for Tax Policy and Administration

TAXATION (Agenda item 18h)
Perez-Navarro, Grace – E/2015/SR.28

## OECD. Development Co-operation Directorate

BRETTON WOODS INSTITUTIONS
Killen, Brenda – E/2015/SR.26

## Open Society Foundations

EBOLA VIRUS DISEASE
Taylor, Aleesha – E/2015/SR.3
SUSTAINABLE DEVELOPMENT (Agenda item 18a)
Taylor, Aleesha – E/2015/SR.3

## Pacific Small Island Developing States

SUSTAINABLE DEVELOPMENT (Agenda item 18a)
Tupouniua, Mahe'uli'uli Sandhurst (Tonga) –
E/2015/SR.43
SUSTAINABLE DEVELOPMENT–HIGH-LEVEL
POLITICAL FORUM (Agenda item 6)
Tupouniua, Mahe'uli'uli Sandhurst (Tonga) –
E/2015/SR.43

## Pakistan

HUMANITARIAN ASSISTANCE (Agenda item 9)
Bokhari, Abdul Moiz – E/2015/SR.37
OPERATIONAL ACTIVITIES–UN (Agenda item 7)
Bhatti, Nauman Bashir – E/2015/SR.6
REGIONAL COOPERATION–ASIA AND THE PACIFIC
(Agenda item 15)
Ammar, Yasar – E/2015/SR.54
UN-WOMEN. EXECUTIVE BOARD–MEMBERS
(Agenda item 4)
Ammar, Yasar – E/2015/SR.23

## Palau

MILLENNIUM DEVELOPMENT GOALS
Otto, Caleb – E/2015/SR.46
SUSTAINABLE DEVELOPMENT GOALS (Agenda item
5c)
Otto, Caleb – E/2015/SR.46

## Panama

OPERATIONAL ACTIVITIES–UN (Agenda item 7)
Franceschi Navarro, Paulina María – E/2015/SR.8
SUSTAINABLE DEVELOPMENT (Agenda item 18a)
Franceschi Navarro, Paulina María – E/2015/SR.19
SUSTAINABLE DEVELOPMENT–HIGH-LEVEL
POLITICAL FORUM (Agenda item 6)
Franceschi Navarro, Paulina María – E/2015/SR.44
UN-WOMEN (Agenda item 7b)
Franceschi Navarro, Paulina María – E/2015/SR.11
UNDP/UNFPA/UNOPS (Agenda item 7b)
Franceschi Navarro, Paulina María – E/2015/SR.11
UNICEF (Agenda item 7b)
Franceschi Navarro, Paulina María – E/2015/SR.11

## Panama (continued)

WORLD FOOD PROGRAMME (Agenda item 7b)
Franceschi Navarro, Paulina María – E/2015/SR.11

## Paraguay

SUSTAINABLE DEVELOPMENT (Agenda item 18a)
González Franco, Federico Alberto – E/2015/SR.19

## Partners in Population and Development

MILLENNIUM DEVELOPMENT GOALS
Alam, Nurul – E/2015/SR.46
SUSTAINABLE DEVELOPMENT GOALS (Agenda item
5c)
Alam, Nurul – E/2015/SR.46

## Philippines

HUMANITARIAN ASSISTANCE (Agenda item 9)
Fos, Enrico T. – E/2015/SR.40
MILLENNIUM DEVELOPMENT GOALS
Balisacan, Arsenio M. – E/2015/SR.48
SUSTAINABLE DEVELOPMENT (Agenda item 18a)
Balisacan, Arsenio M. – E/2015/SR.47(A)
SUSTAINABLE DEVELOPMENT–HIGH-LEVEL
POLITICAL FORUM (Agenda item 6)
Balisacan, Arsenio M. – E/2015/SR.47(A)
SUSTAINABLE DEVELOPMENT GOALS (Agenda item
5c)
Balisacan, Arsenio M. – E/2015/SR.48

## Philippines. Bureau of Internal Revenue

TAXATION (Agenda item 18h)
Jacinto-Henares, Kim S. – E/2015/SR.29

## Poland

HUMANITARIAN ASSISTANCE (Agenda item 9)
Henczel, Remigiusz – E/2015/SR.37

## Republic of Korea

BRETTON WOODS INSTITUTIONS
Oh, Joon – E/2015/SR.27
HUMANITARIAN ASSISTANCE (Agenda item 9)
Choi, Seok-Young – E/2015/SR.37
SOUTH-SOUTH COOPERATION (Agenda item 7c)
Hahn, Choonghee – E/2015/SR.12
SUSTAINABLE DEVELOPMENT (Agenda item 18a)
Hahn, Choonghee – E/2015/SR.19
Lim, Hoon-Min – E/2015/SR.35
Shin, Dong-ik – E/2015/SR.47(A)
SUSTAINABLE DEVELOPMENT–HIGH-LEVEL
POLITICAL FORUM (Agenda item 6)
Shin, Dong-ik – E/2015/SR.47(A)
UN. ECONOMIC AND SOCIAL COUNCIL (2014-2015 :
NEW YORK AND GENEVA)–AGENDA (Agenda item 2)
Lee, Tong-Q – E/2015/SR.2
UN POLICY RECOMMENDATIONS (Agenda item 7a)
Hahn, Choonghee – E/2015/SR.12

## Romania

SOCIAL DEVELOPMENT (Agenda item 19b)
Miculescu, Simona Mirela – E/2015/SR.31
SUSTAINABLE DEVELOPMENT (Agenda item 18a)
Gavrilescu, Gratiela Leocadia – E/2015/SR.43
SUSTAINABLE DEVELOPMENT–HIGH-LEVEL
POLITICAL FORUM (Agenda item 6)
Gavrilescu, Gratiela Leocadia – E/2015/SR.43

## Roundtable on Sustainable Palm Oil

SUSTAINABLE DEVELOPMENT (Agenda item 18a)
Webber, Darrel – E/2015/SR.47(A)

## Roza Otunbayeva Inititative

MILLENNIUM DEVELOPMENT GOALS
Otunbayeva, Roza – E/2015/SR.45
SUSTAINABLE DEVELOPMENT GOALS (Agenda item 5c)
Otunbayeva, Roza – E/2015/SR.45

## Russian Federation

BRETTON WOODS INSTITUTIONS
Ulin, Denis – E/2015/SR.26
DECOLONIZATION (Agenda item 14)
Ravilova-Borovik, Dilyara S. – E/2015/SR.50
EBOLA VIRUS DISEASE
Zagrekov, Victor – E/2015/SR.3
HUMANITARIAN ASSISTANCE (Agenda item 9)
Andreev, Vladimir V. – E/2015/SR.40
MILLENNIUM DEVELOPMENT GOALS
Kononuchenko, Sergei – E/2015/SR.48
NON-COMMUNICABLE DISEASES (Agenda item 12f)
Maksimychev, Dmitry I. – E/2015/SR.33
OPERATIONAL ACTIVITIES–UN (Agenda item 7)
Fotina, Ekaterina V. – E/2015/SR.8
REGIONAL COOPERATION (Agenda item 15)
Kudasova, Yulia N. – E/2015/SR.47(B)
SCIENCE AND TECHNOLOGY–DEVELOPMENT (Agenda item 18b)
Morozov, Anton Y. – E/2015/SR.54
SUSTAINABLE DEVELOPMENT (Agenda item 18a)
Gatilov, Gennadii Mikhailovich – E/2015/SR.43
Maksimychev, Dmitry I. – E/2015/SR.19
Zagrekov, Victor – E/2015/SR.3
SUSTAINABLE DEVELOPMENT–HIGH-LEVEL
POLITICAL FORUM (Agenda item 6)
Gatilov, Gennadii Mikhailovich – E/2015/SR.43
SUSTAINABLE DEVELOPMENT GOALS (Agenda item 5c)
Kononuchenko, Sergei – E/2015/SR.48
TAXATION (Agenda item 18h)
Medvedeva, Irina – E/2015/SR.28
UN POLICY RECOMMENDATIONS (Agenda item 7a)
Maksimychev, Dmitry I. – E/2015/SR.12
UN-WOMEN. EXECUTIVE BOARD–MEMBERS (Agenda item 4)
Khvan, Galina – E/2015/SR.23

## Rwanda

SUSTAINABLE DEVELOPMENT (Agenda item 18a)
Byaje, Jeanne d'Arc – E/2015/SR.19

## Rwanda. President

SUSTAINABLE DEVELOPMENT–MINISTERIAL
MEETING (Agenda item 5a)
Kagame, Paul – E/2015/SR.42

## Sabin Vaccine Institute

NON-COMMUNICABLE DISEASES (Agenda item 12f)
Mistry, Neeraj – E/2015/SR.47(A)
SUSTAINABLE DEVELOPMENT (Agenda item 18a)
Mistry, Neeraj – E/2015/SR.47(A)

## SABMiller (Firm)

TAXATION (Agenda item 18h)
Bales, Vicki – E/2015/SR.29

## San Marino

SUSTAINABLE DEVELOPMENT–HIGH-LEVEL
POLITICAL FORUM (Agenda item 6)
Bodini, Daniele D. – E/2015/SR.44

## Schweizerische Rückversicherungs-Gesellschaft

HUMANITARIAN ASSISTANCE (Agenda item 9)
Liès, Michel – E/2015/SR.38

## Serbia

HUMANITARIAN ASSISTANCE (Agenda item 9)
Zupanjevac, Dragan – E/2015/SR.40
SUSTAINABLE DEVELOPMENT (Agenda item 18a)
Lalic-Smajevic, Katarina – E/2015/SR.19
UN POLICY RECOMMENDATIONS (Agenda item 7a)
Lalic-Smajevic, Katarina – E/2015/SR.12

## Sierra Leone

EBOLA VIRUS DISEASE
Marrah, Kaifala – E/2015/SR.3
SUSTAINABLE DEVELOPMENT (Agenda item 18a)
Marrah, Kaifala – E/2015/SR.3

## Singapore

CRIME PREVENTION (Agenda item 19c)
Li, Wei Adele – E/2015/SR.53

## Social Watch (Organization)

SOCIAL DEVELOPMENT (Agenda item 19b)
Bissio, Roberto – E/2015/SR.31

## Society for International Development

BRETTON WOODS INSTITUTIONS
Prato, Stefano – E/2015/SR.26

## Society of Catholic Medical Missionaries

BRETTON WOODS INSTITUTIONS
Paramundayil, Celine – E/2015/SR.26

## Society to Support Children Suffering from Cancer (Islamic Republic of Iran)

NON-GOVERNMENTAL ORGANIZATIONS (Agenda item 17)
Ghods, Saideh – E/2015/SR.47(A)
SUSTAINABLE DEVELOPMENT (Agenda item 18a)
Ghods, Saideh – E/2015/SR.47(A)

## Soroptimist International

SUSTAINABLE DEVELOPMENT (Agenda item 18a)
Levy, Betty – E/2015/SR.47(A)

## South Africa

HUMAN SETTLEMENTS (Agenda item 18d)
Malawana, Lawrence Xolani – E/2015/SR.55
HUMANITARIAN ASSISTANCE (Agenda item 9)
Makwarela, Mac – E/2015/SR.39; E/2015/SR.40
INSTITUTION BUILDING (Agenda item 5d)
Mxakato-Diseko, Nozipho Joyce – E/2015/SR.49
MILLENNIUM DEVELOPMENT GOALS
Mxakato-Diseko, Nozipho Joyce – E/2015/SR.46
SUSTAINABLE DEVELOPMENT (Agenda item 18a)
Patel, Ebrahim – E/2015/SR.15
SUSTAINABLE DEVELOPMENT GOALS (Agenda item 5c)
Mxakato-Diseko, Nozipho Joyce – E/2015/SR.46

## South Africa. Revenue Service

TAXATION (Agenda item 18h)
Gosai, Nishana – E/2015/SR.29

## Sovereign Military Order of Malta

HUMANITARIAN ASSISTANCE (Agenda item 9)
Pictet-Althann, Marie-Therese – E/2015/SR.40

## Spain

HUMANITARIAN ASSISTANCE (Agenda item 9)
Menéndez Pérez, Ana María – E/2015/SR.40
MILLENNIUM DEVELOPMENT GOALS
Díaz de la Guardia Beuno, Ignacio – E/2015/SR.48
SUSTAINABLE DEVELOPMENT GOALS (Agenda item 5c)
Díaz de la Guardia Beuno, Ignacio – E/2015/SR.48

## Sri Lanka

MILLENNIUM DEVELOPMENT GOALS
Perera, Amrith Rohan – E/2015/SR.44
SUSTAINABLE DEVELOPMENT–HIGH-LEVEL POLITICAL FORUM (Agenda item 6)
Perera, Amrith Rohan – E/2015/SR.44
SUSTAINABLE DEVELOPMENT GOALS (Agenda item 5c)
Perera, Amrith Rohan – E/2015/SR.44

## State of Palestine

DECOLONIZATION (Agenda item 14)
Mansour, Riyad H. – E/2015/SR.50

## Sudan

CRIME PREVENTION (Agenda item 19c)
Elbahi, Mohamed Ibrahim Mohamed – E/2015/SR.53
OPERATIONAL ACTIVITIES–UN (Agenda item 7)
Osman Elnor, Rahamtalla Mohamed – E/2015/SR.6
UN FORUM ON FORESTS (Agenda item 18k)
Ali, Khalid Mohammed – E/2015/SR.55

## Summit Level Group for South-South Consultations and Co-operation

SUSTAINABLE DEVELOPMENT (Agenda item 18a)
Perera, Amrith Rohan (Sri Lanka) – E/2015/SR.43
SUSTAINABLE DEVELOPMENT–HIGH-LEVEL POLITICAL FORUM (Agenda item 6)
Perera, Amrith Rohan (Sri Lanka) – E/2015/SR.43

## Support for Women in Agriculture and Environment (Organization : Uganda)

SUSTAINABLE DEVELOPMENT (Agenda item 18a)
Kenyangi, Gertrude – E/2015/SR.47(A)
SUSTAINABLE DEVELOPMENT–HIGH-LEVEL POLITICAL FORUM (Agenda item 6)
Kenyangi, Gertrude – E/2015/SR.47(A)

## Sweden

BRETTON WOODS INSTITUTIONS
Andersson, Magdalena – E/2015/SR.25
EBOLA VIRUS DISEASE
Thöresson, Per – E/2015/SR.3
HUMANITARIAN ASSISTANCE (Agenda item 9)
Clifford, Katarina – E/2015/SR.37; E/2015/SR.39
MILLENNIUM DEVELOPMENT GOALS
Skoog, Olof – E/2015/SR.48
OPERATIONAL ACTIVITIES–UN (Agenda item 7)
Lennartsson, Magnus – E/2015/SR.5; E/2015/SR.6; E/2015/SR.8; E/2015/SR.9; E/2015/SR.34
SUSTAINABLE DEVELOPMENT (Agenda item 18a)
Nilsson Snellman, Karin – E/2015/SR.15
Thöresson, Per – E/2015/SR.3
SUSTAINABLE DEVELOPMENT–HIGH-LEVEL POLITICAL FORUM (Agenda item 6)
Skoog, Olof – E/2015/SR.44
SUSTAINABLE DEVELOPMENT GOALS (Agenda item 5c)
Skoog, Olof – E/2015/SR.48
UN POLICY RECOMMENDATIONS (Agenda item 7a)
Lennartsson, Magnus – E/2015/SR.9
UN-WOMEN (Agenda item 7b)
Lennartsson, Magnus – E/2015/SR.11
UNDP/UNFPA/UNOPS (Agenda item 7b)
Lennartsson, Magnus – E/2015/SR.11
UNICEF (Agenda item 7b)
Lennartsson, Magnus – E/2015/SR.11
WORLD FOOD PROGRAMME (Agenda item 7b)
Lennartsson, Magnus – E/2015/SR.11

## Sweden. Prime Minister

SUSTAINABLE DEVELOPMENT (Agenda item 18a)
Löfven, Stefan – E/2015/SR.15

## Switzerland

AIDS (Agenda item 12g)
 Zehnder, Olivier Marc – E/2015/SR.22
BRETTON WOODS INSTITUTIONS
 Egli, Patrick – E/2015/SR.26; E/2015/SR.27
HUMANITARIAN ASSISTANCE (Agenda item 9)
 Bessler, Manuel – E/2015/SR.37; E/2015/SR.38;
 E/2015/SR.39
MILLENNIUM DEVELOPMENT GOALS
 Wennubst, Pius – E/2015/SR.48
OPERATIONAL ACTIVITIES–UN (Agenda item 7)
 Egli, Patrick – E/2015/SR.9
 Von Steiger Weber, Tatjana – E/2015/SR.34
 Wennubst, Pius – E/2015/SR.6
SOCIAL DEVELOPMENT (Agenda item 19b)
 Bodenmann, Hannah – E/2015/SR.31
SUSTAINABLE DEVELOPMENT (Agenda item 18a)
 Wennubst, Pius – E/2015/SR.43
 Zehnder, Olivier Marc – E/2015/SR.18
SUSTAINABLE DEVELOPMENT–HIGH-LEVEL
POLITICAL FORUM (Agenda item 6)
 Wennubst, Pius – E/2015/SR.43
SUSTAINABLE DEVELOPMENT–MINISTERIAL
MEETING (Agenda item 5a)
 Seger, Paul – E/2015/SR.42
SUSTAINABLE DEVELOPMENT GOALS (Agenda item
5c)
 Wennubst, Pius – E/2015/SR.48
UN FORUM ON FORESTS (Agenda item 18k)
 Vermont, Sibylle – E/2015/SR.55
UN POLICY RECOMMENDATIONS (Agenda item 7a)
 Egli, Patrick – E/2015/SR.9; E/2015/SR.12
UN-WOMEN (Agenda item 7b)
 Egli, Patrick – E/2015/SR.11
UNDP/UNFPA/UNOPS (Agenda item 7b)
 Egli, Patrick – E/2015/SR.11
UNICEF (Agenda item 7b)
 Egli, Patrick – E/2015/SR.11
WORLD FOOD PROGRAMME (Agenda item 7b)
 Egli, Patrick – E/2015/SR.11

## Syrian Arab Republic

HUMANITARIAN ASSISTANCE (Agenda item 9)
 A'ala, Hussam-edin – E/2015/SR.40
PALESTINIANS–TERRITORIES OCCUPIED BY
ISRAEL–LIVING CONDITIONS (Agenda item 16)
 Ja'afari, Bashar – E/2015/SR.50
UN-WOMEN (Agenda item 7b)
 Jawhara, Rabee – E/2015/SR.11
UNDP/UNFPA/UNOPS (Agenda item 7b)
 Jawhara, Rabee – E/2015/SR.11
UNICEF (Agenda item 7b)
 Jawhara, Rabee – E/2015/SR.11
WORLD FOOD PROGRAMME (Agenda item 7b)
 Jawhara, Rabee – E/2015/SR.11

## Tata Group

SUSTAINABLE DEVELOPMENT (Agenda item 18a)
 Rajan, N.S. – E/2015/SR.20

## Thailand

HUMANITARIAN ASSISTANCE (Agenda item 9)
 Thongphakdi, Thani – E/2015/SR.40
SUSTAINABLE DEVELOPMENT (Agenda item 18a)
 Ganjanarintr, Pornprapai – E/2015/SR.43

## Timor-Leste

OPERATIONAL ACTIVITIES–UN (Agenda item 7)
 Mesquita Borges, Sofia – E/2015/SR.8

## Trinidad and Tobago

SUSTAINABLE DEVELOPMENT (Agenda item 18a)
 Aching, Lizanne – E/2015/SR.19
 Charles, Eden – E/2015/SR.15

## Tunisia

BRETTON WOODS INSTITUTIONS
 Ibrahim, Yassine – E/2015/SR.25
OPERATIONAL ACTIVITIES–UN (Agenda item 7)
 Khiari, Mohamed Khaled – E/2015/SR.8
SUSTAINABLE DEVELOPMENT (Agenda item 18a)
 Khiari, Mohamed Khaled – E/2015/SR.19
UN. ECONOMIC AND SOCIAL COUNCIL (2014-2015 :
NEW YORK AND GENEVA)–AGENDA (Agenda item 2)
 Khiari, Mohamed Khaled – E/2015/SR.14

## Turkey

BRETTON WOODS INSTITUTIONS
 Babacan, Ali – E/2015/SR.25
 Eler, Levent – E/2015/SR.25
HUMAN RIGHTS (Agenda item 19g)
 Canay, Yigit – E/2015/SR.53
HUMANITARIAN ASSISTANCE (Agenda item 9)
 Baran, Berk – E/2015/SR.38
 Çarikçi, Ferden – E/2015/SR.37
LEAST DEVELOPED COUNTRIES–INTERNATIONAL
DECADE (2011-2020) (Agenda item 11b)
 Ünal, Merve Neva – E/2015/SR.56
MILLENNIUM DEVELOPMENT GOALS
 Eler, Levent – E/2015/SR.48
SUSTAINABLE DEVELOPMENT GOALS (Agenda item
5c)
 Eler, Levent – E/2015/SR.48

## Turkmenistan

UN-WOMEN. EXECUTIVE BOARD–MEMBERS
(Agenda item 4)
 Ataeva, Aksoltan T. – E/2015/SR.23

## Uganda

UN-WOMEN. EXECUTIVE BOARD–MEMBERS
(Agenda item 4)
 Muhumuza, Duncan Laki – E/2015/SR.23

## Ukraine

HUMANITARIAN ASSISTANCE (Agenda item 9)
 Kavun, Olha – E/2015/SR.40
SUSTAINABLE DEVELOPMENT (Agenda item 18a)
 Golitsyn, Yaroslav – E/2015/SR.47(A)

## UN. Assistant Secretary-General for Policy Coordination and Inter-Agency Affairs

INSTITUTION BUILDING (Agenda item 5d)
Gass, Thomas – E/2015/SR.49
OPERATIONAL ACTIVITIES–UN (Agenda item 7)
Gass, Thomas – E/2015/SR.5
SUSTAINABLE DEVELOPMENT (Agenda item 18a)
Gass, Thomas – E/2015/SR.20
UN. PERMANENT FORUM ON INDIGENOUS ISSUES
(Agenda item 19h)
Gass, Thomas – E/2015/SR.54
UN CONFERENCES (Agenda item 11)
Gass, Thomas – E/2015/SR.36
UN POLICY RECOMMENDATIONS (Agenda item 7a)
Gass, Thomas – E/2015/SR.13

## UN. Commission for Social Development. Chairman

SOCIAL DEVELOPMENT (Agenda item 19b)
Miculescu, Simona Mirela (Romania) –
E/2015/SR.32

## UN. Commission on Narcotic Drugs. Chair

NARCOTIC DRUGS (Agenda item 19d)
Srisamoot, Arthayudh – E/2015/SR.53

## UN. Commission on Population and Development. Chair

POPULATION–DEVELOPMENT (Agenda item 18f)
Frankinet, Bénédicte – E/2015/SR.55

## UN. Commission on the Status of Women. Chair

WOMEN'S ADVANCEMENT (Agenda item 19a)
Patriota, Antonio de Aguiar – E/2015/SR.32

## UN. Committee for Development Policy. Chair

SUSTAINABLE DEVELOPMENT (Agenda item 18a)
Ocampo, José Antonio – E/2015/SR.35;
E/2015/SR.43
SUSTAINABLE DEVELOPMENT–HIGH-LEVEL
POLITICAL FORUM (Agenda item 6)
Ocampo, José Antonio – E/2015/SR.43

## UN. Committee of Experts on International Cooperation in Tax Matters

TAXATION (Agenda item 18h)
Sollund, Stig B. – E/2015/SR.29

## UN. Committee of Experts on International Cooperation in Tax Matters. Chair

TAXATION (Agenda item 18h)
Yaffar, Armando Lara – E/2015/SR.28;
E/2015/SR.29

## UN. Department of Economic and Social Affairs. Assistant Secretary-General for Economic Development

INTERNATIONAL FINANCIAL INSTITUTIONS (Agenda
item 5b)
Montiel, Lenni – E/2015/SR.46

## UN. Department of Economic and Social Affairs. Division for Social Policy and Development. Director

SOCIAL DEVELOPMENT (Agenda item 19b)
Bas, Daniela – E/2015/SR.32

## UN. Department of Economic and Social Affairs. Financing for Development Office. Director

TAXATION (Agenda item 18h)
Trepelkov, Alexandre – E/2015/SR.28

## UN. Deputy Secretary-General

OPERATIONAL ACTIVITIES–UN (Agenda item 7)
Eliasson, Jan – E/2015/SR.9
SOCIAL DEVELOPMENT (Agenda item 19b)
Eliasson, Jan – E/2015/SR.31
SUSTAINABLE DEVELOPMENT (Agenda item 18a)
Eliasson, Jan – E/2015/SR.15
SUSTAINABLE DEVELOPMENT–MINISTERIAL
MEETING (Agenda item 5a)
Eliasson, Jan – E/2015/SR.42
UN POLICY RECOMMENDATIONS (Agenda item 7a)
Eliasson, Jan – E/2015/SR.9

## UN. Deputy Special Representative of the Secretary-General for Haiti and Humanitarian Coordinator, Resident Coordinator and Resident Representative for UNDP in Haiti

ECONOMIC ASSISTANCE–HAITI (Agenda item 12d)
Wahba, Mourad – E/2015/SR.52

## UN. ECA. Deputy Executive Secretary for Knowledge Generation

EBOLA VIRUS DISEASE
Hamdok, Abdalla – E/2015/SR.3
REGIONAL COOPERATION (Agenda item 15)
Hamdok, Abdalla – E/2015/SR.47(B)
SUSTAINABLE DEVELOPMENT (Agenda item 18a)
Hamdok, Abdalla – E/2015/SR.3

## UN. ECA. Executive Secretary

UN POLICY RECOMMENDATIONS (Agenda item 7a)
Lopes, Carlos – E/2015/SR.13

## UN. ECE. Executive Secretary

REGIONAL COOPERATION (Agenda item 15)
Bach, Christian Friis – E/2015/SR.47(B)

## UN. ECLAC. Executive Secretary

REGIONAL COOPERATION (Agenda item 15)
Bárcena, Alicia – E/2015/SR.47(B)

## UN. Economic and Social Council (2014-2015 : New York and Geneva). President

BRETTON WOODS INSTITUTIONS
Sajdik, Martin (Austria) – E/2015/SR.25;
E/2015/SR.27
EBOLA VIRUS DISEASE
Sajdik, Martin (Austria) – E/2015/SR.3

## UN. Economic and Social Council (2014-2015 : New York and Geneva). President (continued)

OPERATIONAL ACTIVITIES–UN (Agenda item 7)
Sajdik, Martin (Austria) – E/2015/SR.8; E/2015/SR.9
SUSTAINABLE DEVELOPMENT (Agenda item 18a)
Sajdik, Martin (Austria) – E/2015/SR.3
UN. COMMITTEE FOR PROGRAMME AND
COORDINATION–MEMBERS (Agenda item 4)
Sajdik, Martin (Austria) – E/2015/SR.30
UN. ECONOMIC AND SOCIAL COUNCIL (2014-2015 :
NEW YORK AND GENEVA)–AGENDA (Agenda item 2)
Sajdik, Martin (Austria) – E/2015/SR.1; E/2015/SR.2;
E/2015/SR.30
UN. ECONOMIC AND SOCIAL COUNCIL (2014-2015 :
NEW YORK AND GENEVA)–OFFICERS (Agenda item
1)
Sajdik, Martin (Austria) – E/2015/SR.7
UN. STATISTICAL COMMISSION–MEMBERS (Agenda
item 4)
Sajdik, Martin (Austria) – E/2015/SR.30
UN POLICY RECOMMENDATIONS (Agenda item 7a)
Sajdik, Martin (Austria) – E/2015/SR.9;
E/2015/SR.13
UN-HABITAT. GOVERNING COUNCIL–MEMBERS
(Agenda item 4)
Sajdik, Martin (Austria) – E/2015/SR.30

## UN. Economic and Social Council (2014-2015 : New York and Geneva). Secretary

ECONOMIC ASSISTANCE–HAITI (Agenda item 12d)
Sharma, Sangeeta – E/2015/SR.52
REGIONAL COOPERATION–ASIA AND THE PACIFIC
(Agenda item 15)
Gustafik, Otto – E/2015/SR.54
UN. ECONOMIC AND SOCIAL COUNCIL (2014-2015 :
NEW YORK AND GENEVA)–AGENDA (Agenda item 2)
De Laurentis, Jennifer – E/2015/SR.1
UN FORUM ON FORESTS (Agenda item 18k)
Gustafik, Otto – E/2015/SR.55
UN-HABITAT. GOVERNING COUNCIL–MEMBERS
(Agenda item 4)
De Laurentis, Jennifer – E/2015/SR.24
UN-WOMEN. EXECUTIVE BOARD–MEMBERS
(Agenda item 4)
De Laurentis, Jennifer – E/2015/SR.24

## UN. Economic and Social Council (2014-2015 : New York and Geneva). Vice-President

INSTITUTION BUILDING (Agenda item 5d)
Drobnjak, Vladimir (Croatia) – E/2015/SR.49
MILLENNIUM DEVELOPMENT GOALS
Oh, Joon (Republic of Korea) – E/2015/SR.46;
E/2015/SR.48
OPERATIONAL ACTIVITIES–UN (Agenda item 7)
Mejía Vélez, María Emma (Colombia) –
E/2015/SR.5; E/2015/SR.34
RACIAL DISCRIMINATION–PROGRAMME OF ACTION
(Agenda item 19f)
Oh, Joon (Republic of Korea) – E/2015/SR.53
SOCIAL DEVELOPMENT (Agenda item 19b)
Oh, Joon (Republic of Korea) – E/2015/SR.31

## UN. Economic and Social Council (2014-2015 : New York and Geneva). Vice-President (continued)

SUSTAINABLE DEVELOPMENT (Agenda item 18a)
Drobnjak, Vladimir (Croatia) – E/2015/SR.15;
E/2015/SR.20
SUSTAINABLE DEVELOPMENT–MINISTERIAL
MEETING (Agenda item 5a)
Oh, Joon (Republic of Korea) – E/2015/SR.42
SUSTAINABLE DEVELOPMENT GOALS (Agenda item
5c)
Oh, Joon (Republic of Korea) – E/2015/SR.46;
E/2015/SR.48
TAXATION (Agenda item 18h)
Drobnjak, Vladimir (Croatia) – E/2015/SR.28
UN POLICY RECOMMENDATIONS (Agenda item 7a)
Mejía Vélez, María Emma (Colombia) –
E/2015/SR.12
UN-HABITAT. GOVERNING COUNCIL–MEMBERS
(Agenda item 4)
Oh, Joon (Republic of Korea) – E/2015/SR.24
UN-WOMEN. EXECUTIVE BOARD–MEMBERS
(Agenda item 4)
Oh, Joon (Republic of Korea) – E/2015/SR.24

## UN. Economic and Social Council. Ad Hoc Advisory Group on Haiti. Chair

ECONOMIC ASSISTANCE–HAITI (Agenda item 12d)
Norman, Giles Andrew (Canada) – E/2015/SR.52

## UN. Economic and Social Council. Committee of Experts on Public Administration. Chair

PUBLIC ADMINISTRATION (Agenda item 18g)
Saner, Margaret – E/2015/SR.54

## UN. Economic and Social Council. Committee of Experts on Public Administration. Vice-Chair

INSTITUTION BUILDING (Agenda item 5d)
Bethel, Rowena G. – E/2015/SR.49

## UN. ESCAP. Executive Secretary

REGIONAL COOPERATION (Agenda item 15)
Akhtar, Shamshad – E/2015/SR.47(B)

## UN. ESCWA

DECOLONIZATION (Agenda item 14)
Alami, Tarik – E/2015/SR.50

## UN. ESCWA. Executive Secretary

REGIONAL COOPERATION (Agenda item 15)
Khalaf, Rima – E/2015/SR.47(B)
SUSTAINABLE DEVELOPMENT–MINISTERIAL
MEETING (Agenda item 5a)
Khalaf, Rima – E/2015/SR.42

## UN. General Assembly (69th sess. : 2014-2015). President

EBOLA VIRUS DISEASE
Kutesa, Sam K. (Uganda) – E/2015/SR.3
HUMANITARIAN ASSISTANCE (Agenda item 9)
Kutesa, Sam K. (Uganda) – E/2015/SR.37
SUSTAINABLE DEVELOPMENT (Agenda item 18a)
Kutesa, Sam K. (Uganda) – E/2015/SR.3
SUSTAINABLE DEVELOPMENT–MINISTERIAL
MEETING (Agenda item 5a)
Kutesa, Sam K. (Uganda) – E/2015/SR.42

## UN. General Assembly (69th sess. : 2014-2015). Vice-President

HUMANITARIAN ASSISTANCE (Agenda item 9)
Khiari, Mohamed Khaled (Tunisia) – E/2015/SR.37
MILLENNIUM DEVELOPMENT GOALS
Khiari, Mohamed Khaled (Tunisia) – E/2015/SR.45
SUSTAINABLE DEVELOPMENT (Agenda item 18a)
Gunnarsson, Einar (Iceland) – E/2015/SR.15
SUSTAINABLE DEVELOPMENT GOALS (Agenda item 5c)
Khiari, Mohamed Khaled (Tunisia) – E/2015/SR.45

## UN. Group of African States

HUMANITARIAN ASSISTANCE (Agenda item 9)
Bugingo Rugema, Moses Keneth (Rwanda) –
E/2015/SR.37
SUSTAINABLE DEVELOPMENT (Agenda item 18a)
Sana, Maboneza (Rwanda) – E/2015/SR.43
SUSTAINABLE DEVELOPMENT–HIGH-LEVEL
POLITICAL FORUM (Agenda item 6)
Sana, Maboneza (Rwanda) – E/2015/SR.43

## UN. High Representative of the Secretary-General for the Least Developed Countries, Landlocked Developing Countries and Small Island Developing States

LEAST DEVELOPED COUNTRIES–INTERNATIONAL
DECADE (2011-2020) (Agenda item 11b)
Acharya, Gyan Chandra – E/2015/SR.50

## UN. Office for ECOSOC Support and Coordination. Director

OPERATIONAL ACTIVITIES–UN (Agenda item 7)
Hanif, Navid – E/2015/SR.34
UN. ECONOMIC AND SOCIAL COUNCIL (2014-2015 :
NEW YORK AND GENEVA)–AGENDA (Agenda item 2)
Hanif, Navid – E/2015/SR.1

## UN. Office for South-South Cooperation. Director

SOUTH-SOUTH COOPERATION (Agenda item 7c)
Zhou, Yiping – E/2015/SR.12

## UN. Office of the High Commissioner for Human Rights. New York Office. Global Issues and Intergovernmental Section. Chief

HUMAN RIGHTS (Agenda item 19g)
Radcliffe, Charles – E/2015/SR.53

## UN. Office of the Resident Coordinator (Brazil)

SOUTH-SOUTH COOPERATION (Agenda item 7c)
Chediek, Jorge – E/2015/SR.12

## UN. Office of the Resident Coordinator and Humanitarian Coordinator (Mozambique)

OPERATIONAL ACTIVITIES–UN (Agenda item 7)
Topping, Jennifer – E/2015/SR.6

## UN. Peacebuilding Commission. Vice-Chair

ECONOMIC ASSISTANCE–HAITI (Agenda item 12d)
Patriota, Antonio de Aguiar (Brazil) – E/2015/SR.52
POST-CONFLICT RECONSTRUCTION–AFRICA
(Agenda item 12e)
Patriota, Antonio de Aguiar (Brazil) – E/2015/SR.52

## UN. Permanent Forum on Indigenous Issues. Chair

UN. PERMANENT FORUM ON INDIGENOUS ISSUES
(Agenda item 19h)
Davis, Megan – E/2015/SR.54

## UN. Regional Commissions New York Office

DANGEROUS GOODS TRANSPORT (Agenda item 18l)
Simioni, Daniela – E/2015/SR.32

## UN. Regional Commissions New York Office. Director

REGIONAL COOPERATION (Agenda item 15)
Nour, Amr – E/2015/SR.54

## UN. Secretary-General

BRETTON WOODS INSTITUTIONS
Ban, Ki-moon, 1944- – E/2015/SR.25
EBOLA VIRUS DISEASE
Ban, Ki-moon, 1944- – E/2015/SR.3
SUSTAINABLE DEVELOPMENT (Agenda item 18a)
Ban, Ki-moon, 1944- – E/2015/SR.3
SUSTAINABLE DEVELOPMENT–MINISTERIAL
MEETING (Agenda item 5a)
Ban, Ki-moon, 1944- – E/2015/SR.42
SUSTAINABLE DEVELOPMENT GOALS (Agenda item 5c)
Ban, Ki-moon, 1944- – E/2015/SR.49

## UN. Secretary-General's MDG Advocacy Group. Co-Chair

SUSTAINABLE DEVELOPMENT–MINISTERIAL
MEETING (Agenda item 5a)
Kagame, Paul – E/2015/SR.42
Solberg, Erna – E/2015/SR.42

## UN. Special Adviser to the Secretary-General for Community-based Medicine and Lessons from Haiti

EBOLA VIRUS DISEASE
Farmer, Paul (Paul Edward) – E/2015/SR.3
SUSTAINABLE DEVELOPMENT (Agenda item 18a)
Farmer, Paul (Paul Edward) – E/2015/SR.3

**UN. Special Adviser to the Secretary-General on Change Implementation**

UN–TRAINING AND RESEARCH INSTITUTIONS (Agenda item 20)
Kim, Won-soo – E/2015/SR.33

**UN. Special Adviser to the Secretary-General on Interregional Policy Cooperation**

SOCIAL DEVELOPMENT (Agenda item 19b)
Somavía, Juan – E/2015/SR.31

**UN. Special Adviser to the Secretary-General on Post-2015 Development Planning**

OPERATIONAL ACTIVITIES–UN (Agenda item 7)
Mohammed, Amina J. – E/2015/SR.6

**UN. Special Adviser to the Secretary-General on the Millennium Development Goals**

MILLENNIUM DEVELOPMENT GOALS
Sachs, Jeffrey – E/2015/SR.45
SUSTAINABLE DEVELOPMENT–MINISTERIAL MEETING (Agenda item 5a)
Sachs, Jeffrey – E/2015/SR.42
SUSTAINABLE DEVELOPMENT GOALS (Agenda item 5c)
Sachs, Jeffrey – E/2015/SR.45

**UN. Special Committee of 24. Acting Chair**

PALESTINIANS–TERRITORIES OCCUPIED BY ISRAEL–LIVING CONDITIONS (Agenda item 16)
Percaya, Desra (Indonesia) – E/2015/SR.50

**UN. Special Envoy of the Secretary-General on Ebola**

EBOLA VIRUS DISEASE
Nabarro, David – E/2015/SR.3
SUSTAINABLE DEVELOPMENT (Agenda item 18a)
Nabarro, David – E/2015/SR.3

**UN. Statistical Commission. Chair**

STATISTICS (Agenda item 18c)
Pullinger, John (United Kingdom) – E/2015/SR.35

**UN. Statistics Division. Director**

CARTOGRAPHY (Agenda item 18i)
Schweinfest, Stefan – E/2015/SR.55

**UN. Under-Secretary-General and Special Adviser on Africa**

EBOLA VIRUS DISEASE
Abdelaziz, Maged Abdelfattah – E/2015/SR.3
SUSTAINABLE DEVELOPMENT (Agenda item 18a)
Abdelaziz, Maged Abdelfattah – E/2015/SR.3

**UN. Under-Secretary-General for Economic and Social Affairs**

BRETTON WOODS INSTITUTIONS
Wu, Hongbo – E/2015/SR.26
INSTITUTION BUILDING (Agenda item 5d)
Wu, Hongbo – E/2015/SR.43

**UN. Under-Secretary-General for Economic and Social Affairs (continued)**

MILLENNIUM DEVELOPMENT GOALS
Wu, Hongbo – E/2015/SR.43
OPERATIONAL ACTIVITIES–UN (Agenda item 7)
Wu, Hongbo – E/2015/SR.10
SUSTAINABLE DEVELOPMENT (Agenda item 18a)
Wu, Hongbo – E/2015/SR.43
SUSTAINABLE DEVELOPMENT GOALS (Agenda item 5c)
Wu, Hongbo – E/2015/SR.43
UN POLICY RECOMMENDATIONS (Agenda item 7a)
Wu, Hongbo – E/2015/SR.10

**UN. Under-Secretary-General for Humanitarian Affairs and Emergency Relief Coordinator**

HUMANITARIAN ASSISTANCE (Agenda item 9)
O'Brien, Stephen – E/2015/SR.37; E/2015/SR.38; E/2015/SR.39

**UN Commission on Crime Prevention and Criminal Justice. Chair**

CRIME PREVENTION (Agenda item 19c)
Alba Góngora, Luis Alfonso de (Mexico) – E/2015/SR.53
NARCOTIC DRUGS (Agenda item 19d)
Alba Góngora, Luis Alfonso de (Mexico) – E/2015/SR.53

**UN Development Group. Advisory Group. Chair**

OPERATIONAL ACTIVITIES–UN (Agenda item 7)
Albrectsen, Anne-Birgitte – E/2015/SR.5

**UN Development Group. Chair**

OPERATIONAL ACTIVITIES–UN (Agenda item 7)
Clark, Helen – E/2015/SR.8
UNDP/UNFPA/UNOPS (Agenda item 7b)
Clark, Helen – E/2015/SR.11

**UN Interregional Crime and Justice Research Institute. Board of Trustees. President**

CRIME PREVENTION (Agenda item 19c)
Verville, Elizabeth – E/2015/SR.53

**UN Office on Drugs and Crime. New York Office. Director**

CRIME PREVENTION (Agenda item 19c)
Monasebian, Simone – E/2015/SR.53

**UN System Chief Executives Board for Coordination. High-Level Committee on Management. Vice-Chair**

OPERATIONAL ACTIVITIES–UN (Agenda item 7)
Beagle, Jan – E/2015/SR.5

**UN System Chief Executives Board for Coordination. High-Level Committee on Programmes. Vice-Chair**

OPERATIONAL ACTIVITIES–UN (Agenda item 7)
Stewart, Jane – E/2015/SR.5

## UN System Chief Executives Board for Coordination. Secretariat

COORDINATION-REPORTS (Agenda item 12a)
Petrova, Simona – E/2015/SR.35

## UN System Chief Executives Board for Coordination. Secretary

OPERATIONAL ACTIVITIES–UN (Agenda item 7)
Kim, Won-soo – E/2015/SR.6

## UN System Staff College. Director

SOUTH-SOUTH COOPERATION (Agenda item 7c)
Javan, Jafar – E/2015/SR.13
UN–TRAINING AND RESEARCH INSTITUTIONS (Agenda item 20)
Javan, Jafar – E/2015/SR.33
UN POLICY RECOMMENDATIONS (Agenda item 7a)
Javan, Jafar – E/2015/SR.13

## UN University

UN–TRAINING AND RESEARCH INSTITUTIONS (Agenda item 20)
Caeymaex, Olivia – E/2015/SR.33

## UN-HABITAT

HUMAN SETTLEMENTS (Agenda item 18d)
Djacta, Yamina – E/2015/SR.50
SUSTAINABLE DEVELOPMENT (Agenda item 18a)
Djacta, Yamina – E/2015/SR.19

## UN-Women. Deputy Executive Director

UN-WOMEN (Agenda item 7b)
Puri, Lakshmi – E/2015/SR.11
WOMEN IN DEVELOPMENT (Agenda item 18j)
Puri, Lakshmi – E/2015/SR.32
WOMEN'S ADVANCEMENT (Agenda item 19a)
Puri, Lakshmi – E/2015/SR.32

## UNCTAD

BRETTON WOODS INSTITUTIONS
Piantini Munnigh, Luis Manuel – E/2015/SR.25
SCIENCE AND TECHNOLOGY–DEVELOPMENT (Agenda item 18b)
Wu, Dong – E/2015/SR.54

## UNCTAD. Secretary-General

BRETTON WOODS INSTITUTIONS
Kituyi, Mukhisa – E/2015/SR.26
INTERNATIONAL FINANCIAL INSTITUTIONS (Agenda item 5b)
Kituyi, Mukhisa – E/2015/SR.46

## UNDP. Bureau for Policy and Programme Support

SUSTAINABLE DEVELOPMENT (Agenda item 18a)
Kwain, Stan – E/2015/SR.47(A)
SUSTAINABLE DEVELOPMENT–HIGH-LEVEL POLITICAL FORUM (Agenda item 6)
Kwain, Stan – E/2015/SR.47(A)

## UNDP. Bureau for Policy and Programme Support. Director

BRETTON WOODS INSTITUTIONS
Martínez-Solimán, Magdy – E/2015/SR.26
MILLENNIUM DEVELOPMENT GOALS
Martínez-Solimán, Magdy – E/2015/SR.46
SUSTAINABLE DEVELOPMENT GOALS (Agenda item 5c)
Martínez-Solimán, Magdy – E/2015/SR.46

## UNDP. Bureau of Management. Assistant Administrator and Director

UN POLICY RECOMMENDATIONS (Agenda item 7a)
Wandel, Jens – E/2015/SR.13

## UNDP. Principal Coordinator of Ebola Response

EBOLA VIRUS DISEASE
Saigal, Sunil – E/2015/SR.3
SUSTAINABLE DEVELOPMENT (Agenda item 18a)
Saigal, Sunil – E/2015/SR.3

## UNDP/UNFPA Executive Board. President

OPERATIONAL ACTIVITIES–UN (Agenda item 7)
Thomson, Peter (Fiji) – E/2015/SR.6

## UNDP/UNFPA/UNOPS Executive Board. Chair

UNDP/UNFPA/UNOPS (Agenda item 7b)
Carrera Castro, Fernando (Guatemala) – E/2015/SR.11

## Unesco

SCIENCE AND TECHNOLOGY–DEVELOPMENT (Agenda item 18b)
Guimarães-Pinto, Ricardo de – E/2015/SR.47(A)
SUSTAINABLE DEVELOPMENT (Agenda item 18a)
Guimarães-Pinto, Ricardo de – E/2015/SR.47(A)

## UNFPA

HUMANITARIAN ASSISTANCE (Agenda item 9)
Hamid, Salma – E/2015/SR.40

## UNFPA. Executive Director

UNDP/UNFPA/UNOPS (Agenda item 7b)
Osotimehin, Babatunde – E/2015/SR.11

## UNHCR

HUMANITARIAN ASSISTANCE (Agenda item 9)
Türk, Volker – E/2015/SR.40

## UNHCR. New York Liaison Office. Deputy Director

REFUGEES (Agenda item 19e)
Eriksson, Anne Christine – E/2015/SR.53

## UNI Global Union

SUSTAINABLE DEVELOPMENT (Agenda item 18a)
Jennings, Philip – E/2015/SR.15

## UNICEF

HUMANITARIAN ASSISTANCE (Agenda item 9)
Khan, Afshan – E/2015/SR.39; E/2015/SR.40

## UNICEF. Executive Director

UNICEF (Agenda item 7b)
Lake, Anthony – E/2015/SR.11

## UNICEF. Public Partnerships Division. Director

OPERATIONAL ACTIVITIES–UN (Agenda item 7)
Kjorven, Olav – E/2015/SR.10
UN POLICY RECOMMENDATIONS (Agenda item 7a)
Kjorven, Olav – E/2015/SR.10

## UNIDO

SUSTAINABLE DEVELOPMENT (Agenda item 18a)
Maseli, Paul – E/2015/SR.19

## UNITAR. Executive Director

UN–TRAINING AND RESEARCH INSTITUTIONS
(Agenda item 20)
Fegan-Wyles, Sally – E/2015/SR.33

## United Cities and Local Governments

SUSTAINABLE DEVELOPMENT (Agenda item 18a)
Celik, Aliye Pekin – E/2015/SR.47(A)

## United Kingdom

EBOLA VIRUS DISEASE
Cleobury, Simon – E/2015/SR.3
HUMANITARIAN ASSISTANCE (Agenda item 9)
Saez, Patrick – E/2015/SR.38; E/2015/SR.39
INSTITUTION BUILDING (Agenda item 5d)
Wilson, Peter – E/2015/SR.44
NON-GOVERNMENTAL ORGANIZATIONS (Agenda
item 17)
Shearman, Martin – E/2015/SR.51
OPERATIONAL ACTIVITIES–UN (Agenda item 7)
Ritchie, Fiona – E/2015/SR.34
Shearman, Martin – E/2015/SR.8; E/2015/SR.9
SOUTH-SOUTH COOPERATION (Agenda item 7c)
Shearman, Martin – E/2015/SR.12
SUSTAINABLE DEVELOPMENT (Agenda item 18a)
Cleobury, Simon – E/2015/SR.3
Shearman, Martin – E/2015/SR.18
UN POLICY RECOMMENDATIONS (Agenda item 7a)
Shearman, Martin – E/2015/SR.9; E/2015/SR.12

## United Republic of Tanzania. President

SUSTAINABLE DEVELOPMENT (Agenda item 18a)
Kikwete, Jakaya – E/2015/SR.15

## United States

BRETTON WOODS INSTITUTIONS
Thier, Alex – E/2015/SR.26
COORDINATION-REPORTS (Agenda item 12a)
Derderian, Jill – E/2015/SR.35
DECOLONIZATION (Agenda item 14)
Derderian, Jill – E/2015/SR.50
EBOLA VIRUS DISEASE
Cousens, Elizabeth M. – E/2015/SR.3
HUMANITARIAN ASSISTANCE (Agenda item 9)
Campbell, Elizabeth – E/2015/SR.39
Nyman, Elisha – E/2015/SR.37

## United States (continued)

MILLENNIUM DEVELOPMENT GOALS
Erdman, Richard – E/2015/SR.48
NON-GOVERNMENTAL ORGANIZATIONS (Agenda
item 17)
Sison, Michele J. – E/2015/SR.51
OPERATIONAL ACTIVITIES–UN (Agenda item 7)
Dunn, David – E/2015/SR.8; E/2015/SR.9
Erdman, Richard – E/2015/SR.34
Robl, Teri – E/2015/SR.6
Sloane, Esther Pan – E/2015/SR.5
PALESTINIANS–TERRITORIES OCCUPIED BY
ISRAEL–LIVING CONDITIONS (Agenda item 16)
Derderian, Jill – E/2015/SR.50
POST-CONFLICT RECONSTRUCTION–AFRICA
(Agenda item 12e)
Dugan, Hugh – E/2015/SR.52
REGIONAL COOPERATION (Agenda item 15)
Dugan, Hugh – E/2015/SR.54
SCIENCE AND TECHNOLOGY–DEVELOPMENT
(Agenda item 18b)
Reynolds, Andrew – E/2015/SR.54
SUSTAINABLE DEVELOPMENT (Agenda item 18a)
Cousens, Elizabeth M. – E/2015/SR.3
Fox, Sarah – E/2015/SR.18
SUSTAINABLE DEVELOPMENT–HIGH-LEVEL
POLITICAL FORUM (Agenda item 6)
Pipa, Tony – E/2015/SR.44
SUSTAINABLE DEVELOPMENT GOALS (Agenda item
5c)
Erdman, Richard – E/2015/SR.48
TAXATION (Agenda item 18h)
Sloane, Esther Pan – E/2015/SR.28
UN–TRAINING AND RESEARCH INSTITUTIONS
(Agenda item 20)
Dugan, Hugh – E/2015/SR.33
UN. ECONOMIC AND SOCIAL COUNCIL (2014-2015 :
NEW YORK AND GENEVA)–AGENDA (Agenda item 2)
Robl, Teri – E/2015/SR.1
UN. PERMANENT FORUM ON INDIGENOUS ISSUES
(Agenda item 19h)
Phipps, Laurie Shestack – E/2015/SR.54
UN FORUM ON FORESTS (Agenda item 18k)
Reynolds, Andrew – E/2015/SR.55
UN POLICY RECOMMENDATIONS (Agenda item 7a)
Dunn, David – E/2015/SR.9
Robl, Teri – E/2015/SR.13

## University of California (Los Angeles). School of Law

TAXATION (Agenda item 18h)
Zolt, Eric M. – E/2015/SR.29

## UNRWA. Commissioner-General

HUMANITARIAN ASSISTANCE (Agenda item 9)
Krähenbühl, Pierre – E/2015/SR.39

## Uruguay

SUSTAINABLE DEVELOPMENT–HIGH-LEVEL
POLITICAL FORUM (Agenda item 6)
Koncke, Gonzalo – E/2015/SR.44

## Viet Nam

MILLENNIUM DEVELOPMENT GOALS
Nguyen, Phuong Nga – E/2015/SR.44
OPERATIONAL ACTIVITIES–UN (Agenda item 7)
Do, Hung Viet – E/2015/SR.6
Nguyen, Phuong Nga – E/2015/SR.8
SUSTAINABLE DEVELOPMENT (Agenda item 18a)
Do, Hung Viet – E/2015/SR.15
Nguyen, Phuong Nga – E/2015/SR.44
SUSTAINABLE DEVELOPMENT GOALS (Agenda item 5c)
Nguyen, Phuong Nga – E/2015/SR.44
UN POLICY RECOMMENDATIONS (Agenda item 7a)
Nguyen, Phuong Nga – E/2015/SR.13

## WHO

EBOLA VIRUS DISEASE
Chan, Margaret – E/2015/SR.3
NON-COMMUNICABLE DISEASES (Agenda item 12f)
Menabde, Natela – E/2015/SR.33
SUSTAINABLE DEVELOPMENT (Agenda item 18a)
Chan, Margaret – E/2015/SR.3

## World Bank Group

BRETTON WOODS INSTITUTIONS
Villeroché, Hervé de – E/2015/SR.26
EBOLA VIRUS DISEASE
Walker, Melanie – E/2015/SR.3
SUSTAINABLE DEVELOPMENT (Agenda item 18a)
Walker, Melanie – E/2015/SR.3
TAXATION (Agenda item 18h)
Moreno-Dodson, Blanca – E/2015/SR.29

## World Energy Council

SUSTAINABLE DEVELOPMENT (Agenda item 18a)
Nadeau, Marie-José – E/2015/SR.20

## World Federation for Mental Health

SUSTAINABLE DEVELOPMENT (Agenda item 18a)
Wallace, Nancy E. – E/2015/SR.47(A)

## World Food Programme

POST-CONFLICT RECONSTRUCTION–AFRICA (Agenda item 12e)
Luma, Joyce – E/2015/SR.52

## World Food Programme. Deputy Executive Director

WORLD FOOD PROGRAMME (Agenda item 7b)
Abdulla, Amir Mahmoud – E/2015/SR.11

## World Jewellery Confederation

SUSTAINABLE DEVELOPMENT (Agenda item 18a)
Marzotto, Matteo – E/2015/SR.47(A)

## World Trade Organization. Deputy Director-General

BRETTON WOODS INSTITUTIONS
Yi, Xiaozhun – E/2015/SR.25
INTERNATIONAL FINANCIAL INSTITUTIONS (Agenda item 5b)
Agah, Yonov Frederick – E/2015/SR.46

## World Vision International

HUMANITARIAN ASSISTANCE (Agenda item 9)
Jenkins, Kevin – E/2015/SR.38

## Yale University (New Haven, Conn.)

SUSTAINABLE DEVELOPMENT (Agenda item 18a)
Shiller, Robert J. – E/2015/SR.20

## Yemen

UN-WOMEN (Agenda item 7b)
Al-Hamdani, Raiman – E/2015/SR.11
UNDP/UNFPA/UNOPS (Agenda item 7b)
Al-Hamdani, Raiman – E/2015/SR.11
UNICEF (Agenda item 7b)
Al-Hamdani, Raiman – E/2015/SR.11
WORLD FOOD PROGRAMME (Agenda item 7b)
Al-Hamdani, Raiman – E/2015/SR.11

## Zambia

MILLENNIUM DEVELOPMENT GOALS
Mvunga, Christopher Mphanza – E/2015/SR.48
SUSTAINABLE DEVELOPMENT–HIGH-LEVEL POLITICAL FORUM (Agenda item 6)
Mvunga, Christopher Mphanza – E/2015/SR.47(A)
SUSTAINABLE DEVELOPMENT GOALS (Agenda item 5c)
Mvunga, Christopher Mphanza – E/2015/SR.48

## Zimbabwe

AIDS (Agenda item 12g)
Mushayavanhu, Taonga – E/2015/SR.22
HUMANITARIAN ASSISTANCE (Agenda item 9)
Mushayavanhu, Taonga – E/2015/SR.40
SUSTAINABLE DEVELOPMENT (Agenda item 18a)
Shava, Frederick Musiiwa Makamure – E/2015/SR.18

**A'ala, Hussam-edin (Syrian Arab Republic)**

HUMANITARIAN ASSISTANCE (Agenda item 9)
E/2015/SR.40

**Abdelaziz, Maged Abdelfattah (UN. Under-Secretary-General and Special Adviser on Africa)**

EBOLA VIRUS DISEASE
E/2015/SR.3
SUSTAINABLE DEVELOPMENT (Agenda item 18a)
E/2015/SR.3

**Abdrakhmanov, Kairat (Kazakhstan)**

INSTITUTION BUILDING (Agenda item 5d)
E/2015/SR.44
SUSTAINABLE DEVELOPMENT (Agenda item 18a)
E/2015/SR.18; E/2015/SR.44
SUSTAINABLE DEVELOPMENT–HIGH-LEVEL
POLITICAL FORUM (Agenda item 6)
E/2015/SR.44

**Abdulla, Amir Mahmoud (World Food Programme. Deputy Executive Director)**

WORLD FOOD PROGRAMME (Agenda item 7b)
E/2015/SR.11

**Aboulatta, Amr Abdellatif (Egypt)**

MILLENNIUM DEVELOPMENT GOALS
E/2015/SR.44
SUSTAINABLE DEVELOPMENT–HIGH-LEVEL
POLITICAL FORUM (Agenda item 6)
E/2015/SR.44
SUSTAINABLE DEVELOPMENT GOALS (Agenda item 5c)
E/2015/SR.44

**Acharya, Gyan Chandra (UN. High Representative of the Secretary-General for the Least Developed Countries, Landlocked Developing Countries and Small Island Developing States)**

LEAST DEVELOPED COUNTRIES–INTERNATIONAL
DECADE (2011-2020) (Agenda item 11b)
E/2015/SR.50

**Aching, Lizanne (Trinidad and Tobago)**

SUSTAINABLE DEVELOPMENT (Agenda item 18a)
E/2015/SR.19

**Adams, Barbara (Global Policy Forum)**

OPERATIONAL ACTIVITIES–UN (Agenda item 7)
E/2015/SR.6

**Adhikari, Sewa Lamsal (Nepal)**

INSTITUTION BUILDING (Agenda item 5d)
E/2015/SR.44

**Agah, Yonov Frederick (World Trade Organization. Deputy Director-General)**

INTERNATIONAL FINANCIAL INSTITUTIONS (Agenda item 5b)
E/2015/SR.46

**Aguirre, Patricio (Chile)**

UN. ECONOMIC AND SOCIAL COUNCIL (2014-2015 :
NEW YORK AND GENEVA)–AGENDA (Agenda item 2)
E/2015/SR.1

**Ahsan, M. Shameem (Bangladesh)**

HUMANITARIAN ASSISTANCE (Agenda item 9)
E/2015/SR.40

**Akhtar, Shamshad (UN. ESCAP. Executive Secretary)**

REGIONAL COOPERATION (Agenda item 15)
E/2015/SR.47(B)

**Aklilu, Bisrat (Centre for International Forestry Research)**

OPERATIONAL ACTIVITIES–UN (Agenda item 7)
E/2015/SR.5

**Al-Hamdani, Raiman (Yemen)**

UN-WOMEN (Agenda item 7b)
E/2015/SR.11
UNDP/UNFPA/UNOPS (Agenda item 7b)
E/2015/SR.11
UNICEF (Agenda item 7b)
E/2015/SR.11
WORLD FOOD PROGRAMME (Agenda item 7b)
E/2015/SR.11

**Al-Sharrah, Abdullah Ahmad (Kuwait)**

UN–TRAINING AND RESEARCH INSTITUTIONS
(Agenda item 20)
E/2015/SR.33

**Alam, Nurul (Partners in Population and Development)**

MILLENNIUM DEVELOPMENT GOALS
E/2015/SR.46
SUSTAINABLE DEVELOPMENT GOALS (Agenda item 5c)
E/2015/SR.46

**Alami, Tarik (UN. ESCWA)**

DECOLONIZATION (Agenda item 14)
E/2015/SR.50

**Alamilla, Lisel (Belize) (Caribbean Community)**

SUSTAINABLE DEVELOPMENT (Agenda item 18a)
E/2015/SR.43
SUSTAINABLE DEVELOPMENT–HIGH-LEVEL
POLITICAL FORUM (Agenda item 6)
E/2015/SR.43

**Alba Góngora, Luis Alfonso de (Mexico)**

CRIME PREVENTION (Agenda item 19c)
E/2015/SR.53
NARCOTIC DRUGS (Agenda item 19d)
E/2015/SR.53

**Alba Góngora, Luis Alfonso de (Mexico) (UN Commission on Crime Prevention and Criminal Justice. Chair)**

CRIME PREVENTION (Agenda item 19c)
E/2015/SR.53
NARCOTIC DRUGS (Agenda item 19d)
E/2015/SR.53

**Albrectsen, Anne-Birgitte (UN Development Group. Advisory Group. Chair)**

OPERATIONAL ACTIVITIES–UN (Agenda item 7)
E/2015/SR.5

**Alderson, Helen (International Committee of the Red Cross)**

HUMANITARIAN ASSISTANCE (Agenda item 9)
E/2015/SR.38

**Ali, Khalid Mohammed (Sudan)**

UN FORUM ON FORESTS (Agenda item 18k)
E/2015/SR.55

**Alsaleh, Faeqa Saeed (Bahrain)**

SUSTAINABLE DEVELOPMENT (Agenda item 18a)
E/2015/SR.43

**Ammar, Yasar (Pakistan)**

REGIONAL COOPERATION–ASIA AND THE PACIFIC (Agenda item 15)
E/2015/SR.54
UN-WOMEN. EXECUTIVE BOARD–MEMBERS (Agenda item 4)
E/2015/SR.23

**Andersson, Magdalena (Sweden)**

BRETTON WOODS INSTITUTIONS
E/2015/SR.25

**Andreev, Vladimir V. (Russian Federation)**

HUMANITARIAN ASSISTANCE (Agenda item 9)
E/2015/SR.40

**Ataeva, Aksoltan T. (Turkmenistan)**

UN-WOMEN. EXECUTIVE BOARD–MEMBERS (Agenda item 4)
E/2015/SR.23

**Auajjar, Mohamed (Morocco)**

HUMANITARIAN ASSISTANCE (Agenda item 9)
E/2015/SR.37

**Babacan, Ali (Turkey)**

BRETTON WOODS INSTITUTIONS
E/2015/SR.25

**Bach, Christian Friis (UN. ECE. Executive Secretary)**

REGIONAL COOPERATION (Agenda item 15)
E/2015/SR.47(B)

**Badenoch, Charles (World Vision) (Beyond 2015 (Organization : Brussels))**

SUSTAINABLE DEVELOPMENT (Agenda item 18a)
E/2015/SR.47(A)

**Bales, Vicki (SABMiller (Firm))**

TAXATION (Agenda item 18h)
E/2015/SR.29

**Balisacan, Arsenio M. (Philippines)**

MILLENNIUM DEVELOPMENT GOALS
E/2015/SR.48
SUSTAINABLE DEVELOPMENT (Agenda item 18a)
E/2015/SR.47(A)
SUSTAINABLE DEVELOPMENT–HIGH-LEVEL POLITICAL FORUM (Agenda item 6)
E/2015/SR.47(A)
SUSTAINABLE DEVELOPMENT GOALS (Agenda item 5c)
E/2015/SR.48

**Ban, Ki-moon, 1944- (UN. Secretary-General)**

BRETTON WOODS INSTITUTIONS
E/2015/SR.25
EBOLA VIRUS DISEASE
E/2015/SR.3
SUSTAINABLE DEVELOPMENT (Agenda item 18a)
E/2015/SR.3
SUSTAINABLE DEVELOPMENT–MINISTERIAL MEETING (Agenda item 5a)
E/2015/SR.42
SUSTAINABLE DEVELOPMENT GOALS (Agenda item 5c)
E/2015/SR.49

**Baran, Berk (Turkey)**

HUMANITARIAN ASSISTANCE (Agenda item 9)
E/2015/SR.38

**Bárcena, Alicia (UN. ECLAC. Executive Secretary)**

REGIONAL COOPERATION (Agenda item 15)
E/2015/SR.47(B)

**Bargawi, Omar (European Union)**

OPERATIONAL ACTIVITIES–UN (Agenda item 7)
E/2015/SR.5; E/2015/SR.8
UN. ECONOMIC AND SOCIAL COUNCIL (2014-2015 : NEW YORK AND GENEVA)–AGENDA (Agenda item 2)
E/2015/SR.1; E/2015/SR.2

**Bartoli, Fabienne (France)**

EBOLA VIRUS DISEASE
E/2015/SR.3
SUSTAINABLE DEVELOPMENT (Agenda item 18a)
E/2015/SR.3

**Bas, Daniela (UN. Department of Economic and Social Affairs. Division for Social Policy and Development. Director)**

SOCIAL DEVELOPMENT (Agenda item 19b)
E/2015/SR.32

**Beagle, Jan (Joint United Nations Programme on HIV/AIDS. Deputy Executive Director)**

AIDS (Agenda item 12g)
E/2015/SR.22
OPERATIONAL ACTIVITIES–UN (Agenda item 7)
E/2015/SR.5

**Beagle, Jan (UN System Chief Executives Board for Coordination. High-Level Committee on Management. Vice-Chair)**

OPERATIONAL ACTIVITIES–UN (Agenda item 7)
E/2015/SR.5

**Bedas, Bernard (France)**

SUSTAINABLE DEVELOPMENT (Agenda item 18a)
E/2015/SR.18

**Bensouda, Fatou (International Criminal Court. Prosecutor)**

HUMANITARIAN ASSISTANCE (Agenda item 9)
E/2015/SR.39

**Bessler, Manuel (Switzerland)**

HUMANITARIAN ASSISTANCE (Agenda item 9)
E/2015/SR.37; E/2015/SR.38; E/2015/SR.39

**Bethel, Rowena G. (Bahamas. National Insurance Board)**

INSTITUTION BUILDING (Agenda item 5d)
E/2015/SR.49

**Bethel, Rowena G. (UN. Economic and Social Council. Committee of Experts on Public Administration. Vice-Chair)**

INSTITUTION BUILDING (Agenda item 5d)
E/2015/SR.49

**Beviglia Zampetti, Americo (European Union)**

UN FORUM ON FORESTS (Agenda item 18k)
E/2015/SR.55
UN POLICY RECOMMENDATIONS (Agenda item 7a)
E/2015/SR.13

**Bhatti, Nauman Bashir (Pakistan)**

OPERATIONAL ACTIVITIES–UN (Agenda item 7)
E/2015/SR.6

**Bibalou, Marianne Odette (Gabon)**

UN FORUM ON FORESTS (Agenda item 18k)
E/2015/SR.55

**Bishnoi, Bhagwant Singh (India)**

SOUTH-SOUTH COOPERATION (Agenda item 7c)
E/2015/SR.12
UN POLICY RECOMMENDATIONS (Agenda item 7a)
E/2015/SR.12
UNDP/UNFPA/UNOPS (Agenda item 7b)
E/2015/SR.12

**Bissio, Roberto (Social Watch (Organization))**

SOCIAL DEVELOPMENT (Agenda item 19b)
E/2015/SR.31

**Blakely, Delois (New Future Foundation (New York))**

EBOLA VIRUS DISEASE
E/2015/SR.3
SUSTAINABLE DEVELOPMENT (Agenda item 18a)
E/2015/SR.3

**Bodenmann, Hannah (Switzerland)**

SOCIAL DEVELOPMENT (Agenda item 19b)
E/2015/SR.31

**Bodini, Daniele D. (San Marino)**

SUSTAINABLE DEVELOPMENT–HIGH-LEVEL POLITICAL FORUM (Agenda item 6)
E/2015/SR.44

**Bogdan-Martin, Doreen (ITU)**

SUSTAINABLE DEVELOPMENT (Agenda item 18a)
E/2015/SR.47(A)

**Bokhari, Abdul Moiz (Pakistan)**

HUMANITARIAN ASSISTANCE (Agenda item 9)
E/2015/SR.37

**Bugingo Rugema, Moses Keneth (Rwanda) (UN. Group of African States)**

HUMANITARIAN ASSISTANCE (Agenda item 9)
E/2015/SR.37

**Burrow, Sharan (International Trade Union Confederation)**

SUSTAINABLE DEVELOPMENT (Agenda item 18a)
E/2015/SR.15

**Busuttil, John (European Union)**

TAXATION (Agenda item 18h)
E/2015/SR.28; E/2015/SR.56

**Byaje, Jeanne d'Arc (Rwanda)**

SUSTAINABLE DEVELOPMENT (Agenda item 18a)
E/2015/SR.19

**Cabezas, Fernando Arturo (Chile)**

ECONOMIC ASSISTANCE–HAITI (Agenda item 12d)
E/2015/SR.52

**Caeymaex, Olivia (UN University)**

UN–TRAINING AND RESEARCH INSTITUTIONS (Agenda item 20)
E/2015/SR.33

**Calvo Calvo, William José (Costa Rica)**

OPERATIONAL ACTIVITIES–UN (Agenda item 7)
E/2015/SR.5

**Camacho, Sara Luna (Mexico)**

REGIONAL COOPERATION (Agenda item 15)
E/2015/SR.47(B)
UN. ECONOMIC AND SOCIAL COUNCIL (2014-2015 :
NEW YORK AND GENEVA)–AGENDA (Agenda item 2)
E/2015/SR.1

**Campbell, Elizabeth (United States)**

HUMANITARIAN ASSISTANCE (Agenda item 9)
E/2015/SR.39

**Canay, Yigit (Turkey)**

HUMAN RIGHTS (Agenda item 19g)
E/2015/SR.53

**Cardenas Santamaria, Mauricio (Colombia)**

BRETTON WOODS INSTITUTIONS
E/2015/SR.25

**Cardi, Sebastiano (Italy)**

SUSTAINABLE DEVELOPMENT (Agenda item 18a)
E/2015/SR.19

**Cardona, Ricardo (Honduras)**

SUSTAINABLE DEVELOPMENT (Agenda item 18a)
E/2015/SR.43

**Çarikçi, Ferden (Turkey)**

HUMANITARIAN ASSISTANCE (Agenda item 9)
E/2015/SR.37

**Carrera Castro, Fernando (Guatemala)**

ECONOMIC ASSISTANCE–HAITI (Agenda item 12d)
E/2015/SR.52
NARCOTIC DRUGS (Agenda item 19d)
E/2015/SR.53
OPERATIONAL ACTIVITIES–UN (Agenda item 7)
E/2015/SR.5; E/2015/SR.6; E/2015/SR.8;
E/2015/SR.34
REGIONAL COOPERATION (Agenda item 15)
E/2015/SR.47(B)

**Carrera Castro, Fernando (Guatemala) (UNDP/UNFPA/UNOPS Executive Board. Chair)**

UNDP/UNFPA/UNOPS (Agenda item 7b)
E/2015/SR.11

**Carroll, Erica (United Kingdom) (European Union)**

PALESTINIANS–TERRITORIES OCCUPIED BY
ISRAEL–LIVING CONDITIONS (Agenda item 16)
E/2015/SR.50

**Celik, Aliye Pekin (United Cities and Local Governments)**

SUSTAINABLE DEVELOPMENT (Agenda item 18a)
E/2015/SR.47(A)

**Chan, Margaret (WHO)**

EBOLA VIRUS DISEASE
E/2015/SR.3

**Chan, Margaret (WHO) (continued)**

SUSTAINABLE DEVELOPMENT (Agenda item 18a)
E/2015/SR.3

**Chandra, Purnomo Ahmad (Indonesia)**

OPERATIONAL ACTIVITIES–UN (Agenda item 7)
E/2015/SR.34

**Chanthaboury, Kikeo (Lao People's Democratic Republic)**

OPERATIONAL ACTIVITIES–UN (Agenda item 7)
E/2015/SR.10
UN POLICY RECOMMENDATIONS (Agenda item 7a)
E/2015/SR.10; E/2015/SR.13

**Charles, Eden (Trinidad and Tobago)**

SUSTAINABLE DEVELOPMENT (Agenda item 18a)
E/2015/SR.15

**Chediek, Jorge (UN. Office of the Resident Coordinator (Brazil))**

SOUTH-SOUTH COOPERATION (Agenda item 7c)
E/2015/SR.12

**Chir, Kamel (Algeria)**

HUMANITARIAN ASSISTANCE (Agenda item 9)
E/2015/SR.38

**Choesni, Tubagus A. (Indonesia)**

SOUTH-SOUTH COOPERATION (Agenda item 7c)
E/2015/SR.12; E/2015/SR.13
UN POLICY RECOMMENDATIONS (Agenda item 7a)
E/2015/SR.13

**Choi, Seok-Young (Republic of Korea)**

HUMANITARIAN ASSISTANCE (Agenda item 9)
E/2015/SR.37

**Chowdhury, Saber (Inter-Parliamentary Union)**

INSTITUTION BUILDING (Agenda item 5d)
E/2015/SR.49
MILLENNIUM DEVELOPMENT GOALS
E/2015/SR.46
SUSTAINABLE DEVELOPMENT GOALS (Agenda item 5c)
E/2015/SR.46

**Christie, Perry G. (Bahamas) (Caribbean Community)**

SUSTAINABLE DEVELOPMENT (Agenda item 18a)
E/2015/SR.15

**Chu, Guang (China)**

UN-WOMEN. EXECUTIVE BOARD–MEMBERS (Agenda item 4)
E/2015/SR.23

**Clark, Helen (UN Development Group. Chair)**

OPERATIONAL ACTIVITIES–UN (Agenda item 7)
E/2015/SR.8

**Clark, Helen (UN Development Group. Chair) (continued)**

UNDP/UNFPA/UNOPS (Agenda item 7b)
E/2015/SR.11

**Cleobury, Simon (United Kingdom)**

EBOLA VIRUS DISEASE
E/2015/SR.3
SUSTAINABLE DEVELOPMENT (Agenda item 18a)
E/2015/SR.3

**Clifford, Katarina (Sweden)**

HUMANITARIAN ASSISTANCE (Agenda item 9)
E/2015/SR.37; E/2015/SR.39

**Colassis, Laurent (International Committee of the Red Cross)**

HUMANITARIAN ASSISTANCE (Agenda item 9)
E/2015/SR.39

**Colín Ortega, Gabriela (Mexico)**

OPERATIONAL ACTIVITIES–UN (Agenda item 7)
E/2015/SR.9
SOUTH-SOUTH COOPERATION (Agenda item 7c)
E/2015/SR.12
UN POLICY RECOMMENDATIONS (Agenda item 7a)
E/2015/SR.9; E/2015/SR.12
UNDP/UNFPA/UNOPS (Agenda item 7b)
E/2015/SR.12

**Cottani, Giammarco (Italy. Revenue Agency)**

TAXATION (Agenda item 18h)
E/2015/SR.29

**Cotte, Walter (International Federation of Red Cross and Red Crescent Societies)**

HUMANITARIAN ASSISTANCE (Agenda item 9)
E/2015/SR.40

**Cousens, Elizabeth M. (United States)**

EBOLA VIRUS DISEASE
E/2015/SR.3
SUSTAINABLE DEVELOPMENT (Agenda item 18a)
E/2015/SR.3

**Crilchuk, Guido (Argentina)**

OPERATIONAL ACTIVITIES–UN (Agenda item 7)
E/2015/SR.34

**Crippa, Leonardo A. (National Congress of American Indians (United States))**

UN. PERMANENT FORUM ON INDIGENOUS ISSUES (Agenda item 19h)
E/2015/SR.54

**Cuk, Vladimir (European Disability Forum)**

SUSTAINABLE DEVELOPMENT (Agenda item 18a)
E/2015/SR.47(A)

**Cuk, Vladimir (International Disability Alliance)**

SUSTAINABLE DEVELOPMENT–MINISTERIAL MEETING (Agenda item 5a)
E/2015/SR.42

**Dabbashi, Ibrahim O.A. (Libya)**

SUSTAINABLE DEVELOPMENT–HIGH-LEVEL POLITICAL FORUM (Agenda item 6)
E/2015/SR.44

**Dalcero, Pedro Luiz (Brazil)**

HUMANITARIAN ASSISTANCE (Agenda item 9)
E/2015/SR.40

**Daly, Louis A. (CLIPSAS (Organization))**

SUSTAINABLE DEVELOPMENT (Agenda item 18a)
E/2015/SR.47(A)

**Dávila, María Paulina (Colombia)**

UN-WOMEN (Agenda item 7b)
E/2015/SR.11
UNDP/UNFPA/UNOPS (Agenda item 7b)
E/2015/SR.11
UNICEF (Agenda item 7b)
E/2015/SR.11
WORLD FOOD PROGRAMME (Agenda item 7b)
E/2015/SR.11

**Davis, Joan (Gray Panthers (Organization))**

SUSTAINABLE DEVELOPMENT (Agenda item 18a)
E/2015/SR.15

**Davis, Megan (UN. Permanent Forum on Indigenous Issues. Chair)**

UN. PERMANENT FORUM ON INDIGENOUS ISSUES (Agenda item 19h)
E/2015/SR.54

**De Laurentis, Jennifer (UN. Economic and Social Council (2014-2015 : New York and Geneva). Secretary)**

UN. ECONOMIC AND SOCIAL COUNCIL (2014-2015 : NEW YORK AND GENEVA)–AGENDA (Agenda item 2)
E/2015/SR.1
UN-HABITAT. GOVERNING COUNCIL–MEMBERS (Agenda item 4)
E/2015/SR.24
UN-WOMEN. EXECUTIVE BOARD–MEMBERS (Agenda item 4)
E/2015/SR.24

**Dehghani, Gholamhossein (Iran (Islamic Republic of))**

UN. COMMISSION ON NARCOTIC DRUGS– MEMBERS (Agenda item 4)
E/2015/SR.21

## Delattre, François (France)

SUSTAINABLE DEVELOPMENT–HIGH-LEVEL
POLITICAL FORUM (Agenda item 6)
E/2015/SR.44

## Derderian, Jill (United States)

COORDINATION-REPORTS (Agenda item 12a)
E/2015/SR.35
DECOLONIZATION (Agenda item 14)
E/2015/SR.50
PALESTINIANS–TERRITORIES OCCUPIED BY
ISRAEL–LIVING CONDITIONS (Agenda item 16)
E/2015/SR.50

## Dhakiri, Hanif (Indonesia)

SUSTAINABLE DEVELOPMENT (Agenda item 18a)
E/2015/SR.16

## Dhital, Deepak (Nepal)

HUMANITARIAN ASSISTANCE (Agenda item 9)
E/2015/SR.40

## Di Luca, Sebastián (Argentina)

SUSTAINABLE DEVELOPMENT (Agenda item 18a)
E/2015/SR.19

## Diare, Mohamed (Guinea)

EBOLA VIRUS DISEASE
E/2015/SR.3
SUSTAINABLE DEVELOPMENT (Agenda item 18a)
E/2015/SR.3

## Díaz de la Guardia Beuno, Ignacio (Spain)

MILLENNIUM DEVELOPMENT GOALS
E/2015/SR.48
SUSTAINABLE DEVELOPMENT GOALS (Agenda item 5c)
E/2015/SR.48

## Djacta, Larbi (Algeria)

UN–TRAINING AND RESEARCH INSTITUTIONS
(Agenda item 20)
E/2015/SR.33

## Djacta, Yamina (UN-HABITAT)

HUMAN SETTLEMENTS (Agenda item 18d)
E/2015/SR.50
SUSTAINABLE DEVELOPMENT (Agenda item 18a)
E/2015/SR.19

## Do, Hung Viet (Viet Nam)

OPERATIONAL ACTIVITIES–UN (Agenda item 7)
E/2015/SR.6
SUSTAINABLE DEVELOPMENT (Agenda item 18a)
E/2015/SR.15

## Donaldson, Kirstin (Australia)

SUSTAINABLE DEVELOPMENT–HIGH-LEVEL
POLITICAL FORUM (Agenda item 6)
E/2015/SR.44

## Donoghue, David (Ireland)

SOCIAL DEVELOPMENT (Agenda item 19b)
E/2015/SR.31

## Dos Santos, Patricia Fatima B. (Angola)

HUMANITARIAN ASSISTANCE (Agenda item 9)
E/2015/SR.39

## Doucouré, Dianguina dit Yaya (Mali)

EBOLA VIRUS DISEASE
E/2015/SR.3
SUSTAINABLE DEVELOPMENT (Agenda item 18a)
E/2015/SR.3

## Drobnjak, Vladimir (Croatia)

BRETTON WOODS INSTITUTIONS
E/2015/SR.27

## Drobnjak, Vladimir (Croatia) (UN. Economic and Social Council (2014-2015 : New York and Geneva). Vice-President)

INSTITUTION BUILDING (Agenda item 5d)
E/2015/SR.49
SUSTAINABLE DEVELOPMENT (Agenda item 18a)
E/2015/SR.15; E/2015/SR.20
TAXATION (Agenda item 18h)
E/2015/SR.28

## Dugan, Hugh (United States)

POST-CONFLICT RECONSTRUCTION–AFRICA
(Agenda item 12e)
E/2015/SR.52
REGIONAL COOPERATION (Agenda item 15)
E/2015/SR.54
UN–TRAINING AND RESEARCH INSTITUTIONS
(Agenda item 20)
E/2015/SR.33

## Dunn, David (United States)

OPERATIONAL ACTIVITIES–UN (Agenda item 7)
E/2015/SR.8; E/2015/SR.9
UN POLICY RECOMMENDATIONS (Agenda item 7a)
E/2015/SR.9

## Dzadzra, Anthony (Ghana)

TAXATION (Agenda item 18h)
E/2015/SR.29

## Eckey, Susan (Norway)

OPERATIONAL ACTIVITIES–UN (Agenda item 7)
E/2015/SR.5; E/2015/SR.6

## Egli, Patrick (Switzerland)

BRETTON WOODS INSTITUTIONS
E/2015/SR.26; E/2015/SR.27
OPERATIONAL ACTIVITIES–UN (Agenda item 7)
E/2015/SR.9
UN POLICY RECOMMENDATIONS (Agenda item 7a)
E/2015/SR.9; E/2015/SR.12

**Egli, Patrick (Switzerland) (continued)**

UN-WOMEN (Agenda item 7b)
E/2015/SR.11
UNDP/UNFPA/UNOPS (Agenda item 7b)
E/2015/SR.11
UNICEF (Agenda item 7b)
E/2015/SR.11
WORLD FOOD PROGRAMME (Agenda item 7b)
E/2015/SR.11

**El Mkhantar, Hassan (Morocco)**

HUMANITARIAN ASSISTANCE (Agenda item 9)
E/2015/SR.39

**El-Keib, Abdurrahim (***)**

INSTITUTION BUILDING (Agenda item 5d)
E/2015/SR.49

**Elbahi, Mohamed Ibrahim Mohamed (Sudan)**

CRIME PREVENTION (Agenda item 19c)
E/2015/SR.53

**Eler, Levent (Turkey)**

BRETTON WOODS INSTITUTIONS
E/2015/SR.25
MILLENNIUM DEVELOPMENT GOALS
E/2015/SR.48
SUSTAINABLE DEVELOPMENT GOALS (Agenda item 5c)
E/2015/SR.48

**Elias, Andalib (Bangladesh)**

REGIONAL COOPERATION–ASIA AND THE PACIFIC (Agenda item 15)
E/2015/SR.54

**Eliasson, Jan (UN. Deputy Secretary-General)**

OPERATIONAL ACTIVITIES–UN (Agenda item 7)
E/2015/SR.9
SOCIAL DEVELOPMENT (Agenda item 19b)
E/2015/SR.31
SUSTAINABLE DEVELOPMENT (Agenda item 18a)
E/2015/SR.15
SUSTAINABLE DEVELOPMENT–MINISTERIAL MEETING (Agenda item 5a)
E/2015/SR.42
UN POLICY RECOMMENDATIONS (Agenda item 7a)
E/2015/SR.9

**Erdman, Richard (United States)**

MILLENNIUM DEVELOPMENT GOALS
E/2015/SR.48
OPERATIONAL ACTIVITIES–UN (Agenda item 7)
E/2015/SR.34
SUSTAINABLE DEVELOPMENT GOALS (Agenda item 5c)
E/2015/SR.48

**Eriksson, Anne Christine (UNHCR. New York Liaison Office. Deputy Director)**

REFUGEES (Agenda item 19e)
E/2015/SR.53

**Eshanta, Abdulmonem A.H. (Libya)**

UN–TRAINING AND RESEARCH INSTITUTIONS (Agenda item 20)
E/2015/SR.33

**Espinosa Garcés, María Fernanda (Ecuador)**

HUMANITARIAN ASSISTANCE (Agenda item 9)
E/2015/SR.40

**Eun, Sung-soo (IBRD)**

BRETTON WOODS INSTITUTIONS
E/2015/SR.26

**Faizunnesa, Sadia (Bangladesh)**

HUMANITARIAN ASSISTANCE (Agenda item 9)
E/2015/SR.38

**Farmer, Paul (Paul Edward) (UN. Special Adviser to the Secretary-General for Community-based Medicine and Lessons from Haiti)**

EBOLA VIRUS DISEASE
E/2015/SR.3
SUSTAINABLE DEVELOPMENT (Agenda item 18a)
E/2015/SR.3

**Favero, Mauricio Fernando Dias (Brazil)**

OPERATIONAL ACTIVITIES–UN (Agenda item 7)
E/2015/SR.5; E/2015/SR.6; E/2015/SR.8
UN. ECONOMIC AND SOCIAL COUNCIL (2014-2015 : NEW YORK AND GENEVA)–AGENDA (Agenda item 2)
E/2015/SR.1; E/2015/SR.2

**Fegan-Wyles, Sally (UNITAR. Executive Director)**

UN–TRAINING AND RESEARCH INSTITUTIONS (Agenda item 20)
E/2015/SR.33

**Ferrell, Kay Alicyn (International Council for Education of People with Visual Impairment)**

SUSTAINABLE DEVELOPMENT (Agenda item 18a)
E/2015/SR.47(A)

**Fink-Hooijer, Florika (European Union)**

HUMANITARIAN ASSISTANCE (Agenda item 9)
E/2015/SR.38; E/2015/SR.39

**Fladby, Berit (Norway)**

OPERATIONAL ACTIVITIES–UN (Agenda item 7)
E/2015/SR.10
UN POLICY RECOMMENDATIONS (Agenda item 7a)
E/2015/SR.10; E/2015/SR.12; E/2015/SR.13

**Fos, Enrico T. (Philippines)**

HUMANITARIAN ASSISTANCE (Agenda item 9)
E/2015/SR.40

**Fossard, Renaud (Financial Transparency Coalition)**

TAXATION (Agenda item 18h)
E/2015/SR.28

**Fotina, Ekaterina V. (Russian Federation)**

OPERATIONAL ACTIVITIES–UN (Agenda item 7)
E/2015/SR.8

**Fowlie, Gary (ITU)**

SUSTAINABLE DEVELOPMENT (Agenda item 18a)
E/2015/SR.19

**Fox, Sarah (United States)**

SUSTAINABLE DEVELOPMENT (Agenda item 18a)
E/2015/SR.18

**Franceschi Navarro, Paulina María (Panama)**

OPERATIONAL ACTIVITIES–UN (Agenda item 7)
E/2015/SR.8
SUSTAINABLE DEVELOPMENT (Agenda item 18a)
E/2015/SR.19
SUSTAINABLE DEVELOPMENT–HIGH-LEVEL
POLITICAL FORUM (Agenda item 6)
E/2015/SR.44
UN-WOMEN (Agenda item 7b)
E/2015/SR.11
UNDP/UNFPA/UNOPS (Agenda item 7b)
E/2015/SR.11
UNICEF (Agenda item 7b)
E/2015/SR.11
WORLD FOOD PROGRAMME (Agenda item 7b)
E/2015/SR.11

**Francis, Tishka H. (Bahamas) (Caribbean Community)**

TAXATION (Agenda item 18h)
E/2015/SR.28

**Frankinet, Bénédicte (Belgium)**

OPERATIONAL ACTIVITIES–UN (Agenda item 7)
E/2015/SR.6
SUSTAINABLE DEVELOPMENT (Agenda item 18a)
E/2015/SR.18

**Frankinet, Bénédicte (UN. Commission on Population and Development. Chair)**

POPULATION–DEVELOPMENT (Agenda item 18f)
E/2015/SR.55

**Frei Montalva, Eduardo (***)**

SOCIAL DEVELOPMENT (Agenda item 19b)
E/2015/SR.31

**Funes de Rioja, Daniel (International Organisation of Employers)**

SUSTAINABLE DEVELOPMENT (Agenda item 18a)
E/2015/SR.15

**Gabrielyan, Vache (Armenia)**

BRETTON WOODS INSTITUTIONS
E/2015/SR.25

**Ganjanarintr, Pornprapai (Thailand)**

SUSTAINABLE DEVELOPMENT (Agenda item 18a)
E/2015/SR.43

**Gass, Thomas (UN. Assistant Secretary-General for Policy Coordination and Inter-Agency Affairs)**

INSTITUTION BUILDING (Agenda item 5d)
E/2015/SR.49
OPERATIONAL ACTIVITIES–UN (Agenda item 7)
E/2015/SR.5
SUSTAINABLE DEVELOPMENT (Agenda item 18a)
E/2015/SR.20
UN. PERMANENT FORUM ON INDIGENOUS ISSUES
(Agenda item 19h)
E/2015/SR.54
UN CONFERENCES (Agenda item 11)
E/2015/SR.36
UN POLICY RECOMMENDATIONS (Agenda item 7a)
E/2015/SR.13

**Gatilov, Gennadii Mikhailovich (Russian Federation)**

SUSTAINABLE DEVELOPMENT (Agenda item 18a)
E/2015/SR.43
SUSTAINABLE DEVELOPMENT–HIGH-LEVEL
POLITICAL FORUM (Agenda item 6)
E/2015/SR.43

**Gave, François (France)**

OPERATIONAL ACTIVITIES–UN (Agenda item 7)
E/2015/SR.34

**Gavrilescu, Gratiela Leocadia (Romania)**

SUSTAINABLE DEVELOPMENT (Agenda item 18a)
E/2015/SR.43
SUSTAINABLE DEVELOPMENT–HIGH-LEVEL
POLITICAL FORUM (Agenda item 6)
E/2015/SR.43

**Gebremedhin, Anna (Finland)**

HUMANITARIAN ASSISTANCE (Agenda item 9)
E/2015/SR.37

**Gedamu, Admasu Nebebe (Ethiopia)**

OPERATIONAL ACTIVITIES–UN (Agenda item 7)
E/2015/SR.8

**Ghods, Saideh (Society to Support Children Suffering from Cancer (Islamic Republic of Iran))**
NON-GOVERNMENTAL ORGANIZATIONS (Agenda item 17)
E/2015/SR.47(A)
SUSTAINABLE DEVELOPMENT (Agenda item 18a)
E/2015/SR.47(A)

**Gies, Andreas (Germany)**
MILLENNIUM DEVELOPMENT GOALS
E/2015/SR.48
SUSTAINABLE DEVELOPMENT GOALS (Agenda item 5c)
E/2015/SR.48

**Godin, Catherine (Canada)**
HUMANITARIAN ASSISTANCE (Agenda item 9)
E/2015/SR.37

**Golitsyn, Yaroslav (Ukraine)**
SUSTAINABLE DEVELOPMENT (Agenda item 18a)
E/2015/SR.47(A)

**Gómez Guifarro, Gilliam Noemi (Honduras)**
HUMANITARIAN ASSISTANCE (Agenda item 9)
E/2015/SR.40

**González Franco, Federico Alberto (Paraguay)**
SUSTAINABLE DEVELOPMENT (Agenda item 18a)
E/2015/SR.19

**Gosai, Nishana (South Africa. Revenue Service)**
TAXATION (Agenda item 18h)
E/2015/SR.29

**Grant, Michael Douglas (Canada)**
BRETTON WOODS INSTITUTIONS
E/2015/SR.26
SUSTAINABLE DEVELOPMENT (Agenda item 18a)
E/2015/SR.19

**Grignon, Koki Muli (Kenya)**
OPERATIONAL ACTIVITIES–UN (Agenda item 7)
E/2015/SR.9
SOUTH-SOUTH COOPERATION (Agenda item 7c)
E/2015/SR.12
UN POLICY RECOMMENDATIONS (Agenda item 7a)
E/2015/SR.9

**Guerra Rodríguez, Yolanda (Cuba)**
EBOLA VIRUS DISEASE
E/2015/SR.3
SUSTAINABLE DEVELOPMENT (Agenda item 18a)
E/2015/SR.3

**Guesalaga, Patricio (Chile)**
HUMANITARIAN ASSISTANCE (Agenda item 9)
E/2015/SR.40

**Guimarães-Pinto, Ricardo de (Unesco)**
SCIENCE AND TECHNOLOGY–DEVELOPMENT (Agenda item 18b)
E/2015/SR.47(A)
SUSTAINABLE DEVELOPMENT (Agenda item 18a)
E/2015/SR.47(A)

**Guindos Talavera, Beatriz de (IBRD)**
BRETTON WOODS INSTITUTIONS
E/2015/SR.27

**Gumende, António (Mozambique)**
OPERATIONAL ACTIVITIES–UN (Agenda item 7)
E/2015/SR.6

**Gunnarsson, Einar (Iceland) (UN. General Assembly (69th sess. : 2014-2015). Vice-President)**
SUSTAINABLE DEVELOPMENT (Agenda item 18a)
E/2015/SR.15

**Gustafik, Otto (UN. Economic and Social Council (2014-2015 : New York and Geneva). Secretary)**
REGIONAL COOPERATION–ASIA AND THE PACIFIC (Agenda item 15)
E/2015/SR.54
UN FORUM ON FORESTS (Agenda item 18k)
E/2015/SR.55

**Gutulo, Belachew Gujubo (Ethiopia)**
OPERATIONAL ACTIVITIES–UN (Agenda item 7)
E/2015/SR.34

**Gyhra, Richard (Holy See)**
HUMANITARIAN ASSISTANCE (Agenda item 9)
E/2015/SR.40

**Habtemariam, Yanit (Ethiopia)**
HUMANITARIAN ASSISTANCE (Agenda item 9)
E/2015/SR.38

**Haddad, Amy (Australia)**
SUSTAINABLE DEVELOPMENT (Agenda item 18a)
E/2015/SR.19

**Hahn, Choonghee (Republic of Korea)**
SOUTH-SOUTH COOPERATION (Agenda item 7c)
E/2015/SR.12
SUSTAINABLE DEVELOPMENT (Agenda item 18a)
E/2015/SR.19
UN POLICY RECOMMENDATIONS (Agenda item 7a)
E/2015/SR.12

**Hamdok, Abdalla (UN. ECA. Deputy Executive Secretary for Knowledge Generation)**
EBOLA VIRUS DISEASE
E/2015/SR.3
REGIONAL COOPERATION (Agenda item 15)
E/2015/SR.47(B)
SUSTAINABLE DEVELOPMENT (Agenda item 18a)
E/2015/SR.3

**Hamid, Salma (UNFPA)**

HUMANITARIAN ASSISTANCE (Agenda item 9)
E/2015/SR.40

**Hanfstaengl, Eva (Bread for the World (Organization))**

BRETTON WOODS INSTITUTIONS
E/2015/SR.27

**Hanif, Navid (UN. Office for ECOSOC Support and Coordination. Director)**

OPERATIONAL ACTIVITIES–UN (Agenda item 7)
E/2015/SR.34
UN. ECONOMIC AND SOCIAL COUNCIL (2014-2015 : NEW YORK AND GENEVA)–AGENDA (Agenda item 2)
E/2015/SR.1

**Haynes, Rueanna (Trinidad and Tobago) (Caribbean Community)**

OPERATIONAL ACTIVITIES–UN (Agenda item 7)
E/2015/SR.9
UN POLICY RECOMMENDATIONS (Agenda item 7a)
E/2015/SR.9

**Helbling, Thomas (IMF)**

BRETTON WOODS INSTITUTIONS
E/2015/SR.27

**Henczel, Remigiusz (Poland)**

HUMANITARIAN ASSISTANCE (Agenda item 9)
E/2015/SR.37

**Henderson, Nathan (Australia)**

REGIONAL COOPERATION–ASIA AND THE PACIFIC (Agenda item 15)
E/2015/SR.54
UN FORUM ON FORESTS (Agenda item 18k)
E/2015/SR.55

**Hentic, Isabelle (Canada)**

OPERATIONAL ACTIVITIES–UN (Agenda item 7)
E/2015/SR.6

**Hilale, Omar (Morocco)**

REGIONAL COOPERATION (Agenda item 15)
E/2015/SR.54

**Holtz, Aaron (United Kingdom) (European Union)**

GENDER MAINSTREAMING–UN SYSTEM (Agenda item 12c)
E/2015/SR.36

**Hoscheit, Jean-Marc (Luxembourg)**

HUMANITARIAN ASSISTANCE (Agenda item 9)
E/2015/SR.40

**Hoxha, Ferit (Albania)**

NON-GOVERNMENTAL ORGANIZATIONS (Agenda item 17)
E/2015/SR.51
OPERATIONAL ACTIVITIES–UN (Agenda item 7)
E/2015/SR.8

**Huffines, Jeffery (CIVICUS)**

NON-GOVERNMENTAL ORGANIZATIONS (Agenda item 17)
E/2015/SR.47(A)
SUSTAINABLE DEVELOPMENT (Agenda item 18a)
E/2015/SR.47(A)
SUSTAINABLE DEVELOPMENT–HIGH-LEVEL POLITICAL FORUM (Agenda item 6)
E/2015/SR.47(A)

**Hullman, Christiane (Germany)**

NON-GOVERNMENTAL ORGANIZATIONS (Agenda item 17)
E/2015/SR.51

**Ibrahim, Yassine (Tunisia)**

BRETTON WOODS INSTITUTIONS
E/2015/SR.25

**Ibrahimova, Khanim (Azerbaijan)**

BRETTON WOODS INSTITUTIONS
E/2015/SR.26

**Isbister, Jamie (Australia)**

HUMANITARIAN ASSISTANCE (Agenda item 9)
E/2015/SR.37

**Izam, Fatime Abdoulaye (***)**

HUMANITARIAN ASSISTANCE (Agenda item 9)
E/2015/SR.37

**Ja'afari, Bashar (Syrian Arab Republic)**

PALESTINIANS–TERRITORIES OCCUPIED BY ISRAEL–LIVING CONDITIONS (Agenda item 16)
E/2015/SR.50

**Jacinto-Henares, Kim S. (Philippines. Bureau of Internal Revenue)**

TAXATION (Agenda item 18h)
E/2015/SR.29

**Jansons, Raimonds (Latvia) (European Union)**

HUMANITARIAN ASSISTANCE (Agenda item 9)
E/2015/SR.37

**Javan, Jafar (UN System Staff College. Director)**

SOUTH-SOUTH COOPERATION (Agenda item 7c)
E/2015/SR.13
UN–TRAINING AND RESEARCH INSTITUTIONS (Agenda item 20)
E/2015/SR.33
UN POLICY RECOMMENDATIONS (Agenda item 7a)
E/2015/SR.13

**Jawhara, Rabee (Syrian Arab Republic)**

UN-WOMEN (Agenda item 7b)
E/2015/SR.11
UNDP/UNFPA/UNOPS (Agenda item 7b)
E/2015/SR.11
UNICEF (Agenda item 7b)
E/2015/SR.11
WORLD FOOD PROGRAMME (Agenda item 7b)
E/2015/SR.11

**Jenkins, Kevin (World Vision International)**

HUMANITARIAN ASSISTANCE (Agenda item 9)
E/2015/SR.38

**Jenks, Bruce (Dag Hammarskjöld Foundation (Uppsala, Sweden))**

OPERATIONAL ACTIVITIES–UN (Agenda item 7)
E/2015/SR.5

**Jennings, Philip (UNI Global Union)**

SUSTAINABLE DEVELOPMENT (Agenda item 18a)
E/2015/SR.15

**Johnson, Omobola (Nigeria)**

SCIENCE AND TECHNOLOGY–DEVELOPMENT
(Agenda item 18b)
E/2015/SR.54

**Joshi, Mayank (India)**

EBOLA VIRUS DISEASE
E/2015/SR.3
SUSTAINABLE DEVELOPMENT (Agenda item 18a)
E/2015/SR.3

**Jourdan, Marc (Global Foundation for Democracy and Development)**

SUSTAINABLE DEVELOPMENT (Agenda item 18a)
E/2015/SR.47(A)

**Kabaev, Kuban (Kyrgyzstan)**

REGIONAL COOPERATION (Agenda item 15)
E/2015/SR.47(B)

**Kagame, Paul (Rwanda. President)**

SUSTAINABLE DEVELOPMENT–MINISTERIAL
MEETING (Agenda item 5a)
E/2015/SR.42

**Kagame, Paul (UN. Secretary-General's MDG Advocacy Group. Co-Chair)**

SUSTAINABLE DEVELOPMENT–MINISTERIAL
MEETING (Agenda item 5a)
E/2015/SR.42

**Kage, Stephanie (Germany)**

INSTITUTION BUILDING (Agenda item 5d)
E/2015/SR.49
SUSTAINABLE DEVELOPMENT (Agenda item 18a)
E/2015/SR.15; E/2015/SR.20
TAXATION (Agenda item 18h)
E/2015/SR.28

**Kaji, Misako (Japan)**

HUMANITARIAN ASSISTANCE (Agenda item 9)
E/2015/SR.37

**Kane, Mitchell (New York University)**

TAXATION (Agenda item 18h)
E/2015/SR.29

**Kantrow, Louise (International Chamber of Commerce)**

BRETTON WOODS INSTITUTIONS
E/2015/SR.25

**Karau, Stephen Ndungu (Kenya)**

HUMANITARIAN ASSISTANCE (Agenda item 9)
E/2015/SR.40

**Karimsakov, Murat (Eurasian Economic Club of Scientists Association (Kazakhstan))**

BRETTON WOODS INSTITUTIONS
E/2015/SR.25

**Karimsakov, Murat (Kazakhstan)**

BRETTON WOODS INSTITUTIONS
E/2015/SR.25

**Karmakar, Sudhangshu (International Committee for Arab-Israeli Reconciliation)**

SUSTAINABLE DEVELOPMENT (Agenda item 18a)
E/2015/SR.47(A)

**Karybaeva, Mira (Kyrgyzstan)**

OPERATIONAL ACTIVITIES–UN (Agenda item 7)
E/2015/SR.8

**Kavun, Olha (Ukraine)**

HUMANITARIAN ASSISTANCE (Agenda item 9)
E/2015/SR.40

**Kebret, Negash (Ethiopia)**

HUMANITARIAN ASSISTANCE (Agenda item 9)
E/2015/SR.40

**Kelly, Alan (Ireland)**

SUSTAINABLE DEVELOPMENT (Agenda item 18a)
E/2015/SR.43
SUSTAINABLE DEVELOPMENT–HIGH-LEVEL
POLITICAL FORUM (Agenda item 6)
E/2015/SR.43

**Köhler, Pit (European Union)**

SOCIAL DEVELOPMENT (Agenda item 19b)
E/2015/SR.31

**Kohonen, Matti (Christian Aid (Organization))**

BRETTON WOODS INSTITUTIONS
E/2015/SR.27

**Koncke, Gonzalo (Uruguay)**

SUSTAINABLE DEVELOPMENT–HIGH-LEVEL
POLITICAL FORUM (Agenda item 6)
E/2015/SR.44

**Kononuchenko, Sergei (Russian Federation)**

MILLENNIUM DEVELOPMENT GOALS
E/2015/SR.48
SUSTAINABLE DEVELOPMENT GOALS (Agenda item 5c)
E/2015/SR.48

**Kostzer, Daniel (IBRD)**

BRETTON WOODS INSTITUTIONS
E/2015/SR.27

**Kouyialis, Nicos (Cyprus)**

SUSTAINABLE DEVELOPMENT (Agenda item 18a)
E/2015/SR.43
SUSTAINABLE DEVELOPMENT–HIGH-LEVEL
POLITICAL FORUM (Agenda item 6)
E/2015/SR.43

**Krähenbühl, Pierre (UNRWA. Commissioner-General)**

HUMANITARIAN ASSISTANCE (Agenda item 9)
E/2015/SR.39

**Krapp, Reinhard (Germany)**

SOUTH-SOUTH COOPERATION (Agenda item 7c)
E/2015/SR.13
UN POLICY RECOMMENDATIONS (Agenda item 7a)
E/2015/SR.13

**Kudasova, Yulia N. (Russian Federation)**

REGIONAL COOPERATION (Agenda item 15)
E/2015/SR.47(B)

**Kull, Daniel (IBRD)**

HUMANITARIAN ASSISTANCE (Agenda item 9)
E/2015/SR.38

**Kumar, Ajit (India)**

HUMANITARIAN ASSISTANCE (Agenda item 9)
E/2015/SR.40

**Kutesa, Sam K. (Uganda) (UN. General Assembly (69th sess. : 2014-2015). President)**

EBOLA VIRUS DISEASE
E/2015/SR.3
HUMANITARIAN ASSISTANCE (Agenda item 9)
E/2015/SR.37
SUSTAINABLE DEVELOPMENT (Agenda item 18a)
E/2015/SR.3
SUSTAINABLE DEVELOPMENT–MINISTERIAL
MEETING (Agenda item 5a)
E/2015/SR.42

**Kvalsoren, Anne Heidi (Norway)**

SUSTAINABLE DEVELOPMENT (Agenda item 18a)
E/2015/SR.15

**Kwain, Stan (UNDP. Bureau for Policy and Programme Support)**

SUSTAINABLE DEVELOPMENT (Agenda item 18a)
E/2015/SR.47(A)
SUSTAINABLE DEVELOPMENT–HIGH-LEVEL
POLITICAL FORUM (Agenda item 6)
E/2015/SR.47(A)

**Kydyrov, Talaibek (Kyrgyzstan)**

SUSTAINABLE DEVELOPMENT (Agenda item 18a)
E/2015/SR.18

**Laatu, Riikka (Finland)**

SUSTAINABLE DEVELOPMENT (Agenda item 18a)
E/2015/SR.43
SUSTAINABLE DEVELOPMENT–HIGH-LEVEL
POLITICAL FORUM (Agenda item 6)
E/2015/SR.43

**Lagumdzija, Zlatko (\*\*\*)**

MILLENNIUM DEVELOPMENT GOALS
E/2015/SR.46
SUSTAINABLE DEVELOPMENT GOALS (Agenda item 5c)
E/2015/SR.46

**Lake, Anthony (UNICEF. Executive Director)**

UNICEF (Agenda item 7b)
E/2015/SR.11

**Lalic-Smajevic, Katarina (Serbia)**

SUSTAINABLE DEVELOPMENT (Agenda item 18a)
E/2015/SR.19
UN POLICY RECOMMENDATIONS (Agenda item 7a)
E/2015/SR.12

**Lambertini, Inigo (Italy)**

UN–TRAINING AND RESEARCH INSTITUTIONS
(Agenda item 20)
E/2015/SR.33

**Lara Rangel, Salvador de (Mexico)**

LEAST DEVELOPED COUNTRIES–INTERNATIONAL
DECADE (2011-2020) (Agenda item 11b)
E/2015/SR.50

**Lasso Mendoza, Xavier (Ecuador) (Community of
Latin American and Caribbean States)**

BRETTON WOODS INSTITUTIONS
E/2015/SR.25

**Lee, Tong-Q (Republic of Korea)**

UN. ECONOMIC AND SOCIAL COUNCIL (2014-2015 :
NEW YORK AND GENEVA)–AGENDA (Agenda item 2)
E/2015/SR.2

**Lennartsson, Magnus (Sweden)**

OPERATIONAL ACTIVITIES–UN (Agenda item 7)
E/2015/SR.5; E/2015/SR.6; E/2015/SR.8;
E/2015/SR.9; E/2015/SR.34
UN POLICY RECOMMENDATIONS (Agenda item 7a)
E/2015/SR.9
UN-WOMEN (Agenda item 7b)
E/2015/SR.11
UNDP/UNFPA/UNOPS (Agenda item 7b)
E/2015/SR.11
UNICEF (Agenda item 7b)
E/2015/SR.11
WORLD FOOD PROGRAMME (Agenda item 7b)
E/2015/SR.11

**Levy, Betty (Soroptimist International)**

SUSTAINABLE DEVELOPMENT (Agenda item 18a)
E/2015/SR.47(A)

**Li, Wei Adele (Singapore)**

CRIME PREVENTION (Agenda item 19c)
E/2015/SR.53

**Liès, Michel (Schweizerische Rückversicherungs-
Gesellschaft)**

HUMANITARIAN ASSISTANCE (Agenda item 9)
E/2015/SR.38

**Lim, Hoon-Min (Republic of Korea)**

SUSTAINABLE DEVELOPMENT (Agenda item 18a)
E/2015/SR.35

**Löfven, Stefan (Sweden. Prime Minister)**

SUSTAINABLE DEVELOPMENT (Agenda item 18a)
E/2015/SR.15

**Lomónaco Tonda, Jorge (Mexico)**

HUMANITARIAN ASSISTANCE (Agenda item 9)
E/2015/SR.37

**Londoño Soto, Beatriz (Colombia)**

HUMANITARIAN ASSISTANCE (Agenda item 9)
E/2015/SR.40

**Lopes, Carlos (UN. ECA. Executive Secretary)**

UN POLICY RECOMMENDATIONS (Agenda item 7a)
E/2015/SR.13

**Lucas, Sylvie (Luxembourg) (European Union)**

NON-GOVERNMENTAL ORGANIZATIONS (Agenda
item 17)
E/2015/SR.51

**Luma, Joyce (World Food Programme)**

POST-CONFLICT RECONSTRUCTION–AFRICA
(Agenda item 12e)
E/2015/SR.52

**Lynn, Htin (Myanmar)**

SUSTAINABLE DEVELOPMENT (Agenda item 18a)
E/2015/SR.35

**Mabri Toikeusse, Albert (Côte d'Ivoire)**

OPERATIONAL ACTIVITIES–UN (Agenda item 7)
E/2015/SR.9
UN POLICY RECOMMENDATIONS (Agenda item 7a)
E/2015/SR.9

**Mahmood, Moazam (ILO)**

BRETTON WOODS INSTITUTIONS
E/2015/SR.26

**Majali, Saja Sattam Habes (Jordan)**

HUMANITARIAN ASSISTANCE (Agenda item 9)
E/2015/SR.40

**Maksimychev, Dmitry I. (Russian Federation)**

NON-COMMUNICABLE DISEASES (Agenda item 12f)
E/2015/SR.33
SUSTAINABLE DEVELOPMENT (Agenda item 18a)
E/2015/SR.19
UN POLICY RECOMMENDATIONS (Agenda item 7a)
E/2015/SR.12

**Makwarela, Mac (South Africa)**

HUMANITARIAN ASSISTANCE (Agenda item 9)
E/2015/SR.39; E/2015/SR.40

**Malawana, Lawrence Xolani (South Africa)**

HUMAN SETTLEMENTS (Agenda item 18d)
E/2015/SR.55

**Malawana, Lawrence Xolani (South Africa) (Group
of 77)**

UN FORUM ON FORESTS (Agenda item 18k)
E/2015/SR.55

**Mamabolo, Jeremiah Nyamane Kingsley (South Africa) (Group of 77)**

BRETTON WOODS INSTITUTIONS
E/2015/SR.25
SOUTH-SOUTH COOPERATION (Agenda item 7c)
E/2015/SR.12
SUSTAINABLE DEVELOPMENT (Agenda item 18a)
E/2015/SR.43
SUSTAINABLE DEVELOPMENT–HIGH-LEVEL
POLITICAL FORUM (Agenda item 6)
E/2015/SR.43
UN POLICY RECOMMENDATIONS (Agenda item 7a)
E/2015/SR.12
UNDP/UNFPA/UNOPS (Agenda item 7b)
E/2015/SR.12

**Mansour, Riyad H. (State of Palestine)**

DECOLONIZATION (Agenda item 14)
E/2015/SR.50

**Maope, Kelebone (Lesotho)**

INSTITUTION BUILDING (Agenda item 5d)
E/2015/SR.44
SUSTAINABLE DEVELOPMENT–HIGH-LEVEL
POLITICAL FORUM (Agenda item 6)
E/2015/SR.44

**Marais, Lincoln (African Tax Administration Forum)**

TAXATION (Agenda item 18h)
E/2015/SR.28

**Marobe, Simon Poni (South Africa) (Group of 77)**

BRETTON WOODS INSTITUTIONS
E/2015/SR.26
OPERATIONAL ACTIVITIES–UN (Agenda item 7)
E/2015/SR.34
PALESTINIANS–TERRITORIES OCCUPIED BY
ISRAEL–LIVING CONDITIONS (Agenda item 16)
E/2015/SR.50
TAXATION (Agenda item 18h)
E/2015/SR.56

**Marrah, Kaifala (Sierra Leone)**

EBOLA VIRUS DISEASE
E/2015/SR.3
SUSTAINABLE DEVELOPMENT (Agenda item 18a)
E/2015/SR.3

**Martin, Christophe (International Committee of the Red Cross)**

HUMANITARIAN ASSISTANCE (Agenda item 9)
E/2015/SR.40

**Martínez-Solimán, Magdy (UNDP. Bureau for Policy and Programme Support. Director)**

BRETTON WOODS INSTITUTIONS
E/2015/SR.26
MILLENNIUM DEVELOPMENT GOALS
E/2015/SR.46
SUSTAINABLE DEVELOPMENT GOALS (Agenda item 5c)
E/2015/SR.46

**Marzotto, Matteo (World Jewellery Confederation)**

SUSTAINABLE DEVELOPMENT (Agenda item 18a)
E/2015/SR.47(A)

**Maseli, Paul (UNIDO)**

SUSTAINABLE DEVELOPMENT (Agenda item 18a)
E/2015/SR.19

**Maze, Kerry (International Organization for Migration)**

HUMANITARIAN ASSISTANCE (Agenda item 9)
E/2015/SR.40

**Mazzeo, Gonzalo Sebastián (Argentina)**

DECOLONIZATION (Agenda item 14)
E/2015/SR.50

**McArthur, John W. (Brookings Institution (Washington, D.C.))**

MILLENNIUM DEVELOPMENT GOALS
E/2015/SR.46
SUSTAINABLE DEVELOPMENT GOALS (Agenda item 5c)
E/2015/SR.46

**McDonald, Calvin A. (IMF)**

BRETTON WOODS INSTITUTIONS
E/2015/SR.25

**Medvedeva, Irina (Russian Federation)**

TAXATION (Agenda item 18h)
E/2015/SR.28

**Meitzad, Hadas Ester (Israel)**

PALESTINIANS–TERRITORIES OCCUPIED BY
ISRAEL–LIVING CONDITIONS (Agenda item 16)
E/2015/SR.50

**Mejía Vélez, María Emma (Colombia)**

BRETTON WOODS INSTITUTIONS
E/2015/SR.27
INSTITUTION BUILDING (Agenda item 5d)
E/2015/SR.44
SOCIAL DEVELOPMENT (Agenda item 19b)
E/2015/SR.31
SUSTAINABLE DEVELOPMENT (Agenda item 18a)
E/2015/SR.16

**Monasebian, Simone (UN Office on Drugs and Crime. New York Office. Director)**

CRIME PREVENTION (Agenda item 19c)
E/2015/SR.53

**Montaño, Jorge (Mexico) (Group of Friends of the World Conference on Indigenous Peoples)**

UN. PERMANENT FORUM ON INDIGENOUS ISSUES (Agenda item 19h)
E/2015/SR.54

**Montiel, Lenni (UN. Department of Economic and Social Affairs. Assistant Secretary-General for Economic Development)**

INTERNATIONAL FINANCIAL INSTITUTIONS (Agenda item 5b)
E/2015/SR.46

**Mora Delgado, Alexander (Costa Rica)**

SUSTAINABLE DEVELOPMENT (Agenda item 18a)
E/2015/SR.20

**Morales López, Carlos Arturo (Colombia)**

NARCOTIC DRUGS (Agenda item 19d)
E/2015/SR.53

**Moreno-Dodson, Blanca (World Bank Group)**

TAXATION (Agenda item 18h)
E/2015/SR.29

**Morozov, Anton Y. (Russian Federation)**

SCIENCE AND TECHNOLOGY–DEVELOPMENT (Agenda item 18b)
E/2015/SR.54

**Muhumuza, Duncan Laki (Uganda)**

UN-WOMEN. EXECUTIVE BOARD–MEMBERS (Agenda item 4)
E/2015/SR.23

**Mukerji, Asoke Kumar (India)**

SUSTAINABLE DEVELOPMENT (Agenda item 18a)
E/2015/SR.19
SUSTAINABLE DEVELOPMENT–HIGH-LEVEL POLITICAL FORUM (Agenda item 6)
E/2015/SR.44

**Murniningtyas, Endah (Indonesia)**

SUSTAINABLE DEVELOPMENT (Agenda item 18a)
E/2015/SR.43
SUSTAINABLE DEVELOPMENT–HIGH-LEVEL POLITICAL FORUM (Agenda item 6)
E/2015/SR.43

**Mushayavanhu, Taonga (Zimbabwe)**

AIDS (Agenda item 12g)
E/2015/SR.22
HUMANITARIAN ASSISTANCE (Agenda item 9)
E/2015/SR.40

**Mvunga, Christopher Mphanza (Zambia)**

MILLENNIUM DEVELOPMENT GOALS
E/2015/SR.48
SUSTAINABLE DEVELOPMENT–HIGH-LEVEL POLITICAL FORUM (Agenda item 6)
E/2015/SR.47(A)
SUSTAINABLE DEVELOPMENT GOALS (Agenda item 5c)
E/2015/SR.48

**Mxakato-Diseko, Nozipho Joyce (South Africa)**

INSTITUTION BUILDING (Agenda item 5d)
E/2015/SR.49
MILLENNIUM DEVELOPMENT GOALS
E/2015/SR.46
SUSTAINABLE DEVELOPMENT GOALS (Agenda item 5c)
E/2015/SR.46

**Nabarro, David (UN. Special Envoy of the Secretary-General on Ebola)**

EBOLA VIRUS DISEASE
E/2015/SR.3
SUSTAINABLE DEVELOPMENT (Agenda item 18a)
E/2015/SR.3

**Nabulsi, Tarek (League of Arab States)**

SUSTAINABLE DEVELOPMENT (Agenda item 18a)
E/2015/SR.47(A)

**Nadeau, Marie-José (World Energy Council)**

SUSTAINABLE DEVELOPMENT (Agenda item 18a)
E/2015/SR.20

**Nakane, Kazuyuki (Japan)**

MILLENNIUM DEVELOPMENT GOALS
E/2015/SR.44; E/2015/SR.48
SUSTAINABLE DEVELOPMENT GOALS (Agenda item 5c)
E/2015/SR.44; E/2015/SR.48

**Nanxi, Liu (***)**

MILLENNIUM DEVELOPMENT GOALS
E/2015/SR.45
SUSTAINABLE DEVELOPMENT GOALS (Agenda item 5c)
E/2015/SR.45

**Nell, Christian (Germany)**

EBOLA VIRUS DISEASE
E/2015/SR.3
SUSTAINABLE DEVELOPMENT (Agenda item 18a)
E/2015/SR.3

**Nguyen, Phuong Nga (Viet Nam)**

MILLENNIUM DEVELOPMENT GOALS
E/2015/SR.44
OPERATIONAL ACTIVITIES–UN (Agenda item 7)
E/2015/SR.8
SUSTAINABLE DEVELOPMENT (Agenda item 18a)
E/2015/SR.44
SUSTAINABLE DEVELOPMENT GOALS (Agenda item 5c)
E/2015/SR.44
UN POLICY RECOMMENDATIONS (Agenda item 7a)
E/2015/SR.13

**Nilsson Snellman, Karin (Sweden)**

SUSTAINABLE DEVELOPMENT (Agenda item 18a)
E/2015/SR.15

**Niyazalieva, Damira (Kyrgyzstan)**

MILLENNIUM DEVELOPMENT GOALS
E/2015/SR.48
SUSTAINABLE DEVELOPMENT–HIGH-LEVEL
POLITICAL FORUM (Agenda item 6)
E/2015/SR.44
SUSTAINABLE DEVELOPMENT GOALS (Agenda item 5c)
E/2015/SR.48

**Norman, Giles Andrew (Canada) (UN. Economic and Social Council. Ad Hoc Advisory Group on Haiti. Chair)**

ECONOMIC ASSISTANCE–HAITI (Agenda item 12d)
E/2015/SR.52

**Notutela, Ncumisa (South Africa) (Group of 77)**

HUMANITARIAN ASSISTANCE (Agenda item 9)
E/2015/SR.37

**Nour, Amr (UN. Regional Commissions New York Office. Director)**

REGIONAL COOPERATION (Agenda item 15)
E/2015/SR.54

**Ntwaagae, Charles (Botswana)**

SUSTAINABLE DEVELOPMENT (Agenda item 18a)
E/2015/SR.44
SUSTAINABLE DEVELOPMENT–HIGH-LEVEL
POLITICAL FORUM (Agenda item 6)
E/2015/SR.44

**Nyembe, Raymond Thulane (South Africa) (Group of 77)**

OPERATIONAL ACTIVITIES–UN (Agenda item 7)
E/2015/SR.41

**Nyman, Elisha (United States)**

HUMANITARIAN ASSISTANCE (Agenda item 9)
E/2015/SR.37

**O'Brien, Patricia (Ireland)**

HUMANITARIAN ASSISTANCE (Agenda item 9)
E/2015/SR.40

**O'Brien, Stephen (UN. Under-Secretary-General for Humanitarian Affairs and Emergency Relief Coordinator)**

HUMANITARIAN ASSISTANCE (Agenda item 9)
E/2015/SR.37; E/2015/SR.38; E/2015/SR.39

**Ocampo, José Antonio (UN. Committee for Development Policy. Chair)**

SUSTAINABLE DEVELOPMENT (Agenda item 18a)
E/2015/SR.35; E/2015/SR.43
SUSTAINABLE DEVELOPMENT–HIGH-LEVEL
POLITICAL FORUM (Agenda item 6)
E/2015/SR.43

**Oh, Joon (Republic of Korea)**

BRETTON WOODS INSTITUTIONS
E/2015/SR.27

**Oh, Joon (Republic of Korea) (UN. Economic and Social Council (2014-2015 : New York and Geneva). Vice-President)**

MILLENNIUM DEVELOPMENT GOALS
E/2015/SR.46; E/2015/SR.48
RACIAL DISCRIMINATION–PROGRAMME OF ACTION (Agenda item 19f)
E/2015/SR.53
SOCIAL DEVELOPMENT (Agenda item 19b)
E/2015/SR.31
SUSTAINABLE DEVELOPMENT–MINISTERIAL
MEETING (Agenda item 5a)
E/2015/SR.42
SUSTAINABLE DEVELOPMENT GOALS (Agenda item 5c)
E/2015/SR.46; E/2015/SR.48
UN-HABITAT. GOVERNING COUNCIL–MEMBERS (Agenda item 4)
E/2015/SR.24
UN-WOMEN. EXECUTIVE BOARD–MEMBERS (Agenda item 4)
E/2015/SR.24

**Onano, Vivian (***)**

MILLENNIUM DEVELOPMENT GOALS
E/2015/SR.46
SUSTAINABLE DEVELOPMENT GOALS (Agenda item 5c)
E/2015/SR.46

**Onishi, Tomoko (Japan)**

REGIONAL COOPERATION–ASIA AND THE PACIFIC (Agenda item 15)
E/2015/SR.54

**Perceval, María Cristina (Argentina)**

OPERATIONAL ACTIVITIES–UN (Agenda item 7)
E/2015/SR.8
SOCIAL DEVELOPMENT (Agenda item 19b)
E/2015/SR.31
SOUTH-SOUTH COOPERATION (Agenda item 7c)
E/2015/SR.13
SUSTAINABLE DEVELOPMENT (Agenda item 18a)
E/2015/SR.15
UN POLICY RECOMMENDATIONS (Agenda item 7a)
E/2015/SR.13

**Perera, Amrith Rohan (Sri Lanka)**

MILLENNIUM DEVELOPMENT GOALS
E/2015/SR.44
SUSTAINABLE DEVELOPMENT–HIGH-LEVEL
POLITICAL FORUM (Agenda item 6)
E/2015/SR.44
SUSTAINABLE DEVELOPMENT GOALS (Agenda item 5c)
E/2015/SR.44

**Perera, Amrith Rohan (Sri Lanka) (Summit Level Group for South-South Consultations and Co-operation)**

SUSTAINABLE DEVELOPMENT (Agenda item 18a)
E/2015/SR.43
SUSTAINABLE DEVELOPMENT–HIGH-LEVEL
POLITICAL FORUM (Agenda item 6)
E/2015/SR.43

**Pérez Alvarez, Claudia (Cuba)**

HUMANITARIAN ASSISTANCE (Agenda item 9)
E/2015/SR.39; E/2015/SR.40

**Pérez Rulfo Torres, David (Corporativa de Fundaciones (Organization : Mexico))**

NON-GOVERNMENTAL ORGANIZATIONS (Agenda item 17)
E/2015/SR.47(A)
SUSTAINABLE DEVELOPMENT (Agenda item 18a)
E/2015/SR.47(A)

**Perez-Navarro, Grace (OECD. Centre for Tax Policy and Administration)**

TAXATION (Agenda item 18h)
E/2015/SR.28

**Perry, Victoria J. (IMF. Fiscal Affairs Department)**

TAXATION (Agenda item 18h)
E/2015/SR.28; E/2015/SR.29

**Petersen, Ib (Denmark)**

SUSTAINABLE DEVELOPMENT–HIGH-LEVEL
POLITICAL FORUM (Agenda item 6)
E/2015/SR.44

**Petrova, Simona (UN System Chief Executives Board for Coordination. Secretariat)**

COORDINATION-REPORTS (Agenda item 12a)
E/2015/SR.35

**Pfeil, Andreas (Germany)**

OPERATIONAL ACTIVITIES–UN (Agenda item 7)
E/2015/SR.5

**Phipps, Laurie Shestack (United States)**

UN. PERMANENT FORUM ON INDIGENOUS ISSUES (Agenda item 19h)
E/2015/SR.54

**Piantini Munnigh, Luis Manuel (UNCTAD)**

BRETTON WOODS INSTITUTIONS
E/2015/SR.25

**Picco, Isabelle F. (Monaco)**

MILLENNIUM DEVELOPMENT GOALS
E/2015/SR.44
SUSTAINABLE DEVELOPMENT–HIGH-LEVEL
POLITICAL FORUM (Agenda item 6)
E/2015/SR.44
SUSTAINABLE DEVELOPMENT GOALS (Agenda item 5c)
E/2015/SR.44

**Pictet-Althann, Marie-Therese (Sovereign Military Order of Malta)**

HUMANITARIAN ASSISTANCE (Agenda item 9)
E/2015/SR.40

**Pinheiro, Vinícius Carvalho (ILO)**

SOCIAL DEVELOPMENT (Agenda item 19b)
E/2015/SR.31

**Pipa, Tony (United States)**

SUSTAINABLE DEVELOPMENT–HIGH-LEVEL
POLITICAL FORUM (Agenda item 6)
E/2015/SR.44

**Ploumen, Lilianne (Netherlands)**

BRETTON WOODS INSTITUTIONS
E/2015/SR.26

**Pokharel, Shatrudhwan P.S. (Nepal)**

BRETTON WOODS INSTITUTIONS
E/2015/SR.26

**Potgieter-Gqubule, Febe (African Union. Commission)**

EBOLA VIRUS DISEASE
E/2015/SR.3
SUSTAINABLE DEVELOPMENT (Agenda item 18a)
E/2015/SR.3

**Poulsen, Jan Pirouz (European Union)**

EBOLA VIRUS DISEASE
E/2015/SR.3
SUSTAINABLE DEVELOPMENT (Agenda item 18a)
E/2015/SR.3

**Prato, Stefano (Society for International Development)**

BRETTON WOODS INSTITUTIONS
E/2015/SR.26

**Prizreni, Ingrit (Albania)**

SUSTAINABLE DEVELOPMENT (Agenda item 18a)
E/2015/SR.19

**Prosor, Ron (Israel)**

INSTITUTION BUILDING (Agenda item 5d)
E/2015/SR.44
SUSTAINABLE DEVELOPMENT (Agenda item 18a)
E/2015/SR.44

**Pullinger, John (United Kingdom) (UN. Statistical Commission. Chair)**

STATISTICS (Agenda item 18c)
E/2015/SR.35

**Puri, Lakshmi (UN-Women. Deputy Executive Director)**

UN-WOMEN (Agenda item 7b)
E/2015/SR.11
WOMEN IN DEVELOPMENT (Agenda item 18j)
E/2015/SR.32
WOMEN'S ADVANCEMENT (Agenda item 19a)
E/2015/SR.32

**Quest, Richard (Cable News Network (United States))**

SUSTAINABLE DEVELOPMENT (Agenda item 18a)
E/2015/SR.15

**Qureshi, Zia (IBRD)**

BRETTON WOODS INSTITUTIONS
E/2015/SR.26

**Radcliffe, Charles (UN. Office of the High Commissioner for Human Rights. New York Office. Global Issues and Intergovernmental Section. Chief)**

HUMAN RIGHTS (Agenda item 19g)
E/2015/SR.53

**Rahman, Mustafizur (Bangladesh)**

TAXATION (Agenda item 18h)
E/2015/SR.28; E/2015/SR.29

**Raja Zaib Shah, Raja Reza bin (Malaysia)**

MILLENNIUM DEVELOPMENT GOALS
E/2015/SR.48
SUSTAINABLE DEVELOPMENT GOALS (Agenda item 5c)
E/2015/SR.48

**Rajan, N.S. (Tata Group)**

SUSTAINABLE DEVELOPMENT (Agenda item 18a)
E/2015/SR.20

**Rakhmatia, Nara Masista (Indonesia)**

REGIONAL COOPERATION–ASIA AND THE PACIFIC (Agenda item 15)
E/2015/SR.54

**Rattray, Courtenay (Jamaica)**

OPERATIONAL ACTIVITIES–UN (Agenda item 7)
E/2015/SR.9
SUSTAINABLE DEVELOPMENT–MINISTERIAL MEETING (Agenda item 5a)
E/2015/SR.42
UN POLICY RECOMMENDATIONS (Agenda item 7a)
E/2015/SR.9

**Ravilova-Borovik, Dilyara S. (Russian Federation)**

DECOLONIZATION (Agenda item 14)
E/2015/SR.50

**Reaich, Carl Allan (New Zealand)**

HUMANITARIAN ASSISTANCE (Agenda item 9)
E/2015/SR.37; E/2015/SR.39

**Reiffenstuel, Anke (Germany)**

HUMANITARIAN ASSISTANCE (Agenda item 9)
E/2015/SR.37; E/2015/SR.38

**Reyes Zúñiga, Luisa Emilia (Equidad de Género : Ciudadanía, Trabajo y Familia, A.C. (Mexico))**

BRETTON WOODS INSTITUTIONS
E/2015/SR.27

**Reynolds, Andrew (United States)**

SCIENCE AND TECHNOLOGY–DEVELOPMENT (Agenda item 18b)
E/2015/SR.54
UN FORUM ON FORESTS (Agenda item 18k)
E/2015/SR.55

**Ribeiro, Adriana Telles (Brazil)**

UN-WOMEN (Agenda item 7b)
E/2015/SR.11
UNDP/UNFPA/UNOPS (Agenda item 7b)
E/2015/SR.11
UNICEF (Agenda item 7b)
E/2015/SR.11
WORLD FOOD PROGRAMME (Agenda item 7b)
E/2015/SR.11

**Richards, Mercedes (International Federation for Family Development)**

SUSTAINABLE DEVELOPMENT (Agenda item 18a)
E/2015/SR.47(A)

**Ríos Sánchez, Bruno (Mexico)**

NON-GOVERNMENTAL ORGANIZATIONS (Agenda item 17)
E/2015/SR.51
SOCIAL DEVELOPMENT (Agenda item 19b)
E/2015/SR.32

**Ritchie, Fiona (United Kingdom)**

OPERATIONAL ACTIVITIES–UN (Agenda item 7)
E/2015/SR.34

**Robl, Teri (United States)**

OPERATIONAL ACTIVITIES–UN (Agenda item 7)
E/2015/SR.6
UN. ECONOMIC AND SOCIAL COUNCIL (2014-2015 : NEW YORK AND GENEVA)–AGENDA (Agenda item 2)
E/2015/SR.1
UN POLICY RECOMMENDATIONS (Agenda item 7a)
E/2015/SR.13

**Rodríguez Abascal, Ana Silvia (Cuba)**

UN. ECONOMIC AND SOCIAL COUNCIL (2014-2015 : NEW YORK AND GENEVA)–AGENDA (Agenda item 2)
E/2015/SR.1

**Roet, David Yitshak (Israel)**

NON-GOVERNMENTAL ORGANIZATIONS (Agenda item 17)
E/2015/SR.51
SUSTAINABLE DEVELOPMENT (Agenda item 18a)
E/2015/SR.19

**Roostiavati, Agus Prihono (Indonesia)**

SUSTAINABLE DEVELOPMENT (Agenda item 18a)
E/2015/SR.18

**Rosdi, Mustapha Kamal (Malaysia)**

CRIME PREVENTION (Agenda item 19c)
E/2015/SR.53

**Ruíz Blanco, Miguel Camilo (Colombia)**

SOUTH-SOUTH COOPERATION (Agenda item 7c)
E/2015/SR.12
UN. ECONOMIC AND SOCIAL COUNCIL (2014-2015 : NEW YORK AND GENEVA)–AGENDA (Agenda item 2)
E/2015/SR.1

**Ryder, Guy (ILO. Director-General)**

SUSTAINABLE DEVELOPMENT (Agenda item 18a)
E/2015/SR.15; E/2015/SR.17; E/2015/SR.20

**Saadat, Peiman (Iran (Islamic Republic of))**

MILLENNIUM DEVELOPMENT GOALS
E/2015/SR.44
SUSTAINABLE DEVELOPMENT–HIGH-LEVEL POLITICAL FORUM (Agenda item 6)
E/2015/SR.44
SUSTAINABLE DEVELOPMENT GOALS (Agenda item 5c)
E/2015/SR.44

**Sachs, Jeffrey (UN. Special Adviser to the Secretary-General on the Millennium Development Goals)**

MILLENNIUM DEVELOPMENT GOALS
E/2015/SR.45
SUSTAINABLE DEVELOPMENT–MINISTERIAL MEETING (Agenda item 5a)
E/2015/SR.42
SUSTAINABLE DEVELOPMENT GOALS (Agenda item 5c)
E/2015/SR.45

**Saez, Patrick (United Kingdom)**

HUMANITARIAN ASSISTANCE (Agenda item 9)
E/2015/SR.38; E/2015/SR.39

**Saigal, Sunil (UNDP. Principal Coordinator of Ebola Response)**

EBOLA VIRUS DISEASE
E/2015/SR.3
SUSTAINABLE DEVELOPMENT (Agenda item 18a)
E/2015/SR.3

**Sajdik, Martin (Austria) (UN. Economic and Social Council (2014-2015 : New York and Geneva). President)**

BRETTON WOODS INSTITUTIONS
E/2015/SR.25; E/2015/SR.27
EBOLA VIRUS DISEASE
E/2015/SR.3
OPERATIONAL ACTIVITIES–UN (Agenda item 7)
E/2015/SR.8; E/2015/SR.9
SUSTAINABLE DEVELOPMENT (Agenda item 18a)
E/2015/SR.3
UN. COMMITTEE FOR PROGRAMME AND COORDINATION–MEMBERS (Agenda item 4)
E/2015/SR.30
UN. ECONOMIC AND SOCIAL COUNCIL (2014-2015 : NEW YORK AND GENEVA)–AGENDA (Agenda item 2)
E/2015/SR.1; E/2015/SR.2; E/2015/SR.30
UN. ECONOMIC AND SOCIAL COUNCIL (2014-2015 : NEW YORK AND GENEVA)–OFFICERS (Agenda item 1)
E/2015/SR.7
UN. STATISTICAL COMMISSION–MEMBERS (Agenda item 4)
E/2015/SR.30

**Sajdik, Martin (Austria) (UN. Economic and Social Council (2014-2015 : New York and Geneva). President) (continued)**

UN POLICY RECOMMENDATIONS (Agenda item 7a)
E/2015/SR.9; E/2015/SR.13
UN-HABITAT. GOVERNING COUNCIL–MEMBERS (Agenda item 4)
E/2015/SR.30

**Saleh, Idriss Moussa (\*\*\*)**

HUMANITARIAN ASSISTANCE (Agenda item 9)
E/2015/SR.37; E/2015/SR.39

**Samar, Sima (Afghanistan. Human Rights Commission)**

HUMANITARIAN ASSISTANCE (Agenda item 9)
E/2015/SR.39

**Samuels, Barbara (Global Clearinghouse for Development Finance)**

BRETTON WOODS INSTITUTIONS
E/2015/SR.26

**Sana, Maboneza (Rwanda) (UN. Group of African States)**

SUSTAINABLE DEVELOPMENT (Agenda item 18a)
E/2015/SR.43
SUSTAINABLE DEVELOPMENT–HIGH-LEVEL POLITICAL FORUM (Agenda item 6)
E/2015/SR.43

**Saner, Margaret (UN. Economic and Social Council. Committee of Experts on Public Administration. Chair)**

PUBLIC ADMINISTRATION (Agenda item 18g)
E/2015/SR.54

**Santala, Satu (IBRD)**

BRETTON WOODS INSTITUTIONS
E/2015/SR.27

**Santos, Sérgio Rodrigues dos (Brazil)**

UN FORUM ON FORESTS (Agenda item 18k)
E/2015/SR.55

**Sarapuu, Margus (Estonia)**

SUSTAINABLE DEVELOPMENT (Agenda item 18a)
E/2015/SR.43
SUSTAINABLE DEVELOPMENT–HIGH-LEVEL POLITICAL FORUM (Agenda item 6)
E/2015/SR.43

**Sareer, Ahmed (Maldives) (Alliance of Small Island States)**

SUSTAINABLE DEVELOPMENT (Agenda item 18a)
E/2015/SR.43
SUSTAINABLE DEVELOPMENT–HIGH-LEVEL POLITICAL FORUM (Agenda item 6)
E/2015/SR.43

**Schneider, Romain (Luxembourg)**

OPERATIONAL ACTIVITIES–UN (Agenda item 7)
E/2015/SR.9
UN POLICY RECOMMENDATIONS (Agenda item 7a)
E/2015/SR.9

**Schwarzelühr-Sutter, Rita (Germany)**

SUSTAINABLE DEVELOPMENT–HIGH-LEVEL POLITICAL FORUM (Agenda item 6)
E/2015/SR.44

**Schweinfest, Stefan (UN. Statistics Division. Director)**

CARTOGRAPHY (Agenda item 18i)
E/2015/SR.55

**Seger, Paul (Switzerland)**

SUSTAINABLE DEVELOPMENT–MINISTERIAL MEETING (Agenda item 5a)
E/2015/SR.42

**Seilenthal, Jüri (Estonia)**

HUMANITARIAN ASSISTANCE (Agenda item 9)
E/2015/SR.37

**Seksenbay, Tleuzhan S. (Kazakhstan)**

EBOLA VIRUS DISEASE
E/2015/SR.3
OPERATIONAL ACTIVITIES–UN (Agenda item 7)
E/2015/SR.8
SUSTAINABLE DEVELOPMENT (Agenda item 18a)
E/2015/SR.3

**Selk, Vanessa (France)**

UN. PERMANENT FORUM ON INDIGENOUS ISSUES (Agenda item 19h)
E/2015/SR.54

**Serra, Maurizio (Italy)**

HUMANITARIAN ASSISTANCE (Agenda item 9)
E/2015/SR.37

**Shank, Michael (\*\*\*)**

MILLENNIUM DEVELOPMENT GOALS
E/2015/SR.48
SUSTAINABLE DEVELOPMENT GOALS (Agenda item 5c)
E/2015/SR.48

**Sharma, Sangeeta (UN. Economic and Social Council (2014-2015 : New York and Geneva). Secretary)**

ECONOMIC ASSISTANCE–HAITI (Agenda item 12d)
E/2015/SR.52

**Shava, Frederick Musiiwa Makamure (Zimbabwe)**

SUSTAINABLE DEVELOPMENT (Agenda item 18a)
E/2015/SR.18

**Shearman, Martin (United Kingdom)**

NON-GOVERNMENTAL ORGANIZATIONS (Agenda item 17)
E/2015/SR.51
OPERATIONAL ACTIVITIES–UN (Agenda item 7)
E/2015/SR.8; E/2015/SR.9
SOUTH-SOUTH COOPERATION (Agenda item 7c)
E/2015/SR.12
SUSTAINABLE DEVELOPMENT (Agenda item 18a)
E/2015/SR.18
UN POLICY RECOMMENDATIONS (Agenda item 7a)
E/2015/SR.9; E/2015/SR.12

**Shiller, Robert J. (Yale University (New Haven, Conn.))**

SUSTAINABLE DEVELOPMENT (Agenda item 18a)
E/2015/SR.20

**Shin, Dong-ik (Republic of Korea)**

SUSTAINABLE DEVELOPMENT (Agenda item 18a)
E/2015/SR.47(A)
SUSTAINABLE DEVELOPMENT–HIGH-LEVEL
POLITICAL FORUM (Agenda item 6)
E/2015/SR.47(A)

**Siaplay, Mounir (Liberia)**

EBOLA VIRUS DISEASE
E/2015/SR.3
SUSTAINABLE DEVELOPMENT (Agenda item 18a)
E/2015/SR.3

**Silberhorn, Thomas (Germany)**

OPERATIONAL ACTIVITIES–UN (Agenda item 7)
E/2015/SR.9
UN POLICY RECOMMENDATIONS (Agenda item 7a)
E/2015/SR.9

**Simioni, Daniela (UN. Regional Commissions New York Office)**

DANGEROUS GOODS TRANSPORT (Agenda item 18l)
E/2015/SR.32

**Simonyan, Sofya (Armenia)**

BRETTON WOODS INSTITUTIONS
E/2015/SR.26; E/2015/SR.27

**Sipp, Werner (International Narcotics Control Board. President)**

NARCOTIC DRUGS (Agenda item 19d)
E/2015/SR.53

**Sison, Michele J. (United States)**

NON-GOVERNMENTAL ORGANIZATIONS (Agenda item 17)
E/2015/SR.51

**Skoog, Olof (Sweden)**

MILLENNIUM DEVELOPMENT GOALS
E/2015/SR.48

**Skoog, Olof (Sweden) (continued)**

SUSTAINABLE DEVELOPMENT–HIGH-LEVEL
POLITICAL FORUM (Agenda item 6)
E/2015/SR.44
SUSTAINABLE DEVELOPMENT GOALS (Agenda item 5c)
E/2015/SR.48

**Sloane, Esther Pan (United States)**

OPERATIONAL ACTIVITIES–UN (Agenda item 7)
E/2015/SR.5
TAXATION (Agenda item 18h)
E/2015/SR.28

**Snow, Jon (Channel 4 News (London))**

HUMANITARIAN ASSISTANCE (Agenda item 9)
E/2015/SR.39

**Solberg, Erna (Norway. Prime Minister)**

SUSTAINABLE DEVELOPMENT–MINISTERIAL
MEETING (Agenda item 5a)
E/2015/SR.42

**Solberg, Erna (UN. Secretary-General's MDG Advocacy Group. Co-Chair)**

SUSTAINABLE DEVELOPMENT–MINISTERIAL
MEETING (Agenda item 5a)
E/2015/SR.42

**Sollund, Stig B. (UN. Committee of Experts on International Cooperation in Tax Matters)**

TAXATION (Agenda item 18h)
E/2015/SR.29

**Somavía, Juan (Academia Diplomática de Chile)**

REGIONAL COOPERATION (Agenda item 15)
E/2015/SR.47(B)

**Somavía, Juan (UN. Special Adviser to the Secretary-General on Interregional Policy Cooperation)**

SOCIAL DEVELOPMENT (Agenda item 19b)
E/2015/SR.31

**Srisamoot, Arthayudh (UN. Commission on Narcotic Drugs. Chair)**

NARCOTIC DRUGS (Agenda item 19d)
E/2015/SR.53

**Stessl, Sonja (Austria)**

MILLENNIUM DEVELOPMENT GOALS
E/2015/SR.45
SUSTAINABLE DEVELOPMENT GOALS (Agenda item 5c)
E/2015/SR.45

**Steven, David (New York University. Center on International Cooperation)**

OPERATIONAL ACTIVITIES–UN (Agenda item 7)
E/2015/SR.9
UN POLICY RECOMMENDATIONS (Agenda item 7a)
E/2015/SR.9

**Stewart, Jane (UN System Chief Executives Board for Coordination. High-Level Committee on Programmes. Vice-Chair)**

OPERATIONAL ACTIVITIES–UN (Agenda item 7)
E/2015/SR.5

**Stiglitz, Joseph E. (Columbia University (New York))**

SUSTAINABLE DEVELOPMENT (Agenda item 18a)
E/2015/SR.15

**Stokes, Christopher John (Australia)**

OPERATIONAL ACTIVITIES–UN (Agenda item 7)
E/2015/SR.8; E/2015/SR.34
UN-WOMEN (Agenda item 7b)
E/2015/SR.11
UNDP/UNFPA/UNOPS (Agenda item 7b)
E/2015/SR.11
UNICEF (Agenda item 7b)
E/2015/SR.11
WORLD FOOD PROGRAMME (Agenda item 7b)
E/2015/SR.11

**Suazo, Marco Antonio (Honduras)**

OPERATIONAL ACTIVITIES–UN (Agenda item 7)
E/2015/SR.8
SUSTAINABLE DEVELOPMENT (Agenda item 18a)
E/2015/SR.19

**Sukhdev, Pavan (India)**

SUSTAINABLE DEVELOPMENT (Agenda item 18a)
E/2015/SR.20

**Sumi, Junichi (Japan)**

GENDER MAINSTREAMING–UN SYSTEM (Agenda item 12c)
E/2015/SR.36

**Tabah, Joshua (Canada)**

HUMANITARIAN ASSISTANCE (Agenda item 9)
E/2015/SR.39

**Taipale, Pilvi (Finland)**

EBOLA VIRUS DISEASE
E/2015/SR.3
SUSTAINABLE DEVELOPMENT (Agenda item 18a)
E/2015/SR.3

**Talbot, George Wilfred (Guyana)**

BRETTON WOODS INSTITUTIONS
E/2015/SR.26
OPERATIONAL ACTIVITIES–UN (Agenda item 7)
E/2015/SR.10

**Talbot, George Wilfred (Guyana) (continued)**

UN POLICY RECOMMENDATIONS (Agenda item 7a)
E/2015/SR.10

**Tara, Mahama Samuel (Ghana)**

OPERATIONAL ACTIVITIES–UN (Agenda item 7)
E/2015/SR.8

**Taylor, Aleesha (Open Society Foundations)**

EBOLA VIRUS DISEASE
E/2015/SR.3
SUSTAINABLE DEVELOPMENT (Agenda item 18a)
E/2015/SR.3

**Tekeste Meskel, Abraham (Ethiopia)**

BRETTON WOODS INSTITUTIONS
E/2015/SR.25

**Theyer, Hans (Fairtrade International)**

SUSTAINABLE DEVELOPMENT (Agenda item 18a)
E/2015/SR.47(A)

**Thier, Alex (United States)**

BRETTON WOODS INSTITUTIONS
E/2015/SR.26

**Thomas, Mark R. (Mark Roland) (IBRD)**

EBOLA VIRUS DISEASE
E/2015/SR.3
SUSTAINABLE DEVELOPMENT (Agenda item 18a)
E/2015/SR.3

**Thomson, Peter (Fiji) (UNDP/UNFPA Executive Board. President)**

OPERATIONAL ACTIVITIES–UN (Agenda item 7)
E/2015/SR.6

**Thongphakdi, Thani (Thailand)**

HUMANITARIAN ASSISTANCE (Agenda item 9)
E/2015/SR.40

**Thöresson, Per (Sweden)**

EBOLA VIRUS DISEASE
E/2015/SR.3
SUSTAINABLE DEVELOPMENT (Agenda item 18a)
E/2015/SR.3

**Thyssen, Marianne (European Commission. Commissioner for Employment, Social Affairs, Skills and Labour Mobility)**

SUSTAINABLE DEVELOPMENT (Agenda item 18a)
E/2015/SR.15

**Tlapa, Martin (Czech Republic)**

SUSTAINABLE DEVELOPMENT (Agenda item 18a)
E/2015/SR.43
SUSTAINABLE DEVELOPMENT–HIGH-LEVEL POLITICAL FORUM (Agenda item 6)
E/2015/SR.43

**Topping, Jennifer (UN. Office of the Resident Coordinator and Humanitarian Coordinator (Mozambique))**

OPERATIONAL ACTIVITIES–UN (Agenda item 7)
E/2015/SR.6

**Torres, Raymond (ILO)**

INTERNATIONAL FINANCIAL INSTITUTIONS (Agenda item 5b)
E/2015/SR.46

**Touré, Ténin (Action aide aux familles démunies (Mali))**

SUSTAINABLE DEVELOPMENT (Agenda item 18a)
E/2015/SR.47(A)
WOMEN IN DEVELOPMENT (Agenda item 18j)
E/2015/SR.47(A)

**Trepelkov, Alexandre (UN. Department of Economic and Social Affairs. Financing for Development Office. Director)**

TAXATION (Agenda item 18h)
E/2015/SR.28

**Tupouniua, Mahe'uli'uli Sandhurst (Tonga) (Pacific Small Island Developing States)**

SUSTAINABLE DEVELOPMENT (Agenda item 18a)
E/2015/SR.43
SUSTAINABLE DEVELOPMENT–HIGH-LEVEL POLITICAL FORUM (Agenda item 6)
E/2015/SR.43

**Türk, Volker (UNHCR)**

HUMANITARIAN ASSISTANCE (Agenda item 9)
E/2015/SR.40

**Ulin, Denis (Russian Federation)**

BRETTON WOODS INSTITUTIONS
E/2015/SR.26

**Ülker, Cemre (Journalists and Writers Foundation (Turkey))**

SUSTAINABLE DEVELOPMENT (Agenda item 18a)
E/2015/SR.47(A)
WOMEN IN DEVELOPMENT (Agenda item 18j)
E/2015/SR.47(A)

**Ünal, Merve Neva (Turkey)**

LEAST DEVELOPED COUNTRIES–INTERNATIONAL DECADE (2011-2020) (Agenda item 11b)
E/2015/SR.56

**Usui, Masato (Japan)**

OPERATIONAL ACTIVITIES–UN (Agenda item 7)
E/2015/SR.8
UN. ECONOMIC AND SOCIAL COUNCIL (2014-2015 : NEW YORK AND GENEVA)–AGENDA (Agenda item 2)
E/2015/SR.1

**Vadiati, Forouzandeh (Iran (Islamic Republic of))**

NON-GOVERNMENTAL ORGANIZATIONS (Agenda item 17)
E/2015/SR.51

**Valle Pereña, Juan Manuel (Mexican Agency for International Development Cooperation)**

BRETTON WOODS INSTITUTIONS
E/2015/SR.26

**Velikhov, E.P. (International Association of Economic and Social Councils and Similar Institutions)**

INSTITUTION BUILDING (Agenda item 5d)
E/2015/SR.44
MILLENNIUM DEVELOPMENT GOALS
E/2015/SR.44
SUSTAINABLE DEVELOPMENT GOALS (Agenda item 5c)
E/2015/SR.44

**Vella, Karmenu (European Union)**

SUSTAINABLE DEVELOPMENT (Agenda item 18a)
E/2015/SR.43
SUSTAINABLE DEVELOPMENT–HIGH-LEVEL POLITICAL FORUM (Agenda item 6)
E/2015/SR.43

**Velo, Silvia (Italy)**

SUSTAINABLE DEVELOPMENT (Agenda item 18a)
E/2015/SR.43
SUSTAINABLE DEVELOPMENT–HIGH-LEVEL POLITICAL FORUM (Agenda item 6)
E/2015/SR.43

**Velshi, Ali (Al Jazeera America (Television network))**

SUSTAINABLE DEVELOPMENT (Agenda item 18a)
E/2015/SR.20

**Verburg, Gerda (Netherlands) (FAO. Committee on World Food Security. Chair)**

SUSTAINABLE DEVELOPMENT (Agenda item 18a)
E/2015/SR.50

**Verdi, Marco (Inter-American Center of Tax Administrations)**

TAXATION (Agenda item 18h)
E/2015/SR.28; E/2015/SR.29

**Verhoeven, Marijn (IBRD)**

TAXATION (Agenda item 18h)
E/2015/SR.28

**Vermont, Sibylle (Switzerland)**

UN FORUM ON FORESTS (Agenda item 18k)
E/2015/SR.55

**Versegi, Peter Lloyd (Australia)**

UN POLICY RECOMMENDATIONS (Agenda item 7a)
E/2015/SR.12
UNDP/UNFPA/UNOPS (Agenda item 7b)
E/2015/SR.12

**Verville, Elizabeth (UN Interregional Crime and Justice Research Institute. Board of Trustees. President)**

CRIME PREVENTION (Agenda item 19c)
E/2015/SR.53

**Vestrheim, Alf Havard (Norway)**

OPERATIONAL ACTIVITIES–UN (Agenda item 7)
E/2015/SR.34

**Vilas, Paula (Argentina)**

HUMANITARIAN ASSISTANCE (Agenda item 9)
E/2015/SR.39

**Villeroché, Hervé de (World Bank Group)**

BRETTON WOODS INSTITUTIONS
E/2015/SR.26

**Virgill-Rolle, Nicola (Bahamas)**

MILLENNIUM DEVELOPMENT GOALS
E/2015/SR.48
SUSTAINABLE DEVELOPMENT GOALS (Agenda item 5c)
E/2015/SR.48

**Von Steiger Weber, Tatjana (Switzerland)**

OPERATIONAL ACTIVITIES–UN (Agenda item 7)
E/2015/SR.34

**Wagner, Thomas (France)**

HUMANITARIAN ASSISTANCE (Agenda item 9)
E/2015/SR.40

**Wahba, Mourad (UN. Deputy Special Representative of the Secretary-General for Haiti and Humanitarian Coordinator, Resident Coordinator and Resident Representative for UNDP in Haiti)**

ECONOMIC ASSISTANCE–HAITI (Agenda item 12d)
E/2015/SR.52

**Walker, Melanie (World Bank Group)**

EBOLA VIRUS DISEASE
E/2015/SR.3
SUSTAINABLE DEVELOPMENT (Agenda item 18a)
E/2015/SR.3

**Wallace, Nancy E. (World Federation for Mental Health)**

SUSTAINABLE DEVELOPMENT (Agenda item 18a)
E/2015/SR.47(A)

**Wallin, Markku (Finland)**

SUSTAINABLE DEVELOPMENT (Agenda item 18a)
E/2015/SR.15

**Wallin, Stefan (Finland)**

SUSTAINABLE DEVELOPMENT (Agenda item 18a)
E/2015/SR.18

**Wandel, Jens (UNDP. Bureau of Management. Assistant Administrator and Director)**

UN POLICY RECOMMENDATIONS (Agenda item 7a)
E/2015/SR.13

**Wang, Dazhong (China)**

HUMANITARIAN ASSISTANCE (Agenda item 9)
E/2015/SR.37
OPERATIONAL ACTIVITIES–UN (Agenda item 7)
E/2015/SR.9
UN POLICY RECOMMENDATIONS (Agenda item 7a)
E/2015/SR.9

**Wang, Hongbo (China)**

OPERATIONAL ACTIVITIES–UN (Agenda item 7)
E/2015/SR.5; E/2015/SR.8; E/2015/SR.34
SOUTH-SOUTH COOPERATION (Agenda item 7c)
E/2015/SR.12
UN POLICY RECOMMENDATIONS (Agenda item 7a)
E/2015/SR.12
UNDP/UNFPA/UNOPS (Agenda item 7b)
E/2015/SR.12

**Wang, Min (China)**

MILLENNIUM DEVELOPMENT GOALS
E/2015/SR.44
SUSTAINABLE DEVELOPMENT GOALS (Agenda item 5c)
E/2015/SR.44

**Wannous, Chadia (Inter-Agency Secretariat of the ISDR)**

HUMANITARIAN ASSISTANCE (Agenda item 9)
E/2015/SR.40

**Webber, Darrel (Roundtable on Sustainable Palm Oil)**

SUSTAINABLE DEVELOPMENT (Agenda item 18a)
E/2015/SR.47(A)

**Wennubst, Pius (Switzerland)**

MILLENNIUM DEVELOPMENT GOALS
E/2015/SR.48
OPERATIONAL ACTIVITIES–UN (Agenda item 7)
E/2015/SR.6
SUSTAINABLE DEVELOPMENT (Agenda item 18a)
E/2015/SR.43
SUSTAINABLE DEVELOPMENT–HIGH-LEVEL POLITICAL FORUM (Agenda item 6)
E/2015/SR.43
SUSTAINABLE DEVELOPMENT GOALS (Agenda item 5c)
E/2015/SR.48

**Wibowo, Triyono (Indonesia)**

HUMANITARIAN ASSISTANCE (Agenda item 9)
E/2015/SR.40

**Wilcox, Richard (African Union. African Risk Capacity. Insurance Company Limited)**

HUMANITARIAN ASSISTANCE (Agenda item 9)
E/2015/SR.38

**Wilson, Peter (United Kingdom)**

INSTITUTION BUILDING (Agenda item 5d)
E/2015/SR.44

**Wright, Jeffrey (Ebola Survival Fund)**

EBOLA VIRUS DISEASE
E/2015/SR.3
SUSTAINABLE DEVELOPMENT (Agenda item 18a)
E/2015/SR.3

**Wu, Dong (UNCTAD)**

SCIENCE AND TECHNOLOGY–DEVELOPMENT
(Agenda item 18b)
E/2015/SR.54

**Wu, Hongbo (UN. Under-Secretary-General for Economic and Social Affairs)**

BRETTON WOODS INSTITUTIONS
E/2015/SR.26
INSTITUTION BUILDING (Agenda item 5d)
E/2015/SR.43
MILLENNIUM DEVELOPMENT GOALS
E/2015/SR.43
OPERATIONAL ACTIVITIES–UN (Agenda item 7)
E/2015/SR.10
SUSTAINABLE DEVELOPMENT (Agenda item 18a)
E/2015/SR.43
SUSTAINABLE DEVELOPMENT GOALS (Agenda item 5c)
E/2015/SR.43
UN POLICY RECOMMENDATIONS (Agenda item 7a)
E/2015/SR.10

**Yaffar, Armando Lara (UN. Committee of Experts on International Cooperation in Tax Matters. Chair)**

TAXATION (Agenda item 18h)
E/2015/SR.28; E/2015/SR.29

**Yao, Shaojun (China)**

EBOLA VIRUS DISEASE
E/2015/SR.3
SOCIAL DEVELOPMENT (Agenda item 19b)
E/2015/SR.31
SUSTAINABLE DEVELOPMENT (Agenda item 18a)
E/2015/SR.3

**Yassine, Amena Martins (Brazil)**

UN. PERMANENT FORUM ON INDIGENOUS ISSUES
(Agenda item 19h)
E/2015/SR.54

**Yi, Xiaozhun (World Trade Organization. Deputy Director-General)**

BRETTON WOODS INSTITUTIONS
E/2015/SR.25

**Zagrekov, Victor (Russian Federation)**

EBOLA VIRUS DISEASE
E/2015/SR.3
SUSTAINABLE DEVELOPMENT (Agenda item 18a)
E/2015/SR.3

**Zehnder, Olivier Marc (Switzerland)**

AIDS (Agenda item 12g)
E/2015/SR.22
SUSTAINABLE DEVELOPMENT (Agenda item 18a)
E/2015/SR.18

**Zhou, Yiping (UN. Office for South-South Cooperation. Director)**

SOUTH-SOUTH COOPERATION (Agenda item 7c)
E/2015/SR.12

**Zhu, Min (IMF. Deputy Managing Director)**

INTERNATIONAL FINANCIAL INSTITUTIONS (Agenda item 5b)
E/2015/SR.46
SUSTAINABLE DEVELOPMENT (Agenda item 18a)
E/2015/SR.15

**Zinsou, Eric Jean-Marie (Benin)**

BRETTON WOODS INSTITUTIONS
E/2015/SR.26

**Zinsou, Jean-Francis Régis (Benin) (Coordinating Bureau of the Least Developed Countries. Chairman)**

LEAST DEVELOPED COUNTRIES–INTERNATIONAL
DECADE (2011-2020) (Agenda item 11b)
E/2015/SR.56

**Zinsou, Jean-Francis Régis (Benin) (Group of Least Developed Countries)**

BRETTON WOODS INSTITUTIONS
E/2015/SR.25
LEAST DEVELOPED COUNTRIES–INTERNATIONAL
DECADE (2011-2020) (Agenda item 11b)
E/2015/SR.50

**Zolt, Eric M. (University of California (Los Angeles). School of Law)**

TAXATION (Agenda item 18h)
E/2015/SR.29

**Zupanjevac, Dragan (Serbia)**

HUMANITARIAN ASSISTANCE (Agenda item 9)
E/2015/SR.40

## AIDS (Agenda item 12g)

Joint United Nations Programme on HIV/AIDS. Deputy Executive Director
    Beagle, Jan – E/2015/SR.22
Switzerland
    Zehnder, Olivier Marc – E/2015/SR.22
Zimbabwe
    Mushayavanhu, Taonga – E/2015/SR.22

## BRETTON WOODS INSTITUTIONS

Armenia
    Gabrielyan, Vache – E/2015/SR.25
    Simonyan, Sofya – E/2015/SR.26; E/2015/SR.27
Azerbaijan
    Ibrahimova, Khanim – E/2015/SR.26
Bangladesh
    Mitra, Barun Dev – E/2015/SR.26
Benin
    Zinsou, Eric Jean-Marie – E/2015/SR.26
Bread for the World (Organization)
    Hanfstaengl, Eva – E/2015/SR.27
Canada
    Grant, Michael Douglas – E/2015/SR.26
Christian Aid (Organization)
    Kohonen, Matti – E/2015/SR.27
Colombia
    Cardenas Santamaria, Mauricio – E/2015/SR.25
    Mejía Vélez, María Emma – E/2015/SR.27
Community of Latin American and Caribbean States
    Lasso Mendoza, Xavier (Ecuador) – E/2015/SR.25
Croatia
    Drobnjak, Vladimir – E/2015/SR.27
Equidad de Género : Ciudadanía, Trabajo y Familia, A.C. (Mexico)
    Reyes Zúñiga, Luisa Emilia – E/2015/SR.27
Ethiopia
    Tekeste Meskel, Abraham – E/2015/SR.25
Eurasian Economic Club of Scientists Association (Kazakhstan)
    Karimsakov, Murat – E/2015/SR.25
European Union
    Mimica, Neven – E/2015/SR.25
Global Clearinghouse for Development Finance
    Samuels, Barbara – E/2015/SR.26
Group of 77
    Mamabolo, Jeremiah Nyamane Kingsley (South Africa) – E/2015/SR.25
    Marobe, Simon Poni (South Africa) – E/2015/SR.26
Group of Least Developed Countries
    Zinsou, Jean-Francis Régis (Benin) – E/2015/SR.25
Guyana
    Talbot, George Wilfred – E/2015/SR.26
IBRD
    Eun, Sung-soo – E/2015/SR.26
    Guindos Talavera, Beatriz de – E/2015/SR.27
    Kostzer, Daniel – E/2015/SR.27
    Mohieldin, Mahmoud – E/2015/SR.25; E/2015/SR.27
    Qureshi, Zia – E/2015/SR.26
    Santala, Satu – E/2015/SR.27
ILO
    Mahmood, Moazam – E/2015/SR.26

## BRETTON WOODS INSTITUTIONS (continued)

IMF
    Helbling, Thomas – E/2015/SR.27
    McDonald, Calvin A. – E/2015/SR.25
International Chamber of Commerce
    Kantrow, Louise – E/2015/SR.25
Kazakhstan
    Karimsakov, Murat – E/2015/SR.25
Mexican Agency for International Development Cooperation
    Valle Pereña, Juan Manuel – E/2015/SR.26
Nepal
    Pokharel, Shatrudhwan P.S. – E/2015/SR.26
Netherlands
    Ploumen, Lilianne – E/2015/SR.26
Norway
    Pedersen, Geir O. – E/2015/SR.26
OECD. Development Co-operation Directorate
    Killen, Brenda – E/2015/SR.26
Republic of Korea
    Oh, Joon – E/2015/SR.27
Russian Federation
    Ulin, Denis – E/2015/SR.26
Society for International Development
    Prato, Stefano – E/2015/SR.26
Society of Catholic Medical Missionaries
    Paramundayil, Celine – E/2015/SR.26
Sweden
    Andersson, Magdalena – E/2015/SR.25
Switzerland
    Egli, Patrick – E/2015/SR.26; E/2015/SR.27
Tunisia
    Ibrahim, Yassine – E/2015/SR.25
Turkey
    Babacan, Ali – E/2015/SR.25
    Eler, Levent – E/2015/SR.25
UN. Economic and Social Council (2014-2015 : New York and Geneva). President
    Sajdik, Martin (Austria) – E/2015/SR.25; E/2015/SR.27
UN. Secretary-General
    Ban, Ki-moon, 1944- – E/2015/SR.25
UN. Under-Secretary-General for Economic and Social Affairs
    Wu, Hongbo – E/2015/SR.26
UNCTAD
    Piantini Munnigh, Luis Manuel – E/2015/SR.25
UNCTAD. Secretary-General
    Kituyi, Mukhisa – E/2015/SR.26
UNDP. Bureau for Policy and Programme Support. Director
    Martínez-Solimán, Magdy – E/2015/SR.26
United States
    Thier, Alex – E/2015/SR.26
World Bank Group
    Villeroché, Hervé de – E/2015/SR.26
World Trade Organization. Deputy Director-General
    Yi, Xiaozhun – E/2015/SR.25

## CARTOGRAPHY (Agenda item 18i)

UN. Statistics Division. Director
    Schweinfest, Stefan – E/2015/SR.55

## COORDINATION-REPORTS (Agenda item 12a)

UN System Chief Executives Board for Coordination.
Secretariat
 Petrova, Simona – E/2015/SR.35
United States
 Derderian, Jill – E/2015/SR.35

## CRIME PREVENTION (Agenda item 19c)

Malaysia
 Rosdi, Mustapha Kamal – E/2015/SR.53
Mexico
 Alba Góngora, Luis Alfonso de – E/2015/SR.53
Singapore
 Li, Wei Adele – E/2015/SR.53
Sudan
 Elbahi, Mohamed Ibrahim Mohamed –
  E/2015/SR.53
UN Commission on Crime Prevention and Criminal
Justice. Chair
 Alba Góngora, Luis Alfonso de (Mexico) –
  E/2015/SR.53
UN Interregional Crime and Justice Research Institute.
Board of Trustees. President
 Verville, Elizabeth – E/2015/SR.53
UN Office on Drugs and Crime. New York Office.
Director
 Monasebian, Simone – E/2015/SR.53

## DANGEROUS GOODS TRANSPORT (Agenda item 18l)

UN. Regional Commissions New York Office
 Simioni, Daniela – E/2015/SR.32

## DECOLONIZATION (Agenda item 14)

Argentina
 Mazzeo, Gonzalo Sebastián – E/2015/SR.50
Russian Federation
 Ravilova-Borovik, Dilyara S. – E/2015/SR.50
State of Palestine
 Mansour, Riyad H. – E/2015/SR.50
UN. ESCWA
 Alami, Tarik – E/2015/SR.50
United States
 Derderian, Jill – E/2015/SR.50

## EBOLA VIRUS DISEASE

African Union. Commission
 Potgieter-Gqubule, Febe – E/2015/SR.3
ArcelorMittal (Firm)
 Knight, Alan – E/2015/SR.3
Brazil
 Patriota, Antonio de Aguiar – E/2015/SR.3
Center for Global Development (Washington, D.C.)
 Over, A. Mead – E/2015/SR.3
China
 Yao, Shaojun – E/2015/SR.3
Cuba
 Guerra Rodríguez, Yolanda – E/2015/SR.3
Ebola Survival Fund
 Wright, Jeffrey – E/2015/SR.3
European Union
 Poulsen, Jan Pirouz – E/2015/SR.3

## EBOLA VIRUS DISEASE (continued)

Finland
 Taipale, Pilvi – E/2015/SR.3
France
 Bartoli, Fabienne – E/2015/SR.3
Germany
 Nell, Christian – E/2015/SR.3
Guinea
 Diare, Mohamed – E/2015/SR.3
IBRD
 Thomas, Mark R. (Mark Roland) – E/2015/SR.3
India
 Joshi, Mayank – E/2015/SR.3
Kazakhstan
 Seksenbay, Tleuzhan S. – E/2015/SR.3
Liberia
 Siaplay, Mounir – E/2015/SR.3
Mali
 Doucouré, Dianguina dit Yaya – E/2015/SR.3
New Future Foundation (New York)
 Blakely, Delois – E/2015/SR.3
Open Society Foundations
 Taylor, Aleesha – E/2015/SR.3
Russian Federation
 Zagrekov, Victor – E/2015/SR.3
Sierra Leone
 Marrah, Kaifala – E/2015/SR.3
Sweden
 Thöresson, Per – E/2015/SR.3
UN. ECA. Deputy Executive Secretary for Knowledge
Generation
 Hamdok, Abdalla – E/2015/SR.3
UN. Economic and Social Council (2014-2015 : New
York and Geneva). President
 Sajdik, Martin (Austria) – E/2015/SR.3
UN. General Assembly (69th sess. : 2014-2015).
President
 Kutesa, Sam K. (Uganda) – E/2015/SR.3
UN. Secretary-General
 Ban, Ki-moon, 1944- – E/2015/SR.3
UN. Special Adviser to the Secretary-General for
Community-based Medicine and Lessons from Haiti
 Farmer, Paul (Paul Edward) – E/2015/SR.3
UN. Special Envoy of the Secretary-General on Ebola
 Nabarro, David – E/2015/SR.3
UN. Under-Secretary-General and Special Adviser on
Africa
 Abdelaziz, Maged Abdelfattah – E/2015/SR.3
UNDP. Principal Coordinator of Ebola Response
 Saigal, Sunil – E/2015/SR.3
United Kingdom
 Cleobury, Simon – E/2015/SR.3
United States
 Cousens, Elizabeth M. – E/2015/SR.3
WHO
 Chan, Margaret – E/2015/SR.3
World Bank Group
 Walker, Melanie – E/2015/SR.3

## ECONOMIC ASSISTANCE–HAITI (Agenda item 12d)

Chile
 Cabezas, Fernando Arturo – E/2015/SR.52

## ECONOMIC ASSISTANCE–HAITI (Agenda item 12d) (continued)

Guatemala
    Carrera Castro, Fernando – E/2015/SR.52
UN. Deputy Special Representative of the Secretary-General for Haiti and Humanitarian Coordinator, Resident Coordinator and Resident Representative for UNDP in Haiti
    Wahba, Mourad – E/2015/SR.52
UN. Economic and Social Council (2014-2015 : New York and Geneva). Secretary
    Sharma, Sangeeta – E/2015/SR.52
UN. Economic and Social Council. Ad Hoc Advisory Group on Haiti. Chair
    Norman, Giles Andrew (Canada) – E/2015/SR.52
UN. Peacebuilding Commission. Vice-Chair
    Patriota, Antonio de Aguiar (Brazil) – E/2015/SR.52

## GENDER MAINSTREAMING–UN SYSTEM (Agenda item 12c)

European Union
    Holtz, Aaron (United Kingdom) – E/2015/SR.36
Japan
    Sumi, Junichi – E/2015/SR.36

## HUMAN RIGHTS (Agenda item 19g)

Turkey
    Canay, Yigit – E/2015/SR.53
UN. Office of the High Commissioner for Human Rights. New York Office. Global Issues and Intergovernmental Section. Chief
    Radcliffe, Charles – E/2015/SR.53

## HUMAN SETTLEMENTS (Agenda item 18d)

South Africa
    Malawana, Lawrence Xolani – E/2015/SR.55
UN-HABITAT
    Djacta, Yamina – E/2015/SR.50

## HUMANITARIAN ASSISTANCE (Agenda item 9)

\*\*\*
    Izam, Fatime Abdoulaye – E/2015/SR.37
    Saleh, Idriss Moussa – E/2015/SR.37; E/2015/SR.39
Afghanistan. Human Rights Commission
    Samar, Sima – E/2015/SR.39
African Union. African Risk Capacity. Insurance Company Limited
    Wilcox, Richard – E/2015/SR.38
Algeria
    Chir, Kamel – E/2015/SR.38
    Khelif, Hamza – E/2015/SR.37; E/2015/SR.39
Angola
    Dos Santos, Patricia Fatima B. – E/2015/SR.39
Argentina
    Mercado, Julio César – E/2015/SR.40
    Vilas, Paula – E/2015/SR.39
Australia
    Isbister, Jamie – E/2015/SR.37
Bangladesh
    Ahsan, M. Shameem – E/2015/SR.40
    Faizunnesa, Sadia – E/2015/SR.38

## HUMANITARIAN ASSISTANCE (Agenda item 9) (continued)

Brazil
    Dalcero, Pedro Luiz – E/2015/SR.40
Canada
    Godin, Catherine – E/2015/SR.37
    Tabah, Joshua – E/2015/SR.39
Channel 4 News (London)
    Snow, Jon – E/2015/SR.39
Chile
    Guesalaga, Patricio – E/2015/SR.40
China
    Wang, Dazhong – E/2015/SR.37
Colombia
    Londoño Soto, Beatriz – E/2015/SR.40
Cuba
    Pérez Alvarez, Claudia – E/2015/SR.39; E/2015/SR.40
Ecuador
    Espinosa Garcés, María Fernanda – E/2015/SR.40
Estonia
    Seilenthal, Jüri – E/2015/SR.37
Ethiopia
    Habtemariam, Yanit – E/2015/SR.38
    Kebret, Negash – E/2015/SR.40
European Union
    Fink-Hooijer, Florika – E/2015/SR.38; E/2015/SR.39
    Jansons, Raimonds (Latvia) – E/2015/SR.37
Finland
    Gebremedhin, Anna – E/2015/SR.37
France
    Wagner, Thomas – E/2015/SR.40
Germany
    Reiffenstuel, Anke – E/2015/SR.37; E/2015/SR.38
Group of 77
    Notutela, Ncumisa (South Africa) – E/2015/SR.37
Holy See
    Gyhra, Richard – E/2015/SR.40
Honduras
    Gómez Guifarro, Gilliam Noemi – E/2015/SR.40
IBRD
    Kull, Daniel – E/2015/SR.38
India
    Kumar, Ajit – E/2015/SR.40
Indonesia
    Wibowo, Triyono – E/2015/SR.40
Inter-Agency Secretariat of the ISDR
    Wannous, Chadia – E/2015/SR.40
International Committee of the Red Cross
    Alderson, Helen – E/2015/SR.38
    Colassis, Laurent – E/2015/SR.39
    Martin, Christophe – E/2015/SR.40
International Criminal Court. Prosecutor
    Bensouda, Fatou – E/2015/SR.39
International Federation of Red Cross and Red Crescent Societies
    Cotte, Walter – E/2015/SR.40
International Organization for Migration
    Maze, Kerry – E/2015/SR.40
Ireland
    O'Brien, Patricia – E/2015/SR.40
Italy
    Serra, Maurizio – E/2015/SR.37

## HUMANITARIAN ASSISTANCE (Agenda item 9) (continued)

Japan
> Kaji, Misako – E/2015/SR.37

Jordan
> Majali, Saja Sattam Habes – E/2015/SR.40

Kenya
> Karau, Stephen Ndungu – E/2015/SR.40

Luxembourg
> Hoscheit, Jean-Marc – E/2015/SR.40

Mexico
> Lomónaco Tonda, Jorge – E/2015/SR.37

Morocco
> Auajjar, Mohamed – E/2015/SR.37
> El Mkhantar, Hassan – E/2015/SR.39

Nepal
> Dhital, Deepak – E/2015/SR.40

New Zealand
> Reaich, Carl Allan – E/2015/SR.37; E/2015/SR.39

Norway
> Pedersen, Bard Glad – E/2015/SR.38

Pakistan
> Bokhari, Abdul Moiz – E/2015/SR.37

Philippines
> Fos, Enrico T. – E/2015/SR.40

Poland
> Henczel, Remigiusz – E/2015/SR.37

Republic of Korea
> Choi, Seok-Young – E/2015/SR.37

Russian Federation
> Andreev, Vladimir V. – E/2015/SR.40

Schweizerische Rückversicherungs-Gesellschaft
> Liès, Michel – E/2015/SR.38

Serbia
> Zupanjevac, Dragan – E/2015/SR.40

South Africa
> Makwarela, Mac – E/2015/SR.39; E/2015/SR.40

Sovereign Military Order of Malta
> Pictet-Althann, Marie-Therese – E/2015/SR.40

Spain
> Menéndez Pérez, Ana María – E/2015/SR.40

Sweden
> Clifford, Katarina – E/2015/SR.37; E/2015/SR.39

Switzerland
> Bessler, Manuel – E/2015/SR.37; E/2015/SR.38; E/2015/SR.39

Syrian Arab Republic
> A'ala, Hussam-edin – E/2015/SR.40

Thailand
> Thongphakdi, Thani – E/2015/SR.40

Turkey
> Baran, Berk – E/2015/SR.38
> Çarikçi, Ferden – E/2015/SR.37

Ukraine
> Kavun, Olha – E/2015/SR.40

UN. General Assembly (69th sess. : 2014-2015). President
> Kutesa, Sam K. (Uganda) – E/2015/SR.37

UN. General Assembly (69th sess. : 2014-2015). Vice-President
> Khiari, Mohamed Khaled (Tunisia) – E/2015/SR.37

## HUMANITARIAN ASSISTANCE (Agenda item 9) (continued)

UN. Group of African States
> Bugingo Rugema, Moses Keneth (Rwanda) – E/2015/SR.37

UN. Under-Secretary-General for Humanitarian Affairs and Emergency Relief Coordinator
> O'Brien, Stephen – E/2015/SR.37; E/2015/SR.38; E/2015/SR.39

UNFPA
> Hamid, Salma – E/2015/SR.40

UNHCR
> Türk, Volker – E/2015/SR.40

UNICEF
> Khan, Afshan – E/2015/SR.39; E/2015/SR.40

United Kingdom
> Saez, Patrick – E/2015/SR.38; E/2015/SR.39

United States
> Campbell, Elizabeth – E/2015/SR.39
> Nyman, Elisha – E/2015/SR.37

UNRWA. Commissioner-General
> Krähenbühl, Pierre – E/2015/SR.39

World Vision International
> Jenkins, Kevin – E/2015/SR.38

Zimbabwe
> Mushayavanhu, Taonga – E/2015/SR.40

## INSTITUTION BUILDING (Agenda item 5d)

\*\*\*
> El-Keib, Abdurrahim – E/2015/SR.49

Bahamas. National Insurance Board
> Bethel, Rowena G. – E/2015/SR.49

Brazil
> Patriota, Antonio de Aguiar – E/2015/SR.44

Colombia
> Mejía Vélez, María Emma – E/2015/SR.44

Germany
> Kage, Stephanie – E/2015/SR.49

Inter-Parliamentary Union
> Chowdhury, Saber – E/2015/SR.49

International Association of Economic and Social Councils and Similar Institutions
> Velikhov, E.P. – E/2015/SR.44

Israel
> Prosor, Ron – E/2015/SR.44

Kazakhstan
> Abdrakhmanov, Kairat – E/2015/SR.44

Lesotho
> Maope, Kelebone – E/2015/SR.44

Nepal
> Adhikari, Sewa Lamsal – E/2015/SR.44

South Africa
> Mxakato-Diseko, Nozipho Joyce – E/2015/SR.49

UN. Assistant Secretary-General for Policy Coordination and Inter-Agency Affairs
> Gass, Thomas – E/2015/SR.49

UN. Economic and Social Council (2014-2015 : New York and Geneva). Vice-President
> Drobnjak, Vladimir (Croatia) – E/2015/SR.49

UN. Economic and Social Council. Committee of Experts on Public Administration. Vice-Chair
> Bethel, Rowena G. – E/2015/SR.49

## INSTITUTION BUILDING (Agenda item 5d) (continued)

UN. Under-Secretary-General for Economic and Social Affairs
Wu, Hongbo – E/2015/SR.43
United Kingdom
Wilson, Peter – E/2015/SR.44

## INTERNATIONAL FINANCIAL INSTITUTIONS (Agenda item 5b)

IBRD
Panzer, John – E/2015/SR.46
ILO
Torres, Raymond – E/2015/SR.46
IMF. Deputy Managing Director
Zhu, Min – E/2015/SR.46
UN. Department of Economic and Social Affairs. Assistant Secretary-General for Economic Development
Montiel, Lenni – E/2015/SR.46
UNCTAD. Secretary-General
Kituyi, Mukhisa – E/2015/SR.46
World Trade Organization. Deputy Director-General
Agah, Yonov Frederick – E/2015/SR.46

## LEAST DEVELOPED COUNTRIES– INTERNATIONAL DECADE (2011-2020) (Agenda item 11b)

Coordinating Bureau of the Least Developed Countries. Chairman
Zinsou, Jean-Francis Régis (Benin) – E/2015/SR.56
Group of Least Developed Countries
Zinsou, Jean-Francis Régis (Benin) – E/2015/SR.50
Mexico
Lara Rangel, Salvador de – E/2015/SR.50
Turkey
Ünal, Merve Neva – E/2015/SR.56
UN. High Representative of the Secretary-General for the Least Developed Countries, Landlocked Developing Countries and Small Island Developing States
Acharya, Gyan Chandra – E/2015/SR.50

## MILLENNIUM DEVELOPMENT GOALS

\*\*\*
Lagumdzija, Zlatko – E/2015/SR.46
Nanxi, Liu – E/2015/SR.45
Onano, Vivian – E/2015/SR.46
Shank, Michael – E/2015/SR.48
Austria
Stessl, Sonja – E/2015/SR.45
Bahamas
Virgill-Rolle, Nicola – E/2015/SR.48
Brookings Institution (Washington, D.C.)
McArthur, John W. – E/2015/SR.46
China
Wang, Min – E/2015/SR.44
Egypt
Aboulatta, Amr Abdellatif – E/2015/SR.44
Germany
Gies, Andreas – E/2015/SR.48
Indonesia
Percaya, Desra – E/2015/SR.48

## MILLENNIUM DEVELOPMENT GOALS (continued)

Inter-Parliamentary Union
Chowdhury, Saber – E/2015/SR.46
International Association of Economic and Social Councils and Similar Institutions
Velikhov, E.P. – E/2015/SR.44
Iran (Islamic Republic of)
Saadat, Peiman – E/2015/SR.44
Japan
Nakane, Kazuyuki – E/2015/SR.44; E/2015/SR.48
Kyrgyzstan
Niyazalieva, Damira – E/2015/SR.48
Malaysia
Raja Zaib Shah, Raja Reza bin – E/2015/SR.48
Monaco
Picco, Isabelle F. – E/2015/SR.44
Mongolia
Khurelbaatar, Gantsogt – E/2015/SR.48
Palau
Otto, Caleb – E/2015/SR.46
Partners in Population and Development
Alam, Nurul – E/2015/SR.46
Philippines
Balisacan, Arsenio M. – E/2015/SR.48
Roza Otunbayeva Inititative
Otunbayeva, Roza – E/2015/SR.45
Russian Federation
Kononuchenko, Sergei – E/2015/SR.48
South Africa
Mxakato-Diseko, Nozipho Joyce – E/2015/SR.46
Spain
Díaz de la Guardia Beuno, Ignacio – E/2015/SR.48
Sri Lanka
Perera, Amrith Rohan – E/2015/SR.44
Sweden
Skoog, Olof – E/2015/SR.48
Switzerland
Wennubst, Pius – E/2015/SR.48
Turkey
Eler, Levent – E/2015/SR.48
UN. Economic and Social Council (2014-2015 : New York and Geneva). Vice-President
Oh, Joon (Republic of Korea) – E/2015/SR.46; E/2015/SR.48
UN. General Assembly (69th sess. : 2014-2015). Vice-President
Khiari, Mohamed Khaled (Tunisia) – E/2015/SR.45
UN. Special Adviser to the Secretary-General on the Millennium Development Goals
Sachs, Jeffrey – E/2015/SR.45
UN. Under-Secretary-General for Economic and Social Affairs
Wu, Hongbo – E/2015/SR.43
UNDP. Bureau for Policy and Programme Support. Director
Martínez-Solimán, Magdy – E/2015/SR.46
United States
Erdman, Richard – E/2015/SR.48
Viet Nam
Nguyen, Phuong Nga – E/2015/SR.44
Zambia
Mvunga, Christopher Mphanza – E/2015/SR.48

## NARCOTIC DRUGS (Agenda item 19d)

Colombia
  Morales López, Carlos Arturo – E/2015/SR.53
Guatemala
  Carrera Castro, Fernando – E/2015/SR.53
International Narcotics Control Board. President
  Sipp, Werner – E/2015/SR.53
Mexico
  Alba Góngora, Luis Alfonso de – E/2015/SR.53
UN. Commission on Narcotic Drugs. Chair
  Srisamoot, Arthayudh – E/2015/SR.53
UN Commission on Crime Prevention and Criminal
Justice. Chair
  Alba Góngora, Luis Alfonso de (Mexico) –
    E/2015/SR.53

## NON-COMMUNICABLE DISEASES (Agenda item 12f)

Russian Federation
  Maksimychev, Dmitry I. – E/2015/SR.33
Sabin Vaccine Institute
  Mistry, Neeraj – E/2015/SR.47(A)
WHO
  Menabde, Natela – E/2015/SR.33

## NON-GOVERNMENTAL ORGANIZATIONS (Agenda item 17)

Albania
  Hoxha, Ferit – E/2015/SR.51
CIVICUS
  Huffines, Jeffery – E/2015/SR.47(A)
Corporativa de Fundaciones (Organization : Mexico)
  Pérez Rulfo Torres, David – E/2015/SR.47(A)
European Union
  Lucas, Sylvie (Luxembourg) – E/2015/SR.51
Germany
  Hullman, Christiane – E/2015/SR.51
Iran (Islamic Republic of)
  Vadiati, Forouzandeh – E/2015/SR.51
Israel
  Roet, David Yitshak – E/2015/SR.51
Mexico
  Ríos Sánchez, Bruno – E/2015/SR.51
Society to Support Children Suffering from Cancer
(Islamic Republic of Iran)
  Ghods, Saideh – E/2015/SR.47(A)
United Kingdom
  Shearman, Martin – E/2015/SR.51
United States
  Sison, Michele J. – E/2015/SR.51

## OPERATIONAL ACTIVITIES–UN (Agenda item 7)

Albania
  Hoxha, Ferit – E/2015/SR.8
Argentina
  Crilchuk, Guido – E/2015/SR.34
  Perceval, María Cristina – E/2015/SR.8
Australia
  Stokes, Christopher John – E/2015/SR.8;
    E/2015/SR.34

## OPERATIONAL ACTIVITIES–UN (Agenda item 7) (continued)

Belgium
  Frankinet, Bénédicte – E/2015/SR.6
Brazil
  Favero, Mauricio Fernando Dias – E/2015/SR.5;
    E/2015/SR.6; E/2015/SR.8
  Patriota, Antonio de Aguiar – E/2015/SR.34
Canada
  Hentic, Isabelle – E/2015/SR.6
Caribbean Community
  Haynes, Rueanna (Trinidad and Tobago) –
    E/2015/SR.9
Centre for International Forestry Research
  Aklilu, Bisrat – E/2015/SR.5
China
  Wang, Dazhong – E/2015/SR.9
  Wang, Hongbo – E/2015/SR.5; E/2015/SR.8;
    E/2015/SR.34
Costa Rica
  Calvo Calvo, William José – E/2015/SR.5
Côte d'Ivoire
  Mabri Toikeusse, Albert – E/2015/SR.9
Dag Hammarskjöld Foundation (Uppsala, Sweden)
  Jenks, Bruce – E/2015/SR.5
Ethiopia
  Gedamu, Admasu Nebebe – E/2015/SR.8
  Gutulo, Belachew Gujubo – E/2015/SR.34
European Union
  Bargawi, Omar – E/2015/SR.5; E/2015/SR.8
France
  Gave, François – E/2015/SR.34
Germany
  Kern, Ursula Caroline – E/2015/SR.34
  Pfeil, Andreas – E/2015/SR.5
  Silberhorn, Thomas – E/2015/SR.9
Ghana
  Tara, Mahama Samuel – E/2015/SR.8
Global Policy Forum
  Adams, Barbara – E/2015/SR.6
Group of 77
  Marobe, Simon Poni (South Africa) – E/2015/SR.34
  Mminele, Mahlatse (South Africa) – E/2015/SR.8
  Mollinedo Claros, Julio Lázaro (Bolivia (Plurinational
    State of)) – E/2015/SR.5
  Nyembe, Raymond Thulane (South Africa) –
    E/2015/SR.41
Guatemala
  Carrera Castro, Fernando – E/2015/SR.5;
    E/2015/SR.6; E/2015/SR.8; E/2015/SR.34
Guyana
  Talbot, George Wilfred – E/2015/SR.10
Honduras
  Suazo, Marco Antonio – E/2015/SR.8
Indonesia
  Chandra, Purnomo Ahmad – E/2015/SR.34
Jamaica
  Rattray, Courtenay – E/2015/SR.9
Japan
  Minami, Hiroshi – E/2015/SR.34
  Usui, Masato – E/2015/SR.8

**OPERATIONAL ACTIVITIES–UN (Agenda item 7) (continued)**

Joint United Nations Programme on HIV/AIDS. Deputy Executive Director
    Beagle, Jan – E/2015/SR.5
Kazakhstan
    Seksenbay, Tleuzhan S. – E/2015/SR.8
Kenya
    Grignon, Koki Muli – E/2015/SR.9
Kyrgyzstan
    Karybaeva, Mira – E/2015/SR.8
Lao People's Democratic Republic
    Chanthaboury, Kikeo – E/2015/SR.10
Luxembourg
    Schneider, Romain – E/2015/SR.9
Mexico
    Colín Ortega, Gabriela – E/2015/SR.9
Mozambique
    Gumende, António – E/2015/SR.6
New York University. Center on International Cooperation
    Steven, David – E/2015/SR.9
Norway
    Eckey, Susan – E/2015/SR.5; E/2015/SR.6
    Fladby, Berit – E/2015/SR.10
    Vestrheim, Alf Havard – E/2015/SR.34
Pakistan
    Bhatti, Nauman Bashir – E/2015/SR.6
Panama
    Franceschi Navarro, Paulina María – E/2015/SR.8
Russian Federation
    Fotina, Ekaterina V. – E/2015/SR.8
Sudan
    Osman Elnor, Rahamtalla Mohamed – E/2015/SR.6
Sweden
    Lennartsson, Magnus – E/2015/SR.5; E/2015/SR.6; E/2015/SR.8; E/2015/SR.9; E/2015/SR.34
Switzerland
    Egli, Patrick – E/2015/SR.9
    Von Steiger Weber, Tatjana – E/2015/SR.34
    Wennubst, Pius – E/2015/SR.6
Timor-Leste
    Mesquita Borges, Sofia – E/2015/SR.8
Tunisia
    Khiari, Mohamed Khaled – E/2015/SR.8
UN. Assistant Secretary-General for Policy Coordination and Inter-Agency Affairs
    Gass, Thomas – E/2015/SR.5
UN. Deputy Secretary-General
    Eliasson, Jan – E/2015/SR.9
UN. Economic and Social Council (2014-2015 : New York and Geneva). President
    Sajdik, Martin (Austria) – E/2015/SR.8; E/2015/SR.9
UN. Economic and Social Council (2014-2015 : New York and Geneva). Vice-President
    Mejía Vélez, María Emma (Colombia) – E/2015/SR.5; E/2015/SR.34
UN. Office for ECOSOC Support and Coordination. Director
    Hanif, Navid – E/2015/SR.34
UN. Office of the Resident Coordinator and Humanitarian Coordinator (Mozambique)
    Topping, Jennifer – E/2015/SR.6

**OPERATIONAL ACTIVITIES–UN (Agenda item 7) (continued)**

UN. Special Adviser to the Secretary-General on Post-2015 Development Planning
    Mohammed, Amina J. – E/2015/SR.6
UN. Under-Secretary-General for Economic and Social Affairs
    Wu, Hongbo – E/2015/SR.10
UN Development Group. Advisory Group. Chair
    Albrectsen, Anne-Birgitte – E/2015/SR.5
UN Development Group. Chair
    Clark, Helen – E/2015/SR.8
UN System Chief Executives Board for Coordination. High-Level Committee on Management. Vice-Chair
    Beagle, Jan – E/2015/SR.5
UN System Chief Executives Board for Coordination. High-Level Committee on Programmes. Vice-Chair
    Stewart, Jane – E/2015/SR.5
UN System Chief Executives Board for Coordination. Secretary
    Kim, Won-soo – E/2015/SR.6
UNDP/UNFPA Executive Board. President
    Thomson, Peter (Fiji) – E/2015/SR.6
UNICEF. Public Partnerships Division. Director
    Kjorven, Olav – E/2015/SR.10
United Kingdom
    Ritchie, Fiona – E/2015/SR.34
    Shearman, Martin – E/2015/SR.8; E/2015/SR.9
United States
    Dunn, David – E/2015/SR.8; E/2015/SR.9
    Erdman, Richard – E/2015/SR.34
    Robl, Teri – E/2015/SR.6
    Sloane, Esther Pan – E/2015/SR.5
Viet Nam
    Do, Hung Viet – E/2015/SR.6
    Nguyen, Phuong Nga – E/2015/SR.8

**PALESTINIANS–TERRITORIES OCCUPIED BY ISRAEL–LIVING CONDITIONS (Agenda item 16)**

European Union
    Carroll, Erica (United Kingdom) – E/2015/SR.50
Group of 77
    Marobe, Simon Poni (South Africa) – E/2015/SR.50
Israel
    Meitzad, Hadas Ester – E/2015/SR.50
Japan
    Mikami, Yoshiyuki – E/2015/SR.50
Syrian Arab Republic
    Ja'afari, Bashar – E/2015/SR.50
UN. Special Committee of 24. Acting Chair
    Percaya, Desra (Indonesia) – E/2015/SR.50
United States
    Derderian, Jill – E/2015/SR.50

**POPULATION–DEVELOPMENT (Agenda item 18f)**

Brazil
    Patriota, Erika Almeida Watanabe – E/2015/SR.55
UN. Commission on Population and Development. Chair
    Frankinet, Bénédicte – E/2015/SR.55

## POST-CONFLICT RECONSTRUCTION–AFRICA (Agenda item 12e)

UN. Peacebuilding Commission. Vice-Chair
Patriota, Antonio de Aguiar (Brazil) – E/2015/SR.52
United States
Dugan, Hugh – E/2015/SR.52
World Food Programme
Luma, Joyce – E/2015/SR.52

## PUBLIC ADMINISTRATION (Agenda item 18g)

UN. Economic and Social Council. Committee of Experts on Public Administration. Chair
Saner, Margaret – E/2015/SR.54

## RACIAL DISCRIMINATION–PROGRAMME OF ACTION (Agenda item 19f)

UN. Economic and Social Council (2014-2015 : New York and Geneva). Vice-President
Oh, Joon (Republic of Korea) – E/2015/SR.53

## REFUGEES (Agenda item 19e)

UNHCR. New York Liaison Office. Deputy Director
Eriksson, Anne Christine – E/2015/SR.53

## REGIONAL COOPERATION (Agenda item 15)

Academia Diplomática de Chile
Somavía, Juan – E/2015/SR.47(B)
Guatemala
Carrera Castro, Fernando – E/2015/SR.47(B)
Kyrgyzstan
Kabaev, Kuban – E/2015/SR.47(B)
Mexico
Camacho, Sara Luna – E/2015/SR.47(B)
Morocco
Hilale, Omar – E/2015/SR.54
Russian Federation
Kudasova, Yulia N. – E/2015/SR.47(B)
UN. ECA. Deputy Executive Secretary for Knowledge Generation
Hamdok, Abdalla – E/2015/SR.47(B)
UN. ECE. Executive Secretary
Bach, Christian Friis – E/2015/SR.47(B)
UN. ECLAC. Executive Secretary
Bárcena, Alicia – E/2015/SR.47(B)
UN. ESCAP. Executive Secretary
Akhtar, Shamshad – E/2015/SR.47(B)
UN. ESCWA. Executive Secretary
Khalaf, Rima – E/2015/SR.47(B)
UN. Regional Commissions New York Office. Director
Nour, Amr – E/2015/SR.54
United States
Dugan, Hugh – E/2015/SR.54

## REGIONAL COOPERATION–ASIA AND THE PACIFIC (Agenda item 15)

Australia
Henderson, Nathan – E/2015/SR.54
Bangladesh
Elias, Andalib – E/2015/SR.54
European Union
Klausa, Agnieszka – E/2015/SR.54

## REGIONAL COOPERATION–ASIA AND THE PACIFIC (Agenda item 15) (continued)

Indonesia
Rakhmatia, Nara Masista – E/2015/SR.54
Japan
Onishi, Tomoko – E/2015/SR.54
Pakistan
Ammar, Yasar – E/2015/SR.54
UN. Economic and Social Council (2014-2015 : New York and Geneva). Secretary
Gustafik, Otto – E/2015/SR.54

## SCIENCE AND TECHNOLOGY–DEVELOPMENT (Agenda item 18b)

Nigeria
Johnson, Omobola – E/2015/SR.54
Russian Federation
Morozov, Anton Y. – E/2015/SR.54
UNCTAD
Wu, Dong – E/2015/SR.54
Unesco
Guimarães-Pinto, Ricardo de – E/2015/SR.47(A)
United States
Reynolds, Andrew – E/2015/SR.54

## SOCIAL DEVELOPMENT (Agenda item 19b)

***
Frei Montalva, Eduardo – E/2015/SR.31
Argentina
Perceval, María Cristina – E/2015/SR.31
China
Yao, Shaojun – E/2015/SR.31
Colombia
Mejía Vélez, María Emma – E/2015/SR.31
European Union
Köhler, Pit – E/2015/SR.31
ILO
Pinheiro, Vinícius Carvalho – E/2015/SR.31
Ireland
Donoghue, David – E/2015/SR.31
Mexico
Ríos Sánchez, Bruno – E/2015/SR.32
Romania
Miculescu, Simona Mirela – E/2015/SR.31
Social Watch (Organization)
Bissio, Roberto – E/2015/SR.31
Switzerland
Bodenmann, Hannah – E/2015/SR.31
UN. Commission for Social Development. Chairman
Miculescu, Simona Mirela (Romania) – E/2015/SR.32
UN. Department of Economic and Social Affairs. Division for Social Policy and Development. Director
Bas, Daniela – E/2015/SR.32
UN. Deputy Secretary-General
Eliasson, Jan – E/2015/SR.31
UN. Economic and Social Council (2014-2015 : New York and Geneva). Vice-President
Oh, Joon (Republic of Korea) – E/2015/SR.31
UN. Special Adviser to the Secretary-General on Interregional Policy Cooperation
Somavía, Juan – E/2015/SR.31

## SOUTH-SOUTH COOPERATION (Agenda item 7c)

Argentina
  Perceval, María Cristina – E/2015/SR.13
Brazil
  Patriota, Guilherme de Aguiar – E/2015/SR.12;
    E/2015/SR.13
China
  Wang, Hongbo – E/2015/SR.12
Colombia
  Ruíz Blanco, Miguel Camilo – E/2015/SR.12
Germany
  Krapp, Reinhard – E/2015/SR.13
Group of 77
  Mamabolo, Jeremiah Nyamane Kingsley (South
    Africa) – E/2015/SR.12
India
  Bishnoi, Bhagwant Singh – E/2015/SR.12
Indonesia
  Choesni, Tubagus A. – E/2015/SR.12; E/2015/SR.13
Japan
  Momita, Yasuaki – E/2015/SR.12
Kenya
  Grignon, Koki Muli – E/2015/SR.12
Mexico
  Colín Ortega, Gabriela – E/2015/SR.12
Republic of Korea
  Hahn, Choonghee – E/2015/SR.12
UN. Office for South-South Cooperation. Director
  Zhou, Yiping – E/2015/SR.12
UN. Office of the Resident Coordinator (Brazil)
  Chediek, Jorge – E/2015/SR.12
UN System Staff College. Director
  Javan, Jafar – E/2015/SR.13
United Kingdom
  Shearman, Martin – E/2015/SR.12

## STATISTICS (Agenda item 18c)

UN. Statistical Commission. Chair
  Pullinger, John (United Kingdom) – E/2015/SR.35

## SUSTAINABLE DEVELOPMENT (Agenda item 18a)

Action aide aux familles démunies (Mali)
  Touré, Ténin – E/2015/SR.47(A)
African Union. Commission
  Potgieter-Gqubule, Febe – E/2015/SR.3
Al Jazeera America (Television network)
  Velshi, Ali – E/2015/SR.20
Albania
  Prizreni, Ingrit – E/2015/SR.19
Alliance of Small Island States
  Sareer, Ahmed (Maldives) – E/2015/SR.43
ArcelorMittal (Firm)
  Knight, Alan – E/2015/SR.3
Argentina
  Di Luca, Sebastián – E/2015/SR.19
  Oporto, Mario Néstor – E/2015/SR.47(A)
  Perceval, María Cristina – E/2015/SR.15
Australia
  Haddad, Amy – E/2015/SR.19
Bahrain
  Alsaleh, Faeqa Saeed – E/2015/SR.43
Bangladesh
  Momen, Abulkalam Abdul – E/2015/SR.44

## SUSTAINABLE DEVELOPMENT (Agenda item 18a) (continued)

Belgium
  Frankinet, Bénédicte – E/2015/SR.18
Beyond 2015 (Organization : Brussels)
  Badenoch, Charles (World Vision) –
    E/2015/SR.47(A)
Botswana
  Ntwaagae, Charles – E/2015/SR.44
Brazil
  Patriota, Antonio de Aguiar – E/2015/SR.3;
    E/2015/SR.19
Burkina Faso
  Ouedraogo-Boni, Bibiane – E/2015/SR.43
Cable News Network (United States)
  Quest, Richard – E/2015/SR.15
Canada
  Grant, Michael Douglas – E/2015/SR.19
Caribbean Community
  Alamilla, Lisel (Belize) – E/2015/SR.43
  Christie, Perry G. (Bahamas) – E/2015/SR.15
Center for Global Development (Washington, D.C.)
  Over, A. Mead – E/2015/SR.3
China
  Yao, Shaojun – E/2015/SR.3
CIVICUS
  Huffines, Jeffery – E/2015/SR.47(A)
CLIPSAS (Organization)
  Daly, Louis A. – E/2015/SR.47(A)
Colombia
  Mejía Vélez, María Emma – E/2015/SR.16
Columbia University (New York)
  Stiglitz, Joseph E. – E/2015/SR.15
Corporativa de Fundaciones (Organization : Mexico)
  Pérez Rulfo Torres, David – E/2015/SR.47(A)
Costa Rica
  Mora Delgado, Alexander – E/2015/SR.20
Croatia
  Klisovic, Josko – E/2015/SR.43
Cuba
  Guerra Rodríguez, Yolanda – E/2015/SR.3
Cyprus
  Kouyialis, Nicos – E/2015/SR.43
Czech Republic
  Tlapa, Martin – E/2015/SR.43
Ebola Survival Fund
  Wright, Jeffrey – E/2015/SR.3
Estonia
  Sarapuu, Margus – E/2015/SR.43
European Commission. Commissioner for Employment, Social Affairs, Skills and Labour Mobility
  Thyssen, Marianne – E/2015/SR.15
European Disability Forum
  Cuk, Vladimir – E/2015/SR.47(A)
European Union
  Poulsen, Jan Pirouz – E/2015/SR.3
  Vella, Karmenu – E/2015/SR.43
Fairtrade International
  Theyer, Hans – E/2015/SR.47(A)
FAO. Committee on World Food Security. Chair
  Verburg, Gerda (Netherlands) – E/2015/SR.50

## SUSTAINABLE DEVELOPMENT (Agenda item 18a) (continued)

Finland
    Laatu, Riikka – E/2015/SR.43
    Taipale, Pilvi – E/2015/SR.3
    Wallin, Markku – E/2015/SR.15
    Wallin, Stefan – E/2015/SR.18
France
    Bartoli, Fabienne – E/2015/SR.3
    Bedas, Bernard – E/2015/SR.18
Germany
    Kage, Stephanie – E/2015/SR.15; E/2015/SR.20
    Nell, Christian – E/2015/SR.3
Global Foundation for Democracy and Development
    Jourdan, Marc – E/2015/SR.47(A)
Gray Panthers (Organization)
    Davis, Joan – E/2015/SR.15
Group of 77
    Mamabolo, Jeremiah Nyamane Kingsley (South Africa) – E/2015/SR.43
    Patel, Ebrahim (South Africa) – E/2015/SR.18
Guinea
    Diare, Mohamed – E/2015/SR.3
Honduras
    Cardona, Ricardo – E/2015/SR.43
    Suazo, Marco Antonio – E/2015/SR.19
IBRD
    Thomas, Mark R. (Mark Roland) – E/2015/SR.3
ILO. Director-General
    Ryder, Guy – E/2015/SR.15; E/2015/SR.17; E/2015/SR.20
IMF. Deputy Managing Director
    Zhu, Min – E/2015/SR.15
India
    Joshi, Mayank – E/2015/SR.3
    Mukerji, Asoke Kumar – E/2015/SR.19
    Sukhdev, Pavan – E/2015/SR.20
Indonesia
    Dhakiri, Hanif – E/2015/SR.16
    Murniningtyas, Endah – E/2015/SR.43
    Roostiavati, Agus Prihono – E/2015/SR.18
International Committee for Arab-Israeli Reconciliation
    Karmakar, Sudhangshu – E/2015/SR.47(A)
International Council for Education of People with Visual Impairment
    Ferrell, Kay Alicyn – E/2015/SR.47(A)
International Federation for Family Development
    Richards, Mercedes – E/2015/SR.47(A)
International Federation for Home Economics
    Minard, Margaret – E/2015/SR.47(A)
International Organisation of Employers
    Funes de Rioja, Daniel – E/2015/SR.15
International Trade Union Confederation
    Burrow, Sharan – E/2015/SR.15
Ireland
    Kelly, Alan – E/2015/SR.43
Israel
    Prosor, Ron – E/2015/SR.44
    Roet, David Yitshak – E/2015/SR.19
Italy
    Cardi, Sebastiano – E/2015/SR.19
    Velo, Silvia – E/2015/SR.43

## SUSTAINABLE DEVELOPMENT (Agenda item 18a) (continued)

ITU
    Bogdan-Martin, Doreen – E/2015/SR.47(A)
    Fowlie, Gary – E/2015/SR.19
Japan
    Minami, Hiroshi – E/2015/SR.15
Journalists and Writers Foundation (Turkey)
    Ülker, Cemre – E/2015/SR.47(A)
Kazakhstan
    Abdrakhmanov, Kairat – E/2015/SR.18; E/2015/SR.44
    Seksenbay, Tleuzhan S. – E/2015/SR.3
Kyrgyzstan
    Kydyrov, Talaibek – E/2015/SR.18
League of Arab States
    Nabulsi, Tarek – E/2015/SR.47(A)
Legion of Good Will
    Parmegiani, Danilo – E/2015/SR.47(A)
Liberia
    Siaplay, Mounir – E/2015/SR.3
Mali
    Doucouré, Dianguina dit Yaya – E/2015/SR.3
Myanmar
    Lynn, Htin – E/2015/SR.35
New Future Foundation (New York)
    Blakely, Delois – E/2015/SR.3
Norway
    Kvalsoren, Anne Heidi – E/2015/SR.15
Open Society Foundations
    Taylor, Aleesha – E/2015/SR.3
Pacific Small Island Developing States
    Tupouniua, Mahe'uli'uli Sandhurst (Tonga) – E/2015/SR.43
Panama
    Franceschi Navarro, Paulina María – E/2015/SR.19
Paraguay
    González Franco, Federico Alberto – E/2015/SR.19
Philippines
    Balisacan, Arsenio M. – E/2015/SR.47(A)
Republic of Korea
    Hahn, Choonghee – E/2015/SR.19
    Lim, Hoon-Min – E/2015/SR.35
    Shin, Dong-ik – E/2015/SR.47(A)
Romania
    Gavrilescu, Gratiela Leocadia – E/2015/SR.43
Roundtable on Sustainable Palm Oil
    Webber, Darrel – E/2015/SR.47(A)
Russian Federation
    Gatilov, Gennadii Mikhailovich – E/2015/SR.43
    Maksimychev, Dmitry I. – E/2015/SR.19
    Zagrekov, Victor – E/2015/SR.3
Rwanda
    Byaje, Jeanne d'Arc – E/2015/SR.19
Sabin Vaccine Institute
    Mistry, Neeraj – E/2015/SR.47(A)
Serbia
    Lalic-Smajevic, Katarina – E/2015/SR.19
Sierra Leone
    Marrah, Kaifala – E/2015/SR.3
Society to Support Children Suffering from Cancer (Islamic Republic of Iran)
    Ghods, Saideh – E/2015/SR.47(A)

## SUSTAINABLE DEVELOPMENT (Agenda item 18a) (continued)

Soroptimist International
  Levy, Betty – E/2015/SR.47(A)
South Africa
  Patel, Ebrahim – E/2015/SR.15
Summit Level Group for South-South Consultations and Co-operation
  Perera, Amrith Rohan (Sri Lanka) – E/2015/SR.43
Support for Women in Agriculture and Environment (Organization : Uganda)
  Kenyangi, Gertrude – E/2015/SR.47(A)
Sweden
  Nilsson Snellman, Karin – E/2015/SR.15
  Thöresson, Per – E/2015/SR.3
Sweden. Prime Minister
  Löfven, Stefan – E/2015/SR.15
Switzerland
  Wennubst, Pius – E/2015/SR.43
  Zehnder, Olivier Marc – E/2015/SR.18
Tata Group
  Rajan, N.S. – E/2015/SR.20
Thailand
  Ganjanarintr, Pornprapai – E/2015/SR.43
Trinidad and Tobago
  Aching, Lizanne – E/2015/SR.19
  Charles, Eden – E/2015/SR.15
Tunisia
  Khiari, Mohamed Khaled – E/2015/SR.19
Ukraine
  Golitsyn, Yaroslav – E/2015/SR.47(A)
UN. Assistant Secretary-General for Policy Coordination and Inter-Agency Affairs
  Gass, Thomas – E/2015/SR.20
UN. Committee for Development Policy. Chair
  Ocampo, José Antonio – E/2015/SR.35; E/2015/SR.43
UN. Deputy Secretary-General
  Eliasson, Jan – E/2015/SR.15
UN. ECA. Deputy Executive Secretary for Knowledge Generation
  Hamdok, Abdalla – E/2015/SR.3
UN. Economic and Social Council (2014-2015 : New York and Geneva). President
  Sajdik, Martin (Austria) – E/2015/SR.3
UN. Economic and Social Council (2014-2015 : New York and Geneva). Vice-President
  Drobnjak, Vladimir (Croatia) – E/2015/SR.15; E/2015/SR.20
UN. General Assembly (69th sess. : 2014-2015). President
  Kutesa, Sam K. (Uganda) – E/2015/SR.3
UN. General Assembly (69th sess. : 2014-2015). Vice-President
  Gunnarsson, Einar (Iceland) – E/2015/SR.15
UN. Group of African States
  Sana, Maboneza (Rwanda) – E/2015/SR.43
UN. Secretary-General
  Ban, Ki-moon, 1944- – E/2015/SR.3
UN. Special Adviser to the Secretary-General for Community-based Medicine and Lessons from Haiti
  Farmer, Paul (Paul Edward) – E/2015/SR.3

## SUSTAINABLE DEVELOPMENT (Agenda item 18a) (continued)

UN. Special Envoy of the Secretary-General on Ebola
  Nabarro, David – E/2015/SR.3
UN. Under-Secretary-General and Special Adviser on Africa
  Abdelaziz, Maged Abdelfattah – E/2015/SR.3
UN. Under-Secretary-General for Economic and Social Affairs
  Wu, Hongbo – E/2015/SR.43
UN-HABITAT
  Djacta, Yamina – E/2015/SR.19
UNDP. Bureau for Policy and Programme Support
  Kwain, Stan – E/2015/SR.47(A)
UNDP. Principal Coordinator of Ebola Response
  Saigal, Sunil – E/2015/SR.3
Unesco
  Guimarães-Pinto, Ricardo de – E/2015/SR.47(A)
UNI Global Union
  Jennings, Philip – E/2015/SR.15
UNIDO
  Maseli, Paul – E/2015/SR.19
United Cities and Local Governments
  Celik, Aliye Pekin – E/2015/SR.47(A)
United Kingdom
  Cleobury, Simon – E/2015/SR.3
  Shearman, Martin – E/2015/SR.18
United Republic of Tanzania. President
  Kikwete, Jakaya – E/2015/SR.15
United States
  Cousens, Elizabeth M. – E/2015/SR.3
  Fox, Sarah – E/2015/SR.18
Viet Nam
  Do, Hung Viet – E/2015/SR.15
  Nguyen, Phuong Nga – E/2015/SR.44
WHO
  Chan, Margaret – E/2015/SR.3
World Bank Group
  Walker, Melanie – E/2015/SR.3
World Energy Council
  Nadeau, Marie-José – E/2015/SR.20
World Federation for Mental Health
  Wallace, Nancy E. – E/2015/SR.47(A)
World Jewellery Confederation
  Marzotto, Matteo – E/2015/SR.47(A)
Yale University (New Haven, Conn.)
  Shiller, Robert J. – E/2015/SR.20
Zimbabwe
  Shava, Frederick Musiiwa Makamure – E/2015/SR.18

## SUSTAINABLE DEVELOPMENT–HIGH-LEVEL POLITICAL FORUM (Agenda item 6)

Alliance of Small Island States
  Sareer, Ahmed (Maldives) – E/2015/SR.43
Argentina
  Oporto, Mario Néstor – E/2015/SR.47(A)
Australia
  Donaldson, Kirstin – E/2015/SR.44
Botswana
  Ntwaagae, Charles – E/2015/SR.44
Caribbean Community
  Alamilla, Lisel (Belize) – E/2015/SR.43

## SUSTAINABLE DEVELOPMENT–HIGH-LEVEL POLITICAL FORUM (Agenda item 6) (continued)

## SUSTAINABLE DEVELOPMENT–HIGH-LEVEL POLITICAL FORUM (Agenda item 6) (continued)

## SUSTAINABLE DEVELOPMENT–MINISTERIAL MEETING (Agenda item 5a)

## SUSTAINABLE DEVELOPMENT GOALS (Agenda item 5c)

\*\*\*

    Lagumdzija, Zlatko – E/2015/SR.46
    Nanxi, Liu – E/2015/SR.45
    Onano, Vivian – E/2015/SR.46
    Shank, Michael – E/2015/SR.48
Austria
    Stessl, Sonja – E/2015/SR.45
Bahamas
    Virgill-Rolle, Nicola – E/2015/SR.48
Brookings Institution (Washington, D.C.)
    McArthur, John W. – E/2015/SR.46
China
    Wang, Min – E/2015/SR.44
Egypt
    Aboulatta, Amr Abdellatif – E/2015/SR.44
Germany
    Gies, Andreas – E/2015/SR.48
Indonesia
    Percaya, Desra – E/2015/SR.48
Inter-Parliamentary Union
    Chowdhury, Saber – E/2015/SR.46
International Association of Economic and Social Councils and Similar Institutions
    Velikhov, E.P. – E/2015/SR.44
Iran (Islamic Republic of)
    Saadat, Peiman – E/2015/SR.44
Japan
    Nakane, Kazuyuki – E/2015/SR.44; E/2015/SR.48
Kyrgyzstan
    Niyazalieva, Damira – E/2015/SR.48
Malaysia
    Raja Zaib Shah, Raja Reza bin – E/2015/SR.48
Monaco
    Picco, Isabelle F. – E/2015/SR.44
Mongolia
    Khurelbaatar, Gantsogt – E/2015/SR.48
Palau
    Otto, Caleb – E/2015/SR.46
Partners in Population and Development
    Alam, Nurul – E/2015/SR.46
Philippines
    Balisacan, Arsenio M. – E/2015/SR.48
Roza Otunbayeva Inititative
    Otunbayeva, Roza – E/2015/SR.45
Russian Federation
    Kononuchenko, Sergei – E/2015/SR.48
South Africa
    Mxakato-Diseko, Nozipho Joyce – E/2015/SR.46
Spain
    Díaz de la Guardia Beuno, Ignacio – E/2015/SR.48
Sri Lanka
    Perera, Amrith Rohan – E/2015/SR.44
Sweden
    Skoog, Olof – E/2015/SR.48
Switzerland
    Wennubst, Pius – E/2015/SR.48
Turkey
    Eler, Levent – E/2015/SR.48

## SUSTAINABLE DEVELOPMENT GOALS (Agenda item 5c) (continued)

UN. Economic and Social Council (2014-2015 : New York and Geneva). Vice-President
    Oh, Joon (Republic of Korea) – E/2015/SR.46; E/2015/SR.48
UN. General Assembly (69th sess. : 2014-2015). Vice-President
    Khiari, Mohamed Khaled (Tunisia) – E/2015/SR.45
UN. Secretary-General
    Ban, Ki-moon, 1944- – E/2015/SR.49
UN. Special Adviser to the Secretary-General on the Millennium Development Goals
    Sachs, Jeffrey – E/2015/SR.45
UN. Under-Secretary-General for Economic and Social Affairs
    Wu, Hongbo – E/2015/SR.43
UNDP. Bureau for Policy and Programme Support. Director
    Martínez-Solimán, Magdy – E/2015/SR.46
United States
    Erdman, Richard – E/2015/SR.48
Viet Nam
    Nguyen, Phuong Nga – E/2015/SR.44
Zambia
    Mvunga, Christopher Mphanza – E/2015/SR.48

## TAXATION (Agenda item 18h)

African Tax Administration Forum
    Marais, Lincoln – E/2015/SR.28
Bangladesh
    Rahman, Mustafizur – E/2015/SR.28; E/2015/SR.29
Caribbean Community
    Francis, Tishka H. (Bahamas) – E/2015/SR.28
European Union
    Busuttil, John – E/2015/SR.28; E/2015/SR.56
Financial Transparency Coalition
    Fossard, Renaud – E/2015/SR.28
Germany
    Kage, Stephanie – E/2015/SR.28
Ghana
    Dzadzra, Anthony – E/2015/SR.29
Group of 77
    Marobe, Simon Poni (South Africa) – E/2015/SR.56
    Mminele, Mahlatse (South Africa) – E/2015/SR.28; E/2015/SR.33
IBRD
    Verhoeven, Marijn – E/2015/SR.28
IMF. Fiscal Affairs Department
    Perry, Victoria J. – E/2015/SR.28; E/2015/SR.29
Inter-American Center of Tax Administrations
    Verdi, Marco – E/2015/SR.28; E/2015/SR.29
Italy. Revenue Agency
    Cottani, Giammarco – E/2015/SR.29
New York University
    Kane, Mitchell – E/2015/SR.29
OECD. Centre for Tax Policy and Administration
    Perez-Navarro, Grace – E/2015/SR.28
Philippines. Bureau of Internal Revenue
    Jacinto-Henares, Kim S. – E/2015/SR.29
Russian Federation
    Medvedeva, Irina – E/2015/SR.28

## TAXATION (Agenda item 18h) (continued)

SABMiller (Firm)
    Bales, Vicki – E/2015/SR.29
South Africa. Revenue Service
    Gosai, Nishana – E/2015/SR.29
UN. Committee of Experts on International Cooperation in Tax Matters
    Sollund, Stig B. – E/2015/SR.29
UN. Committee of Experts on International Cooperation in Tax Matters. Chair
    Yaffar, Armando Lara – E/2015/SR.28;
        E/2015/SR.29
UN. Department of Economic and Social Affairs. Financing for Development Office. Director
    Trepelkov, Alexandre – E/2015/SR.28
UN. Economic and Social Council (2014-2015 : New York and Geneva). Vice-President
    Drobnjak, Vladimir (Croatia) – E/2015/SR.28
United States
    Sloane, Esther Pan – E/2015/SR.28
University of California (Los Angeles). School of Law
    Zolt, Eric M. – E/2015/SR.29
World Bank Group
    Moreno-Dodson, Blanca – E/2015/SR.29

## UN–TRAINING AND RESEARCH INSTITUTIONS (Agenda item 20)

Algeria
    Djacta, Larbi – E/2015/SR.33
Group of 77
    Mminele, Mahlatse (South Africa) – E/2015/SR.33
Italy
    Lambertini, Inigo – E/2015/SR.33
Kuwait
    Al-Sharrah, Abdullah Ahmad – E/2015/SR.33
Libya
    Eshanta, Abdulmonem A.H. – E/2015/SR.33
UN. Special Adviser to the Secretary-General on Change Implementation
    Kim, Won-soo – E/2015/SR.33
UN System Staff College. Director
    Javan, Jafar – E/2015/SR.33
UN University
    Caeymaex, Olivia – E/2015/SR.33
UNITAR. Executive Director
    Fegan-Wyles, Sally – E/2015/SR.33
United States
    Dugan, Hugh – E/2015/SR.33

## UN. COMMISSION ON NARCOTIC DRUGS– MEMBERS (Agenda item 4)

Iran (Islamic Republic of)
    Dehghani, Gholamhossein – E/2015/SR.21

## UN. COMMITTEE FOR PROGRAMME AND COORDINATION–MEMBERS (Agenda item 4)

UN. Economic and Social Council (2014-2015 : New York and Geneva). President
    Sajdik, Martin (Austria) – E/2015/SR.30

## UN. ECONOMIC AND SOCIAL COUNCIL (2014-2015 : NEW YORK AND GENEVA)–AGENDA (Agenda item 2)

Brazil
    Favero, Mauricio Fernando Dias – E/2015/SR.1;
        E/2015/SR.2
Chile
    Aguirre, Patricio – E/2015/SR.1
Colombia
    Ruíz Blanco, Miguel Camilo – E/2015/SR.1
Cuba
    Rodríguez Abascal, Ana Silvia – E/2015/SR.1
Egypt
    Khalil, Mootaz Ahmadein – E/2015/SR.1
European Union
    Bargawi, Omar – E/2015/SR.1; E/2015/SR.2
Group of 77
    Mollinedo Claros, Julio Lázaro (Bolivia (Plurinational State of)) – E/2015/SR.1; E/2015/SR.2
Iran (Islamic Republic of)
    Momeni, Javad – E/2015/SR.1
Japan
    Usui, Masato – E/2015/SR.1
Mexico
    Camacho, Sara Luna – E/2015/SR.1
Republic of Korea
    Lee, Tong-Q – E/2015/SR.2
Tunisia
    Khiari, Mohamed Khaled – E/2015/SR.14
UN. Economic and Social Council (2014-2015 : New York and Geneva). President
    Sajdik, Martin (Austria) – E/2015/SR.1; E/2015/SR.2;
        E/2015/SR.30
UN. Economic and Social Council (2014-2015 : New York and Geneva). Secretary
    De Laurentis, Jennifer – E/2015/SR.1
UN. Office for ECOSOC Support and Coordination. Director
    Hanif, Navid – E/2015/SR.1
United States
    Robl, Teri – E/2015/SR.1

## UN. ECONOMIC AND SOCIAL COUNCIL (2014-2015 : NEW YORK AND GENEVA)–OFFICERS (Agenda item 1)

UN. Economic and Social Council (2014-2015 : New York and Geneva). President
    Sajdik, Martin (Austria) – E/2015/SR.7

## UN. PERMANENT FORUM ON INDIGENOUS ISSUES (Agenda item 19h)

Brazil
    Yassine, Amena Martins – E/2015/SR.54
France
    Selk, Vanessa – E/2015/SR.54
Group of Friends of the World Conference on Indigenous Peoples
    Montaño, Jorge (Mexico) – E/2015/SR.54
National Congress of American Indians (United States)
    Crippa, Leonardo A. – E/2015/SR.54

## UN. PERMANENT FORUM ON INDIGENOUS ISSUES (Agenda item 19h) (continued)

UN. Assistant Secretary-General for Policy Coordination and Inter-Agency Affairs
   Gass, Thomas – E/2015/SR.54
UN. Permanent Forum on Indigenous Issues. Chair
   Davis, Megan – E/2015/SR.54
United States
   Phipps, Laurie Shestack – E/2015/SR.54

## UN. STATISTICAL COMMISSION–MEMBERS (Agenda item 4)

UN. Economic and Social Council (2014-2015 : New York and Geneva). President
   Sajdik, Martin (Austria) – E/2015/SR.30

## UN CONFERENCES (Agenda item 11)

UN. Assistant Secretary-General for Policy Coordination and Inter-Agency Affairs
   Gass, Thomas – E/2015/SR.36

## UN FORUM ON FORESTS (Agenda item 18k)

Australia
   Henderson, Nathan – E/2015/SR.55
Brazil
   Santos, Sérgio Rodrigues dos – E/2015/SR.55
European Union
   Beviglia Zampetti, Americo – E/2015/SR.55
Gabon
   Bibalou, Marianne Odette – E/2015/SR.55
Group of 77
   Malawana, Lawrence Xolani (South Africa) – E/2015/SR.55
Iran (Islamic Republic of)
   Momeni, Javad – E/2015/SR.55
Japan
   Mikami, Yoshiyuki – E/2015/SR.55
Sudan
   Ali, Khalid Mohammed – E/2015/SR.55
Switzerland
   Vermont, Sibylle – E/2015/SR.55
UN. Economic and Social Council (2014-2015 : New York and Geneva). Secretary
   Gustafik, Otto – E/2015/SR.55
United States
   Reynolds, Andrew – E/2015/SR.55

## UN POLICY RECOMMENDATIONS (Agenda item 7a)

Argentina
   Perceval, María Cristina – E/2015/SR.13
Australia
   Versegi, Peter Lloyd – E/2015/SR.12
Brazil
   Patriota, Guilherme de Aguiar – E/2015/SR.13
Caribbean Community
   Haynes, Rueanna (Trinidad and Tobago) – E/2015/SR.9
China
   Wang, Dazhong – E/2015/SR.9
   Wang, Hongbo – E/2015/SR.12

## UN POLICY RECOMMENDATIONS (Agenda item 7a) (continued)

Côte d'Ivoire
   Mabri Toikeusse, Albert – E/2015/SR.9
European Union
   Beviglia Zampetti, Americo – E/2015/SR.13
Germany
   Krapp, Reinhard – E/2015/SR.13
   Silberhorn, Thomas – E/2015/SR.9
Group of 77
   Mamabolo, Jeremiah Nyamane Kingsley (South Africa) – E/2015/SR.12
Guyana
   Talbot, George Wilfred – E/2015/SR.10
India
   Bishnoi, Bhagwant Singh – E/2015/SR.12
Indonesia
   Choesni, Tubagus A. – E/2015/SR.13
Jamaica
   Rattray, Courtenay – E/2015/SR.9
Kenya
   Grignon, Koki Muli – E/2015/SR.9
Lao People's Democratic Republic
   Chanthaboury, Kikeo – E/2015/SR.10; E/2015/SR.13
Luxembourg
   Schneider, Romain – E/2015/SR.9
Mexico
   Colín Ortega, Gabriela – E/2015/SR.9; E/2015/SR.12
New York University. Center on International Cooperation
   Steven, David – E/2015/SR.9
Norway
   Fladby, Berit – E/2015/SR.10; E/2015/SR.12; E/2015/SR.13
Republic of Korea
   Hahn, Choonghee – E/2015/SR.12
Russian Federation
   Maksimychev, Dmitry I. – E/2015/SR.12
Serbia
   Lalic-Smajevic, Katarina – E/2015/SR.12
Sweden
   Lennartsson, Magnus – E/2015/SR.9
Switzerland
   Egli, Patrick – E/2015/SR.9; E/2015/SR.12
UN. Assistant Secretary-General for Policy Coordination and Inter-Agency Affairs
   Gass, Thomas – E/2015/SR.13
UN. Deputy Secretary-General
   Eliasson, Jan – E/2015/SR.9
UN. ECA. Executive Secretary
   Lopes, Carlos – E/2015/SR.13
UN. Economic and Social Council (2014-2015 : New York and Geneva). President
   Sajdik, Martin (Austria) – E/2015/SR.9; E/2015/SR.13
UN. Economic and Social Council (2014-2015 : New York and Geneva). Vice-President
   Mejía Vélez, María Emma (Colombia) – E/2015/SR.12
UN. Under-Secretary-General for Economic and Social Affairs
   Wu, Hongbo – E/2015/SR.10

## UN POLICY RECOMMENDATIONS (Agenda item 7a) (continued)

UN System Staff College. Director
Javan, Jafar – E/2015/SR.13
UNDP. Bureau of Management. Assistant Administrator and Director
Wandel, Jens – E/2015/SR.13
UNICEF. Public Partnerships Division. Director
Kjorven, Olav – E/2015/SR.10
United Kingdom
Shearman, Martin – E/2015/SR.9; E/2015/SR.12
United States
Dunn, David – E/2015/SR.9
Robl, Teri – E/2015/SR.13
Viet Nam
Nguyen, Phuong Nga – E/2015/SR.13

## UN-HABITAT. GOVERNING COUNCIL–MEMBERS (Agenda item 4)

UN. Economic and Social Council (2014-2015 : New York and Geneva). President
Sajdik, Martin (Austria) – E/2015/SR.30
UN. Economic and Social Council (2014-2015 : New York and Geneva). Secretary
De Laurentis, Jennifer – E/2015/SR.24
UN. Economic and Social Council (2014-2015 : New York and Geneva). Vice-President
Oh, Joon (Republic of Korea) – E/2015/SR.24

## UN-WOMEN (Agenda item 7b)

Australia
Stokes, Christopher John – E/2015/SR.11
Brazil
Ribeiro, Adriana Telles – E/2015/SR.11
Colombia
Dávila, María Paulina – E/2015/SR.11
Japan
Minami, Hiroshi – E/2015/SR.11
Panama
Franceschi Navarro, Paulina María – E/2015/SR.11
Sweden
Lennartsson, Magnus – E/2015/SR.11
Switzerland
Egli, Patrick – E/2015/SR.11
Syrian Arab Republic
Jawhara, Rabee – E/2015/SR.11
UN-Women. Deputy Executive Director
Puri, Lakshmi – E/2015/SR.11
Yemen
Al-Hamdani, Raiman – E/2015/SR.11

## UN-WOMEN. EXECUTIVE BOARD–MEMBERS (Agenda item 4)

China
Chu, Guang – E/2015/SR.23
Pakistan
Ammar, Yasar – E/2015/SR.23
Russian Federation
Khvan, Galina – E/2015/SR.23
Turkmenistan
Ataeva, Aksoltan T. – E/2015/SR.23

## UN-WOMEN. EXECUTIVE BOARD–MEMBERS (Agenda item 4) (continued)

Uganda
Muhumuza, Duncan Laki – E/2015/SR.23
UN. Economic and Social Council (2014-2015 : New York and Geneva). Secretary
De Laurentis, Jennifer – E/2015/SR.24
UN. Economic and Social Council (2014-2015 : New York and Geneva). Vice-President
Oh, Joon (Republic of Korea) – E/2015/SR.24

## UNDP/UNFPA/UNOPS (Agenda item 7b)

Australia
Stokes, Christopher John – E/2015/SR.11
Versegi, Peter Lloyd – E/2015/SR.12
Brazil
Ribeiro, Adriana Telles – E/2015/SR.11
China
Wang, Hongbo – E/2015/SR.12
Colombia
Dávila, María Paulina – E/2015/SR.11
Group of 77
Mamabolo, Jeremiah Nyamane Kingsley (South Africa) – E/2015/SR.12
India
Bishnoi, Bhagwant Singh – E/2015/SR.12
Japan
Minami, Hiroshi – E/2015/SR.11
Mexico
Colín Ortega, Gabriela – E/2015/SR.12
Panama
Franceschi Navarro, Paulina María – E/2015/SR.11
Sweden
Lennartsson, Magnus – E/2015/SR.11
Switzerland
Egli, Patrick – E/2015/SR.11
Syrian Arab Republic
Jawhara, Rabee – E/2015/SR.11
UN Development Group. Chair
Clark, Helen – E/2015/SR.11
UNDP/UNFPA/UNOPS Executive Board. Chair
Carrera Castro, Fernando (Guatemala) – E/2015/SR.11
UNFPA. Executive Director
Osotimehin, Babatunde – E/2015/SR.11
Yemen
Al-Hamdani, Raiman – E/2015/SR.11

## UNICEF (Agenda item 7b)

Australia
Stokes, Christopher John – E/2015/SR.11
Brazil
Ribeiro, Adriana Telles – E/2015/SR.11
Colombia
Dávila, María Paulina – E/2015/SR.11
Japan
Minami, Hiroshi – E/2015/SR.11
Panama
Franceschi Navarro, Paulina María – E/2015/SR.11
Sweden
Lennartsson, Magnus – E/2015/SR.11
Switzerland
Egli, Patrick – E/2015/SR.11

## UNICEF (Agenda item 7b) (continued)

Syrian Arab Republic
    Jawhara, Rabee – E/2015/SR.11
UNICEF. Executive Director
    Lake, Anthony – E/2015/SR.11
Yemen
    Al-Hamdani, Raiman – E/2015/SR.11

## WOMEN IN DEVELOPMENT (Agenda item 18j)

Action aide aux familles démunies (Mali)
    Touré, Ténin – E/2015/SR.47(A)
Journalists and Writers Foundation (Turkey)
    Ülker, Cemre – E/2015/SR.47(A)
UN-Women. Deputy Executive Director
    Puri, Lakshmi – E/2015/SR.32

## WOMEN'S ADVANCEMENT (Agenda item 19a)

UN. Commission on the Status of Women. Chair
    Patriota, Antonio de Aguiar – E/2015/SR.32
UN-Women. Deputy Executive Director
    Puri, Lakshmi – E/2015/SR.32

## WORLD FOOD PROGRAMME (Agenda item 7b)

Australia
    Stokes, Christopher John – E/2015/SR.11
Brazil
    Ribeiro, Adriana Telles – E/2015/SR.11
Colombia
    Dávila, María Paulina – E/2015/SR.11
Japan
    Minami, Hiroshi – E/2015/SR.11
Panama
    Franceschi Navarro, Paulina María – E/2015/SR.11
Sweden
    Lennartsson, Magnus – E/2015/SR.11
Switzerland
    Egli, Patrick – E/2015/SR.11
Syrian Arab Republic
    Jawhara, Rabee – E/2015/SR.11
World Food Programme. Deputy Executive Director
    Abdulla, Amir Mahmoud – E/2015/SR.11
Yemen
    Al-Hamdani, Raiman – E/2015/SR.11

# LIST OF RESOLUTIONS

*Vote reads Yes-No-Abstain*

| E/RES/2015/ | Title | Meeting / Date, 2015 (E/2015/SR.-) | A.I. No. | Vote |
|---|---|---|---|---|
| 1 | Membership of the Economic and Social Council in the Organizational Committee of the Peacebuilding Commission | 14 / 4 Mar. 15 | 2 | without vote |
| 2 | Joint United Nations Programme on HIV/AIDS | 22 / 8 Apr. 15 | 12g | without vote |
| 3 | Social dimensions of the New Partnership for Africa's Development | 32 / 8 June 15 | 19b | without vote |
| 4 | Promoting the rights of persons with disabilities and strengthening the mainstreaming of disability in the post-2015 development agenda | 32 / 8 June 15 | 19b | without vote |
| 5 | Modalities for the 3rd review and appraisal of the Madrid International Plan of Action on Ageing, 2002 | 32 / 8 June 15 | 19b | without vote |
| 6 | Future organization and methods of work of the Commission on the Status of Women | 32 / 8 June 15 | 19a | without vote |
| 7 | Work of the Committee of Experts on the Transport of Dangerous Goods and on the Globally Harmonized System of Classification and Labelling of Chemicals | 32 / 8 June 15 | 18l | without vote |
| 8 | United Nations Inter-Agency Task Force on the Prevention and Control of Non-Communicable Diseases | 33 / 9 June 15 | 12f | without vote |
| 9 | United Nations System Staff College in Turin, Italy | 33 / 9 June 15 | 20 | without vote |
| 10 | 2020 World Population and Housing Census Programme | 35 / 10 June 15 | 18c | without vote |
| 11 | Report of the Committee for Development Policy on its 17th session | 35 / 10 June 15 | 18a | without vote |
| 12 | Mainstreaming a gender perspective into all policies and programmes in the United Nations system | 36 / 10 June 15 | 12c | without vote |
| 13 | Situation of and assistance to Palestinian women | 36 / 10 June 15 | 19a | 16-2-20 |
| 14 | Strengthening of the coordination of emergency humanitarian assistance of the United Nations | 40 / 19 June 15 | 9 | without vote |
| 15 | Progress in the implementation of General Assembly resolution 67/226 on the quadrennial comprehensive policy review of operational activities for development of the United Nations system | 41 / 29 June 15 | 7 | without vote |
| 16 | Support to Non-Self-Governing Territories by the specialized agencies and international institutions associated with the United Nations | 50 / 20 July 15 | 14 | 19-0-25 |
| 17 | Economic and social repercussions of the Israeli occupation on the living conditions of the Palestinian people in the Occupied Palestinian Territory, including East Jerusalem, and the Arab population in the occupied Syrian Golan | 50 / 20 July 15 | 16 | 42-2-2 |

# LIST OF RESOLUTIONS

| E/RES/2015/ | Title | Meeting / Date, 2015 (E/2015/SR.-) | A.I. No. | Vote |
|---|---|---|---|---|
| 18 | Ad Hoc Advisory Group on Haiti | 52 / 21 July 15 | 12d | without vote |
| 19 | Thirteenth United Nations Congress on Crime Prevention and Criminal Justice | 53 / 21 July 15 | 19c | without vote |
| 20 | United Nations Standard Minimum Rules for the Treatment of Prisoners (the Mandela Rules) | 53 / 21 July 15 | 19c | without vote |
| 21 | Taking action against gender-related killing of women and girls | 53 / 21 July 15 | 19c | without vote |
| 22 | Technical assistance for implementing the international conventions and protocols related to counter-terrorism | 53 / 21 July 15 | 19c | without vote |
| 23 | Implementation of the United Nations Global Plan of Action to Combat Trafficking in Persons | 53 / 21 July 15 | 19c | without vote |
| 24 | Improving the quality and availability of statistics on crime and criminal justice for policy development | 53 / 21 July 15 | 19c | without vote |
| 25 | Special session of the General Assembly on the world drug problem to be held in 2016 | 53 / 21 July 15 | 19d | without vote |
| 26 | Assessment of the progress made in the implementation of and follow-up to the outcomes of the World Summit on the Information Society | 54 / 22 July 15 | 18b | without vote |
| 27 | Science, technology and innovation for development | 54 / 22 July 15 | 18b | without vote |
| 28 | Report of the Committee of Experts on Public Administration on its 14th session | 54 / 22 July 15 | 18g | without vote |
| 29 | Admission of Norway to membership in the Economic Commission for Latin America and the Caribbean | 54 / 22 July 15 | 15 | without vote |
| 30 | Restructuring the conference structure of the Economic and Social Commission for Asia and the Pacific to be fit for the evolving post-2015 development agenda | 54 / 22 July 15 | 15 | without vote |
| 31 | Establishment of the Asian and Pacific Centre for the Development of Disaster Information Management | 54 / 22 July 15 | 15 | without vote |
| 32 | Admission of Mauritania to membership in the Economic and Social Commission for Western Asia | 54 / 22 July 15 | 15 | without vote |
| 33 | International arrangement on forests beyond 2015 | 55 / 22 July 15 | 18k | without vote |
| 34 | Human settlements | 55 / 22 July 15 | 18d | without vote |
| 35 | Programme of Action for the Least Developed Countries for the Decade 2011-2020 | 56 / 23 July 15 | 11b | without vote |

# LIST OF DOCUMENTS

NOTE: Languages of corrigenda are indicated only when corrigenda are not issued in all six languages. Documents issued as Supplements to the Official Records of the Economic and Social Council, 2015 are also indicated. The information provided below is current as of the date this Index is submitted for publication.

**General series**

E/2015/1 + Add.1
E/2015/2
E/2015/3 (A/70/61)
E/2015/4 (A/70/62)
E/2015/5 *Symbol not used*
E/2015/6 *Symbol not used*
E/2015/7
E/2015/8
E/2015/9 + Add.1-11
E/2015/10 (A/70/63)
E/2015/11 *Symbol not used*
E/2015/12
E/2015/13 (A/70/82)
E/2015/14
E/2015/15 + Add.1-2
E/2015/16
E/2015/17
E/2015/18
E/2015/19
E/2015/20
E/2015/21
E/2015/22 (E/C.12/2014/3) (ESCOR, 2015, Suppl. no. 2)
E/2015/23 *Symbol not used*
E/2015/24 (E/CN.3/2015/40) (ESCOR, 2015, Suppl. no. 4)
E/2015/25 (E/CN.9/2015/7) (ESCOR, 2015, Suppl. no. 5)
E/2015/26 (E/CN.5/2015/9) (ESCOR, 2015, Suppl. no. 6) + Corr.1
E/2015/27 (E/CN.6/2015/10) (ESCOR, 2015, Suppl. no. 7)
E/2015/28 (E/CN.7/2015/15) (ESCOR, 2015, Suppl. no. 8)
E/2015/28/Add.1 (E/CN.7/2015/15/Add.1) (ESCOR, 2015, Suppl. no. 8A)
E/2015/29 *Symbol not used*
E/2015/30 (E/CN.15/2015/19) (ESCOR, 2015, Suppl. no. 10)
E/2015/30/Add.1 (E/CN.15/2015/19/Add.1) (ESCOR, 2015, Suppl. no. 10A)
E/2015/31 (E/CN.16/2015/4) (ESCOR, 2015, Suppl. no. 11)
E/2015/32 (Part I)
E/2015/32 (Part II)
E/2015/33 (ESCOR, 2015, Suppl. no. 13)
E/2015/34 (Part I) (E/ICEF/2015/7 (Part I))
E/2015/34 (Part II) (E/ICEF/2015/7 (Part II))
E/2015/34/Rev.1 (E/ICEF/2015/7/Rev.1) (ESCOR, 2015, Suppl. no. 14)
E/2015/35 (ESCOR, 2015, Suppl. no. 15)
E/2015/36 (ESCOR, 2015, Suppl. no. 16)
E/2015/37 (E/ECE/1472) (ESCOR, 2015, Suppl. no. 17)
E/2015/38 *Symbol not used*
E/2015/39 (E/ESCAP/71/42) (ESCOR, 2015, Suppl. no. 19)
E/2015/40 *Symbol not used*
E/2015/41 *Symbol not used*

**General series**

E/2015/42 (E/CN.18/2015/14) (ESCOR, 2015, Suppl. no. 22) + Corr.1
E/2015/43 (E/C.19/2015/10) (ESCOR, 2015, Suppl. no. 23)
E/2015/44 (E/C.16/2015/7) (ESCOR, 2015, Suppl. no. 24)
E/2015/45 (E/C.18/2015/6) (ESCOR, 2015, Suppl. no. 25)
E/2015/46 (E/C.20/2015/17) (ESCOR, 2015, Suppl. no. 26)
E/2015/47
E/2015/48 *Symbol not used*
E/2015/49 + Corr.1
E/2015/50
E/2015/51
E/2015/52
E/2015/53
E/2015/54
E/2015/55 (A/70/75)
E/2015/56
E/2015/57 (A/70/76)
E/2015/58
E/2015/59
E/2015/60
E/2015/61
E/2015/62
E/2015/63
E/2015/64 (A/70/77)
E/2015/65
E/2015/66
E/2015/67
E/2015/68
E/2015/69
E/2015/70 (A/7079)
E/2015/71
E/2015/72
E/2015/73
E/2015/74
E/2015/75 (A/70/83)
E/2015/76 (A/70/84)
E/2015/77 (A/70/85)
E/2015/78
E/2015/79 (A/70/87)
E/2015/80
E/2015/81 (A/70/90)
E/2015/82 (A/70/92) + Corr.1
E/2015/83 *Symbol not used*
E/2015/84
E/2015/85
E/2015/86 (A/70/137)
E/2015/87
E/2015/88-98 *Symbols not used*
E/2015/99 (ESCOR, 2015, Suppl. no. 1)
E/2015/100

# LIST OF DOCUMENTS

## Information series

E/2015/INF/1 *Symbol not used*
E/2015/INF/2 + Corr.1
E/2015/INF/3 *Symbol not used*
E/2015/INF/4
E/2015/INF/5

## Limited series

E/2015/L.1 + Rev.1
E/2015/L.2-17
E/2015/L.18 + Rev.1
E/2015/L.19 (E/HLPF/2015/L.2)
E/2015/L.20-25

## Non-governmental organizations series

E/2015/NGO/1-71

## Summary records

E/2015/SR.1-46
E/2015/SR.47(A)
E/2015/SR.47(B)
E/2015/SR.48-56

## Miscellaneous documents

E/HLS/2015/1

## Resolutions and Decisions

E/RES/2015/1-35
   Resolutions have been issued separately, and later
collected in document E/2015/99 (ESCOR, 2015, Suppl.1)

Decisions 2015/200-257
   Decisions are collected in document E/2015/99 (ESCOR,
2015, Suppl.1)

# LIST OF DOCUMENTS

## Supplements to Official Records

**No. 1** E/2015/99
Resolutions and decisions of the Economic and
Social Council : 2015 session
*To be issued*
    - (ESCOR, 2015, Suppl. no. 1).

**No. 2** E/2015/22 (E/C.12/2014/3)
Committee on Economic, Social and Cultural
Rights : report on the 52nd and 53rd sessions (28
April-23 May 2014, 10-28 November 2014). - New
York ; Geneva : UN, 2015.
    iv, 22 p. : tables. - (ESCOR, 2015, Suppl. no.
2).

**No. 3** *Symbol not used.*

**No. 4** E/2015/24 (E/CN.3/2015/40)
Statistical Commission : report on the 46th session
(3-6 March 2015). - New York : UN, 2015.
    49 p. - (ESCOR, 2015, Suppl. no. 4).

**No. 5** E/2015/25 (E/CN.9/2015/7)
Commission on Population and Development :
report on the 48th session (11 April 2014 and 13-
17 April 2015). - New York : UN, 2015.
    23 p. - (ESCOR, 2015, Suppl. no. 5).

**No. 6** E/2015/26 (E/CN.5/2015/9) + Corr.1
Commission for Social Development : report on
the 53rd session (21 February 2014 and 4-13
February 2015). - New York : UN, 2015.
    46 p. - (ESCOR, 2015, Suppl. no. 6).

**No. 7** E/2015/27 (E/CN.6/2015/10)
Commission on the Status of Women : report on
the 59th session (21 March 2014 and 9-20 March
2015). - New York : UN, 2015.
    46 p. - (ESCOR, 2015, Suppl. no. 7).

**No. 8** E/2015/28 (E/CN.7/2015/15)
Commission on Narcotic Drugs : report on the
58th session (5 December 2014 and 9-17 March
2015). - New York : UN, 2015.
    viii, 88 p. - (ESCOR, 2015, Suppl. no. 8).

**No. 8A** E/2015/28/Add.1 (E/CN.7/2015/15/Add.1)
Commission on Narcotic Drugs : report on the
reconvened 58th session (9-11 December 2015). -
New York : UN, 2016.
    iv, 22 p. : table. - (ESCOR, 2015, Suppl. no.
8A).

**No. 9** *Symbol not used.*

**No. 10** E/2015/30 (E/CN.15/2015/19)
Commission on Crime Prevention and Criminal
Justice : report on the 24th session (5 December
2014 and 18-22 May 2015). - New York : UN,
2015.
    vii, 103 p. - (ESCOR, 2015, Suppl. no. 10).

**No. 10A** E/2015/30/Add.1 (E/CN.15/2015/19/Add.1)
Commission on Crime Prevention and Criminal
Justice : report on the reconvened 24th session
(10-11 December 2015). - New York : UN, 2016.
    iii, 15 p. : table. - (ESCOR, 2015, Suppl. no.
10A).

**No. 11** E/2015/31 (E/CN.16/2015/4)
Commission on Science and Technology for
Development : report on the 18th session (4-8
May 2015). - New York : UN, 2015.
    43 p. - (ESCOR, 2015, Suppl. no. 11).

**No. 12** *Symbol not used.*

**No. 13** E/2015/33
Committee for Development Policy : report on the
17th session (23-27 March 2015). - New York :
UN, 2015.
    34 p. : graphs, tables. - (ESCOR, 2015, Suppl.
no. 13).

**No. 14** E/2015/34/Rev.1 (E/ICEF/2015/7/Rev.1)
Executive Board of the United Nations Children's
Fund : report on the 1st and 2nd regular sessions
and annual session of 2015. - New York : UN,
2015.
    81 p. : tables. - (ESCOR, 2015, Suppl. no. 14).

**No. 15** E/2015/35
Executive Board of the United Nations
Development Programme, the United Nations
Population Fund and the United Nations Office for
Project Services : report of the Executive Board on
its work during 2015. - New York : UN, 2015.
    105 p. - (ESCOR, 2015, Suppl. no. 15).

**No. 16** E/2015/36
Executive Board of the World Food Programme :
report on the 1st and 2nd regular sessions and
annual session of 2014. - New York : UN, 2015.
    37 p. - (ESCOR, 2015, Suppl. no. 16).

**No. 17** E/2015/37 (E/ECE/1472)
Economic Commission for Europe : biennial report
(12 April 2013-16 April 2015). - New York ; Geneva
: UN, 2015.
    iv, 73 p. : tables. - (ESCOR, 2015, Suppl. no.
17).

**No. 18** *Symbol not used.*

**No. 19** E/2015/39 (E/ESCAP/71/42)
Economic and Social Commission for Asia and the
Pacific : annual report (9 August 2014-29 May
2015). - New York : UN, 2015.
    vi, 113 p. : tables. - (ESCOR, 2015, Suppl. no.
19).

**No. 20** *Symbol not used.*

**No. 21** *Symbol not used.*

# LIST OF DOCUMENTS

## Supplements to Official Records

**No. 22**   E/2015/42 (E/CN.18/2015/14) + Corr.1
United Nations Forum on Forests : report on the
11th session (19 April 2013 and 4 to 15 May
2015). - New York : UN, 2015.
     48 p. : table. - (ESCOR, 2015, Suppl. no. 22).

**No. 23**   E/2015/43 (E/C.19/2015/10)
Permanent Forum on Indigenous Issues : report
on the 14th session (20 April-1 May 2015). - New
York : UN, 2015.
     17 p. - (ESCOR, 2015, Suppl. no. 23).

**No. 24**   E/2015/44 (E/C.16/2015/7)
Committee of Experts on Public Administration :
report on the 14th session (20-24 April 2015). -
New York : UN, 2015.
     29 p. - (ESCOR, 2015, Suppl. no. 24).

**No. 25**   E/2015/45 (E/C.18/2015/6)
Committee of Experts on International Cooperation
in Tax Matters : report on the 11th session (19-23
October 2015). - New York : UN, 2015.
     28 p. - (ESCOR, 2015, Suppl. no. 25).

**No. 26**   E/2015/46 (E/C.20/2015/17)
Committee of Experts on Global Geospatial
Information Management : report on the 5th
session (5-7 August 2015). - New York : UN, 2015.
     28 p. - (ESCOR, 2015, Suppl. no. 26).

www.ingramcontent.com/pod-product-compliance
Lightning Source LLC
Chambersburg PA
CBHW080618270326
41928CB00016B/3110